LIFE
COLORS

LIFE COLORS

PAMALA OSLIE

NEW WORLD LIBRARY
SAN RAFAEL, CALIFORNIA

Published by New World Library
58 Paul Drive, San Rafael, CA 94903

Cover design: Rick Garcia
Text design: Cassandra Chu
Typography: Typecraft

First printing, September 1991
Printed in the U.S.A. on acid–free paper
ISBN 0-931432-81-2

This book is dedicated to every being
seeking to remember that we are One,
and that we are unlimited creators.
May we all live together in love
and joy and light and harmony.

Acknowledgments

I wish to express my love and gratitude to the following friends who have all been inspirational teachers to me.

My appreciation to the three people who helped me the most with this book:

To Becky Benenate for all her support and devoted time and energy in putting this book together.

To Janet Mills for her friendship and all her lifetimes of love, inspiration and wisdom.

To Bo Fox whom I love and cherish beyond words and who has been a wonderful light in my life.

My deepest love and appreciation to my mother, Beverly, for her encouragement, love and support and to my father, Palmer, for his inspiration and dedicated love.

To my sister, Paula, and my brothers Larry and Scott who have been incredibly loving, patient and supportive toward me. And to their lights Michael, Christine, Kari, Keith, Kory, Kyle, Kalen, Kip and Diane.

To all my wonderful friends who have brought so much love and joy to my experience in this lifetime — Kandis Blakely, Cathe Crest Martinez, Terry and Ehsida Bissett Jaymes, Mary Judge, Rod Lathim, Thom Rollerson, Lori Mazzuca, Carolyn Ringo and Jeff Levens, Rip Riparetti, Rob Robb, Kim Stanwood, Alli Stillman, Anne Stewart, Linda Thornton, Alexis Ells, Lorraine Khosravi, Monica Ryker, Rich and Dinny Harter, Pat Harwell, Tim O'Brien, Peggy O'Toole, Chandler Armstrong, Joyce Johnson, Susan Shaffer, Diane Matsinger, Lisa and David Schenkel, Joan and Mike Clifford, Susan Conger, Kathryn Grove, Lenie Colacino, Lee Bryant, Nancy Fuller, Eva Ein, Kenny Loggins and family,

Diana and Dan Brown, Lynne and Frank Babb, Sandy Park, Glen and Patricia Posner, Lisa Moore, Darai and Jeff Roundy, Barbara Rollinson, John Leonard, Hank McMonigle, Kim Fox Shockley and family and Arthur.

To all my clients who have become such special friends. Thank you for your trust and support.

To Michael Bromley and Barbara Bowers for their willingness to help me awaken my inner abilities.

To Rick Garcia for the cover design and Rich Fuller for the photography.

To my editor Leslie Keenan and my publisher Marc Allen for believing in this book.

To all those who have inspired my awakening, especially Seth, Jane Roberts, Richard Bach and Terry Cole-Whittaker.

Contents

Introduction

What type of personality are you? What are your goals and purposes for being here? How do you process life — physically, mentally, emotionally? What kind of marriage partner is best suited for you? What are your attitudes about career, money, family, sex? What types of occupations are best for you? What is your definition of success? What are your positive qualities and negative tendencies? How do you maintain and enhance your positive characteristics? Where are your weak spots concerning health? These are all questions that interest everyone. Over the years I have discovered that valuable clues and answers to these questions lie hidden in our own personal auras.

I became interested in the aura in 1983, after discovering that I was able to receive clairvoyant information about people. After attending numerous aura workshops led by Dr. Barbara Bowers, who is able to physically see the aura, I noticed that I was receiving psychic information about people that corresponded with her descriptions and data on the various aura colors. Eventually, through my psychic work I also developed the ability to see the various aura colors. I discovered that there are consistent and basic personality traits that coincide with each one of the different aura colors.

The aura is the electromagnetic energy field that radiates from all matter, although some matter is so dense and vibrates so slowly that it is often difficult to detect its aura. Throughout the ages, artists have depicted the aura as a halo or glowing light that appears around the heads or bodies of highly evolved spiritual masters and enlightened saints. Apparently, the auras around these beings were so clear and powerful that others could easily see, feel or sense them. Recently, the aura has been scientifically detected through Kirilian photography.

I see the aura as glowing bands of different luminescent colored lights that completely surround the body. Everyone has an aura that is comprised of many different colored bands of light that radiate or extend approximately six feet out in all directions from the body. I can tell if a person is healthy or ill, happy or frustrated by the intensity and vibrancy of the color, as well as by the expansiveness and size of the aura. One person's aura may be bright, vibrant and expanded, showing a sense of openness, well-being, positive self-esteem and health, while another's may be faded and tightly drawn to the body, showing fear, illness, lack of self-esteem, hopelessness or a perceived need for protection. A dark, densely colored aura usually reveals depression, anger or self-pity. Each colored band in the aura tells a different story. Each color contains information about the person.

Being able to "read" the aura and understand the meaning behind each color has helped me understand the way I process information, my interactions with people, how I handle love relationships, and my purpose in life.

My purpose in writing about the aura is to bring this knowledge and information to others, to enable them to understand how and why they process life in a particular way. This knowledge gives people permission to be themselves, to become more accepting of themselves and others, while also learning effective ways of changing their unwanted behavior and attitudes.

The different colors of an aura are created in much the same manner as sounds are created. With sounds, the faster the vibration, the higher the frequency of sound. The vibration of a bass note on a piano resonates at a slower rate than the "high C" note. As the waves of energy that make up the auric field change their speed of vibration, the colors also change. In the aura, the colors Red and Orange are created by a slower vibration. Faster vibrations create Blue, Violet and Indigo. A bass note is not better than or worse than a high note. They are just different sounds. Likewise, the color Orange in the aura is not better or worse than the color Blue. Different colors signify different desires for a variety of experiences on the planet. Life would be mundane and uninspiring if we all had the same aura colors, just as a song would be quite monotonous if it were composed of only one note.

In writing about the different aura colors, it is not my intention to establish any kind of limitation, separation or "superior" attitudes among readers. There are no good or bad colors. The different colors in the aura reflect one's choices in this lifetime, but do not mean that you are *limited* to a particular goal or way of processing. We are all free to expand, grow, and change in any way we choose. By understanding the attributes of each of the different colors, one can even consciously draw in a color for a specific purpose, such as healing, prosperity or compassion. My goal is to show that while we may all have different methods, goals and purposes, we are all part of the whole. We are each a part of a colorful auric rainbow.

■ **AURA LIFECOLORS**

There are many different colored bands in a person's aura. The band that is closest to the body reveals the person's priorities, methods of processing life and primary purpose for being on the planet. This is the band I focus on in this book. I call it the LifeColor. The other bands of the aura frequently change colors and positions, reflecting what is happening with the person at a given time. However, the band closest to the body, the LifeColor, does not usually change.

For simplification, I have categorized the aura Life-Colors into three different families: the physical colors, the mental colors and the emotional colors.

Those with physical colors process information predominantly through their physical bodies, through touch. The physical colors include Red, Orange, Magenta and Yellow.

Those with mental colors process life intellectually, by first gathering information or data, then analyzing it. The mental colors include Logical Tan, Abstract Tan, Sensitive Tan, Environmental Tan and Green.

Those with the emotional colors — Blue, Violet, Indigo, Lavender and Crystal — process life primarily through their feelings, emotions and intuition.

Some of the LifeColors are predominantly in males, while others are predominantly in females. The use of "he" or "she" throughout the book, however, is usually arbitrary.

A person is not restricted to living only within her LifeColor. Choosing to come into this life with a particular LifeColor does not mean that one cannot experience the qualities, purposes, priorities and methods of the other LifeColors. While we have our original LifeColor, we also continuously add other colors into the outer bands of the aura. Through years of working with people, however, I have discovered that one cannot discard, discount or ignore the attributes of her original LifeColor without experiencing a sense of disconnection, confusion and disharmony within herself. Each person needs to fulfill her LifeColors before she can successfully and harmoniously expand to the other colors. She must first love and accept who she is before she can satisfactorily experience the qualities of the other colors.

Some people are born with one LifeColor; others are born with two LifeColors, which I call Combination Colors. Combination Colors show up as the two bands of color in the aura which are consistently the closest colors around the body. Having two LifeColors can be a powerful combination, giving an additional dimension to one's abilities, or it can create a great deal of inner conflict.

I feel and believe that, on a deep level, we have all chosen our LifeColor, or our Combination Colors. The reasons for choosing two LifeColors vary with each individual. Some people choose two LifeColors because the qualities of the second color add more power, energy, fun or creativity to their main goal in life. Another reason for choosing two LifeColors is to ensure balance, practicality, responsibility or self-reliance.

In a situation where someone has two LifeColors in the same aura family — for example a Blue/Violet combination, which has two LifeColors in the emotional family — this person may be living the equivalent of two lifetimes in this one life. Perhaps she is in a hurry to experience and learn her life lessons, so that she won't have to physically incarnate on this planet again. Or perhaps she didn't learn all the lessons (or receive all the benefits) from her last life, and so has carried them over into this lifetime.

People with this type of Combination Color often *sense* that they are living two lifetimes at once. As they switch over from one life to another (without actually needing to die or change bodies), they usually feel a dramatic shift in their lives. Their personalities may drastically change. The loving Blue who has held marriage and relationships as her main priority her entire life suddenly discovers she has a burning desire to make a strong impact on the planet. She can no longer stay at home and be a housewife and mother. Her familiar relationships, career, priorities and emotions begin to feel alien to her. She feels like an entirely different being.

Living two lifetimes at once only applies to those who have two LifeColors in the same aura family. Many Combination Colors may experience a similar shift in their lives as they move their focus from one of their LifeColors into the other. For example, as a Yellow/Violet Combination Color moves his focus from his Yellow characteristics to his Violet, he may also experience a shift in his career or marital status. To discover if you are one of those who are living two lives in one, first ask yourself if you believe and feel that you are. (Always trust yourself and your own feelings.) After answering the questions in the LifeColor Questionnaire, notice if your two highest scores both appear in the same aura family. If they do, and you feel that you are in the process of shifting — or have already shifted — into being an entirely different person, then chances are you fall into this category.

Frequently, people add another color to their auras sometime during their lifetime, and that color becomes a part of their personality. It's not that important to know whether you were born with certain LifeColors or added them later on in life as long as you are happy and those colors benefit you. For example, if you came here as a Blue and have added Yellow to your aura, and the addition is having a positive influence on your life, then enjoy it. You basically have become a Blue/Yellow personality. If you feel, however, that you were born as a Yellow/Violet, but added Logical Tan to please your parents or to be accepted by society, that extra color may be causing you to suppress who you really are. In this case, you may want to consider letting go of the characteristics of that color and allowing yourself to explore the qualities of your true LifeColors.

The following chapters describe the general attributes, life purposes, goals and qualities that each LifeColor displays when an individual is "in power" (or centered) and "out of power" (or off balance). When a person is "in power," she is living her positive personality and her true potential. When she is "out of power," she is living in fear, self-doubt and hesitancy. She is not living her full potential.

There are methods that show how to regain balance and stay in power when a person finds herself out of power. There are also descriptions of the different colors' characteristics in the areas of relationships, sex and children, problem-solving skills, definitions of success, and occupational interests, as well as the physical problems or weak health areas experienced by each color.

With the descriptions in this book, you will be able to identify your own LifeColor or Colors and use the information to enhance your life.

After reading the descriptions of the various LifeColors, you will also begin to recognize the personalities of your friends and family members. You can refer to the section on relationships to learn about your methods of relating to each other.

1. Identifying Your
Aura LifeColors

There are two ways to determine your LifeColors. The first method is to read through the description of each color, and see which most accurately describes your personality. Most people find it easy to discover their LifeColors or Combination Colors — as well as those of their friends and families — in this way.

The second method is to answer the following questions. Discovering your LifeColors will give you a better understanding of your purpose in life, and why you relate to some people better than others.

Keep in mind that frequently there are only subtle differences between some of the LifeColors. For example, Blues, Yellows and Violets can all exhibit the same emotional qualities, the same desire for a relationship (although for different reasons) and similar desires to help people. They each desire to help people in different ways, however. A Yellow, for example, usually helps people by fixing things for them — their cars, their kitchen sinks or their physical bodies. A Yellow prefers not to get too heavily involved with people's emotional problems while helping them. A Blue usually helps people one to one, on an emotional level — counseling, teaching or nursing. (A Blue nurse often cares about the patient's emotions even more than his

1

physical ailments.) A Violet usually wants to help many people at one time, by inspiring and empowering the masses. Rarely does a Violet have the desire or the patience to help one person at a time.

If you pay close attention to all of the descriptions, you will intuitively feel which one or two colors are most closely aligned with who you really are. It is as common for people to have two LifeColors as it is to have just one. It is also common, however, for people to function primarily out of one of their LifeColors more than the other.

Occasionally, people suppress their natural LifeColors because of family pressures or expectations. For example, a person with a carefree and energetic Yellow LifeColor may have been forced by domineering and controlling parents to behave in a more disciplined fashion. He may have been told that it was not appropriate to be silly, playful or irresponsible. Consequently, the sensitive Yellow loses his natural enthusiasm, his creativity and his desire to make people laugh. Parents frequently raise their children based on their own beliefs and their own LifeColors. They do the best they can given that they are not always aware of the differences in their children's LifeColors, or even of their own purposes and challenges in this lifetime.

To discover your LifeColor(s), first answer the questions in the questionnaire. When answering these questions, be sure to give your "true" answers, not the responses that you think you "should" give. After answering the questions, note the category in which you had the highest number of "yes" responses. This is your LifeColor. Then note which category had the second highest number of "yes" responses. If that number of "yes" responses is close to that of the first category, you probably have a Combination Color. Both of these colors are your LifeColors. If, however, your second category has far fewer "yes" responses than your first, you probably have a single

LifeColor. If three or four colors rate high numbers, you probably have added one or two colors to your aura that have become part of your personality. (For example, adding Violet to a Yellow/Green combination is very common. Violet seems to be one of the colors that can calm down and balance out the conflict that frequently occurs in a Yellow/Green combination.)

Next, read the list of occupations to see which category appeals to you the most. Your chosen category will further reveal your LifeColor(s). When you feel you have discovered your LifeColor(s), read the individual section on those colors for indepth information. Then, if you have two colors, read the section on that particular Combination Color. If you relate to the descriptions in those particular sections, you have discovered your LifeColor(s). Ultimately, you are your own best judge.

There is also a section on relationships to help you understand how you relate to people with other LifeColors. The relationship section is meant to serve as a *guide* to your relationships. There are no "shoulds" or absolutes. It is possible for any relationship to succeed with enough desire, love and commitment. The information can help you discover ways to enhance your relationships and give you insight into areas in which you may experience difficulties.

The last section gives you information that will assist you in learning how to see the human aura and how to add various colors to the outer bands of your aura.

Directions to Identify Your LifeColors

1. Take the test. Choose the one or two categories with the highest number of "yes" responses.

2. Read the career choices. Choose the category of careers to which you are most drawn (or have been drawn).

3. Read the chapters on the specific LifeColors that correspond to your answers.

4. Read the section on the specific "Combination Color" that corresponds to your answers.

5. To see which LifeColors are most compatible with yours, read the relationship sections that involve your Life-Color.

LifeColor Questionnaire

Before taking this test, read all of the questions in each category. This will give you a general feeling of the personality type of each of the particular aura colors. Then, after taking the test, total the number of times that you answer "yes" in each category. Be sure to respond with the answers that are generally true of you, most of the time. Taking the test during an emotionally distraught or traumatic time for you may skew or alter your true answers. Therefore, it is recommended that you don't take the test during emotionally stressful times.

Yes	Sometimes	No	LifeColor #1
___	_____	___	I enjoy tangible physical reality more than discussing spiritual, emotional or mental concepts.
___	_____	___	I enjoy the animalistic, physical pleasures of the body — sex, eating, drinking, etc.
___	_____	___	I often have a quick temper, but get over it quickly and do not hold grudges.
___	_____	___	I enjoy expressing myself through my sexuality and my physical body more than through my emotions or my intellect.
___	_____	___	I prefer work that is physical and has immediate, tangible results.
___	_____	___	I tend to be a loner.
___	_____	___	I have a hard time expressing my feelings to others.
___	_____	___	I am usually powerful, self-confident, independent and practical.
___	_____	___	I enjoy taking physical action on projects rather than theorizing about ideas and plans.
___	_____	___	I tend to believe only in the existence of those things which I can physically touch.
___	_____	___	I am persistent and hard-working and usually keep the rest of the team going.
___	_____	___	I tend to be honest and blunt.
___	_____	___	(Total each column here.)

Yes	Sometimes	No	LifeColor #2
___	_____	___	I tend to be a physical daredevil and risk-taker.
___	_____	___	I relish dangerous, thrilling, physical challenges.
___	_____	___	Having a regular job and a family feels boring to me.
___	_____	___	I prefer to spend time alone.
___	_____	___	I prefer doing individual sports and challenges rather than team sports.
___	_____	___	I enjoy the challenge of going beyond physical limitations.
___	_____	___	I do not need to share my emotional feelings with anyone.
___	_____	___	Spiritual beliefs and concepts do not interest me.
___	_____	___	I prefer occupations which allow me to experience raw, physical courage.
___	_____	___	I am not interested in what other people think about me.
___	_____	___	I tend to use money for daring adventures such as mountain climbing or car racing, rather than for investment.
___	_____	___	People often see me as self-absorbed and aloof.
___	_____	___	(Total each column here.)

Yes	Sometimes	No	LifeColor #3
___	_____	___	I like the bizarre and the unusual.
___	_____	___	I do not usually conform to society's rules or laws.
___	_____	___	Although I love parties and social events, I have trouble keeping friends because my behavior sometimes shocks people.
___	_____	___	I enjoy outrageous artistic expression.
___	_____	___	I do not like being responsible for friends or family.
___	_____	___	I am a quick thinker, but people rarely understand my ideas.
___	_____	___	I love to learn about new things, but I tend to have a short attention span. I often leave things unfinished.
___	_____	___	I feel alone and misunderstood a lot of the time.
___	_____	___	Acting foolish and outrageous is fun and does not embarrass me.
___	_____	___	My lifestyle tends to be flamboyant and eccentric.
___	_____	___	I would enjoy being married several times just for fun.
___	_____	___	I believe controversy is necessary and that it keeps life interesting.
___	_____	___	(Total each column here.)

Yes	*Sometimes*	*No*	LifeColor #4
___	____	___	It is very important to me to be able to play, have fun, exercise and be with people.
___	____	___	I like to laugh and cheer people up.
___	____	___	I have or have had a tendency to regularly overdo at least one of the following: drugs, alcohol, cigarettes, caffeine, sex, exercise, chocolates, sweets or overeating.
___	____	___	When there is conflict, my first impulse is to run away or avoid the situation.
___	____	___	I need physical exercise or dance on a regular basis.
___	____	___	I like to be creative, artistic or work with my hands.
___	____	___	I enjoy physical work.
___	____	___	I tend to look younger than my age.
___	____	___	My feelings can be hurt very easily.
___	____	___	I wish people could just play all the time.
___	____	___	I believe that sex should be fun.
___	____	___	I like to be spontaneous.
___	____	___	(Total each column here.)

Yes	Sometimes	No	LifeColor #5
___	_____	___	I prefer secure, stable jobs which provide regular paychecks.
___	_____	___	I tend to keep my feelings and emotions to myself.
___	_____	___	I prefer to see the proof, logic and data behind ideas.
___	_____	___	I enjoy working with mechanical or electronic gadgets and machines — computers, calculators, appliances, and electronic games.
___	_____	___	I enjoy working with details.
___	_____	___	I am a very analytical, logical, and sequential thinker.
___	_____	___	I am practical with money and prefer secure investments.
___	_____	___	I usually follow the rules and abide by the laws. I prefer structure.
___	_____	___	I tend to take a long time to make a decision. (Take as long as you want to answer this question.)
___	_____	___	I typically follow a regular routine.
___	_____	___	My attitude is "seeing is believing."
___	_____	___	I tend to be a "pack rat," hanging on to things just in case I need them.
_____	_____	_____	(Total each column here.)

Yes	Sometimes	No	LifeColor #6
___	___	___	I enjoy analyzing and measuring the environment.
___	___	___	I am able to judge weight, distance and volume through inner physical senses. (I can tell how much something weighs by holding it in my hand.)
___	___	___	I am a logical and practical thinker.
___	___	___	I am slow to develop friends and usually spend my time alone.
___	___	___	Money is important to me for security and stability.
___	___	___	I am a responsible, dedicated employee who follows directions well.
___	___	___	I perceive reality as logical and three-dimensional.
___	___	___	I am a very private person and keep my feelings to myself.
___	___	___	I am quiet and reserved but independent and strong.
___	___	___	I prefer stable jobs and reliable paychecks.
___	___	___	I tend to be serious and self-controlled.
___	___	___	When raising children, I would be a rational disciplinarian.
___	___	___	(Total each column here.)

Yes	Sometimes	No	LifeColor #7
___	___	___	Home and family are two of my most important priorities.
___	___	___	I feel that supporting community activities and attending functions such as PTA meetings is important.
___	___	___	I am a sensitive, calm, patient and rational thinker.
___	___	___	Having a sense of security and stability in my home is important to me.
___	___	___	I care about people, but enjoy entertaining only a few close friends.
___	___	___	I tend to be quiet, reserved and often shy.
___	___	___	I prefer to understand the logic in a situation, however I am also emotionally supportive of people's needs.
___	___	___	I believe that service to humanity is true spirituality.
___	___	___	I prefer to work in a support role where I take care of the details.
___	___	___	I usually put my family's needs before my own.
___	___	___	I prefer to work in a structured environment.
___	___	___	I usually work out my emotional upsets in a calm, logical and quiet manner.
___	___	___	(Total each column here.)

Yes	Sometimes	No	LifeColor #8
—	————	—	I frequently feel scattered, often forget appointments, or overbook my schedule with conflicting appointments.
—	————	—	I can see all the details that need to be taken care of, but I have difficulty deciding which ones need to be done first.
—	————	—	My possessions are not very important to me so I have trouble taking care of them.
—	————	—	I am constantly misplacing things.
—	————	—	I tend to theorize about emotions rather than actually experience them.
—	————	—	I prefer jobs that allow me to work randomly with all the details of a project.
—	————	—	I enjoy attending social functions where I can talk with a lot of different people.
—	————	—	I get so busy and things get so hectic that I often forget to pay my bills.
—	————	—	I am open, optimistic and very friendly.
—	————	—	I love humanity, but I am often uncomfortable maintaining an intimate relationship.
—	————	—	I usually see numerous solutions to a problem.
—	————	—	I know many acquaintances, but have very few close friends.
—	————	—	(Total each column here.)

Yes	Sometimes	No	LifeColor #9
___	_____	___	I can be a workaholic and have a hard time relaxing.
___	_____	___	I tend to be a perfectionist and I am usually demanding on myself.
___	_____	___	I love to learn and to be intellectually stimulated.
___	_____	___	I can be strong-willed and tenacious.
___	_____	___	It is very important to me to set goals, to know that people respect me and to make a lot of money.
___	_____	___	I enjoy being in charge and delegating responsibilities to others.
___	_____	___	I like things to be organized and well-planned. I frequently write lists.
___	_____	___	I enjoy the challenge of developing plans and ideas, rather than doing detailed work.
___	_____	___	I have high standards in relationships and tend to be bored easily by most other people.
___	_____	___	I can become impatient and frustrated with people if they are not motivated and ambitious.
___	_____	___	People can be intimidated by me.
___	_____	___	I frequently drink caffeinated beverages.
___	_____	___	(Total each column here.)

Yes	Sometimes	No	LifeColor #10
___	_____	___	People frequently turn to me with their emotional problems and I usually lovingly and patiently help them.
___	_____	___	I have been known to cry easily.
___	_____	___	One of my strongest priorities is to be in a loving relationship.
___	_____	___	I feel guilty if I say no to someone.
___	_____	___	God and spirituality are very important to me.
___	_____	___	Money is not a major priority to me.
___	_____	___	I tend to help and take care of everyone.
___	_____	___	I frequently have cold hands and feet.
___	_____	___	When there is conflict, I want everyone to love each other.
___	_____	___	Love and people are the most important elements in my life.
___	_____	___	I tend to feel the emotions of other people.
___	_____	___	I have difficulty letting go of relationships.
___	_____	___	(Total each column here.)

Yes	Sometimes	No	LifeColor #11
___	_____	___	I feel that I have a message to get across to people.
___	_____	___	I have a strong desire to help improve the planet.
___	_____	___	I have always felt that I was going to be famous or do something important.
___	_____	___	I have had a desire to perform to audiences.
___	_____	___	If I had a lot of money, I would travel or become involved in humanitarian causes.
___	_____	___	I am very interested in cosmic and universal concepts.
___	_____	___	I frequently end up in leadership positions or at least at the center of attention.
___	_____	___	I easily visualize future events.
___	_____	___	I am passionate about sex and have a strong sex drive.
___	_____	___	I can become involved in too many projects at the same time.
___	_____	___	Freedom and independence are major priorities to me.
___	_____	___	I would much rather be self-employed.
___	_____	___	(Total each column here.)

Yes	Sometimes	No	LifeColor #12
___	___	___	I enjoy fantasy and make-believe more than the "real" world.
___	___	___	I am quiet, sensitive and spiritual.
___	___	___	I have a difficult time managing money.
___	___	___	I tend to spend a lot of time alone, daydreaming.
___	___	___	I prefer pretty, gentle and fine artistic things and I am uncomfortable with dirt, bugs or harsh environments.
___	___	___	I am often forgetful and frequently "spacey."
___	___	___	People accuse me of being irresponsible and unrealistic.
___	___	___	I have difficulty dealing with everyday responsibilities.
___	___	___	I am an imaginative and creative thinker; however, I usually have trouble following through with my ideas.
___	___	___	I seem to be out of my body more than I am in it.
___	___	___	I tend to want others to solve my problems for me.
___	___	___	I prefer to work in relaxed, low-stress environments.
___	___	___	(Total each column here.)

Yes	Sometimes	No	LifeColor #13
____	_____	____	I often choose to work in quiet, calm and peaceful environments.
____	_____	____	I am extremely sensitive and can be overwhelmed by being around too many people.
____	_____	____	I need to spend a lot of time alone in quiet meditation to replenish myself.
____	_____	____	Spending quiet time reading or being in my garden is therapeutic for me.
____	_____	____	Physical reality often feels cold, harsh and threatening to me.
____	_____	____	I don't always know how to behave in social situations.
____	_____	____	My spirituality and my serene inner connection with God are the most important aspects of my life.
____	_____	____	Frequently, I am unsure of what I am supposed to do on the planet.
____	_____	____	I tend to be withdrawn, quiet and insecure.
____	_____	____	I feel safer and more secure with others taking responsibility and making decisions for me.
____	_____	____	I am careful with money.
____	_____	____	I often feel I have quiet, inner healing powers.
____	_____	____	(Total each column here.)

Yes	Sometimes	No	LifeColor #14
——	——	——	I have difficulty relating to the world in its current condition and often don't feel that I belong here.
——	——	——	I have difficulty relating to my physical body.
——	——	——	I have a highly sensitive physical, emotional and psychological system.
——	——	——	I have no issues regarding sexuality — heterosexuality, homosexuality or bi-sexuality — in myself or in others.
——	——	——	I "know" that there is spiritual energy in all things.
——	——	——	I have a strong curiosity about physical reality as it relates to spirituality.
——	——	——	I am extremely sensitive and compassionate, yet strong and independent.
——	——	——	I tend to question and challenge old, dogmatic beliefs and methods.
——	——	——	I cannot be forced to operate against my beliefs even if it would make others happy.
——	——	——	I feel more creative and spiritually "advanced" than others.
——	——	——	My appearance often seems androgynous.
——	——	——	Waking up suddenly causes me physical pain.
——	——	——	(Total each column here.)

The following is a test to see if you have a "Red Overlay." If you answer "yes" to three or more of these questions, chances are you have a red overlay. Please read the section in Chapter 5 on red overlays for more information.

Yes	*Sometimes*	*No*	LifeColor #15 (not a LifeColor)
___	_____	___	I frequently experience intense, often uncontrollable anger or rage.
___	_____	___	My life seems to be a constant struggle.
___	_____	___	I consistently experience conflict and frustration regarding relationships, health, money and/or career.
___	_____	___	I experienced at least one of the following as a child: a) emotionally, physically or mentally abandoned or rejected (i.e., unwanted child, adopted, alcoholic parent, etc.), b) emotionally, physically or mentally abused, c) life-threatening situation before birth, at birth or at a young age.
___	_____	___	(Total each column here.)

List which LifeColor categories you answered with the most "yes" responses to discover your LifeColors.

Aura category with highest number of "yes" answers: #_____
Aura category with the second highest number of "yes" answers: #_____
Do you have a "Red Overlay?" _____

Identifying Your Aura LifeColor Key

Answers to Questionnaire
#1 = Red
#2 = Orange
#3 = Magenta
#4 = Yellow
#5 = Logical Tan
#6 = Environmental Tan
#7 = Sensitive Tan
#8 = Abstract Tan
#9 = Green
#10 = Blue
#11 = Violet
#12 = Lavender
#13 = Crystal
#14 = Indigo
#15 = Red Overlay (not a LifeColor)

To further help you discover your LifeColors, choose which list of occupations appeals to you the most. Please note that just because you are currently in a particular occupation, it does not necessarily mean that is the "correct" occupation for you. If you are not happy in your line of work, you are probably not in alignment with your LifeColors.

Check the occupation categories which you are most drawn to, or would be if money and family approval were not considerations. (Also check the occupations in which you have worked in the past.) Certain occupations may appear on more than one list. For example, "writer" appears on many lists. Notice which other occupations in those lists you are most attracted to and you will probably discover your real LifeColor(s).

#1	#2	#3
Firefighter	Race car driver	Artist
Rescue worker	Skydiver	Clown
Police work	Hang-glider	Comedian
Military personnel	Wilderness guide	Actor
Football player	River rafter	Art dealer or collector
Boxer	Wild safari hunter	Inventor
Bodyguard	Stuntman	Set designer
Truck driver	Mountain climber	Costume designer
Heavy equipment	Explorer	Photographer
operator	Rescue worker	Publisher (especially
Construction worker	Firefighter	for avant-garde
Repairperson	Police worker	publications)
Mechanic	Detective	Entrepreneur
Furniture mover	Deep sea diver	Salesperson
Shop foreman	Bounty hunter	(especially for
Tractor driver	Trapeze artist	unusual items)
Farmer	Private investigator	
Surgeon	Guard	
Bartender	Lion-tamer	
Waiter/waitress		
Butcher		
Dancer		

#4	#5	#6
Musician	Engineer	Archaeologist
Artist	Architect	Geologist
Comedian	Bookkeeper	Environmental
Writer	Accountant	researcher
Laborer	Computer analyst	Scientist
Gardener	Researcher	Explorer
Bodybuilder	Scientist	Map maker
Lifeguard	Office clerk	Forest ranger
Firefighter	Data processor	Military personnel
Auto mechanic	Factory assembly	Pilot
Athlete	worker	Shipping & receiving
Surfer	Librarian	clerk
House painter	Court reporter	Purchase order clerk
Construction worker	Appliance or	City planner
Bartender	electrical	Developer
Chef	repairperson	Architect
Waiter/waitress	Technician	Computer operator
Massage therapist		Lab technician
Healer		Telephone repairperson
Doctor		Aerospace engineer
Nutritionist		Electrical repairperson
Veterinarian		Farmer
Court jester for the world		

#7

Bookkeeper
Receptionist
Secretary
Office personnel
Accountant
Arbitrator
Counselor
Therapist
Judge
Dentist
Hygienist
Welfare/social worker
Teacher
Child care worker

#8

Teacher
Consultant
City developer
Landscaper
Gardener
Salesperson
Computer
 programmer
Designer

#9

Corporate executive
Business entrepreneur
Banker
Producer
Fundraiser
Organizer
Office manager
Marketing & advertising
 coordinator
Planning and
 investment advisor
Real estate agent
Salesperson (especially
 sales involving
 expensive items such
 as cars, gems,
 insurance and homes)
Stockbroker
Business manager
 or agent
King (or at least
 "owner" of the world)

#10

Teacher
Counselor
Nurse
Child care worker
Assistant or
Director of
 nonprofit
 organizations
Secretary
Volunteer
Nun
Housewife
Mother
Maid
Waitress
Social worker

#11

Performer
Actor
Singer
Musician
Artist
Writer
Designer
Producer
Director
Cameraperson
Teacher
Minister
Psychologist
Consultant
Lecturer
Politician
Lawyer
Corporate officer
Business owner
Developer
Investment broker
Leader
Astronaut
Activist

#12

Storyteller
Mime
Artist (especially
 fantasy)
Writer (especially
 children's books)
Dancer
Actor
Costume designer
Interior decorator
Teacher

#13	#14	#15 *(not a LifeColor)*
Librarian	Artist	No List
Secretary	Writer	
Receptionist	Musician	
Massage therapist	Designer	
Healer/medicine	Day care worker	
Dental assistant	Animal caretaker	
Artist	Social worker	
Interior decorator		
Florist		
Herb grower		
Physical therapist		

#16	#17	#18
Actor	Lawyer	Writer
Musician	Computer operator	Producer
Singer	Politician	Director
Artist	Physicist	Manager
Comedian	Mediator	Station owner
Performer	Scientist	Performer
Dancer	Government	Business owner
Doctor	personnel	Seminar and workshop
Acupuncturist	Space research &	leader
Psychotherapist	development	Speaker
Physical therapist	personnel	Coordinator
Massage therapist	Public speaker	Publisher
Dentist	News broadcaster	Bank owner or manager
Chiropractor	Journalist	Financial broker
Beautician	Station manager	Stock market investor
Environmentalist	Psychologist	or advisor
	Printer	Corporation president
	Publisher	or owner
	Editor	Entrepreneur
	Writer	Politician
	Land developer	Business consultant
	Investment broker	Real estate agent
	Businessman	Advertising & marketing
	Social agency	
	worker	
	Minister	

#19

Teacher
Psychologist
Minister
Missionary
Musician
Actress
Photographer
Writer
Artist
Travel agent
Tour guide
Director
Foreign language
  interpreter
Speech therapist
Social agency
  director
Volunteer for
  political or
  environmental causes

#20

Writer
Producer
Inventor
Doctor
Pilot
Chiropractor
Entrepreneur
Musician/composer
Jeweler
Car salesperson
Professional
  athlete
Owner/manager of:
  Restaurants
  Sport teams
  Health clubs
  Auto repair garages
  Construction companies
Attorney
Teacher

#21

Accountant
Insurance broker
Banker
Investment consultant
Employee in large
  business firm
Executive
Tax analyst
Civil servant
Governmental & county
  office jobs
Researcher

#22

Architect
Engineer
Draftsman
Designer
Doctor
Dentist
Chef
Medical technician
Pilot
Postal worker
Graphic artist
Mechanic
Technician
Electrician
Musician
Writer

#23

Artist
Dancer
Actor
Aerobics instructor
Hair dresser
Manicurist
Facialist
Florist
Waitress
Ski instructor
Elementary or
  pre-school teacher
Physical therapist
Massage therapist
Art teacher
Writer
Flight attendant

#24

Director for nonprofit
  or service organization
Fundraiser
Personnel director
Career counselor
Hospital administrator
Real estate agent
Office manager
Loan officer
Event coordinator
Store owner
Public relations director
Business consultant

Which category had the types of occupations to which you
are the most drawn? _____

Refer to the key to discover your LifeColor(s). If you were drawn to more than one category, refer to the key to see if there is a consistency in the colors. For example, if you were drawn to the Yellow category and the Blue category, as well as the Blue/Yellow category and the Yellow/Violet category, you are most likely a Blue/Yellow who has added a bit of Violet to the outer bands of your aura. Blue and Yellow seem to be your predominant choices. Refer to your answers in the first part of the questionnaire to see if your responses coincide with your career preferences. Whichever descriptions you feel most aligned with are probably your LifeColors.

(Did you notice any occupation from your past or present which caused you to feel unhappy or unfulfilled? Were you going against your real LifeColors?)

Key to List of Occupations

#1 = Red
#2 = Orange
#3 = Magenta
#4 = Yellow
#5 = Logical Tan
#6 = Environmental Tan
#7 = Sensitive Tan
#8 = Abstract Tan
#9 = Green
#10 = Blue
#11 = Violet
#12 = Lavender
#13 = Crystal
#14 = Indigo
#15 = Red Overlay — no list
#16 = Violet/Yellow
#17 = Violet/Tan
#18 = Violet/Green
#19 = Blue/Violet
#20= Yellow/Green
#21 = Tan/Green
#22 = Tan/Yellow
#23 = Blue/Yellow
#24 = Blue/Green

2. Physical LifeColors

Following are descriptions of all the aura LifeColors, and the most common Combination Colors. I hope that reading these descriptions will help you understand and accept yourself as you are, and also help you learn how you can stay in power and balanced. It is useful to note that many people have covered up one or both of their original LifeColors at a young age because they felt that their true identity was wrong, inadequate or inappropriate. For example, because Yellows are such an energetic handful for their parents, they may subdue their energies and learn to become responsible Tan personalities instead. Violet children often learn to hold back on their incredible power in order to not overwhelm or displease their conventional or quieter parents. Many children are raised to be Tan or Blue personalities because that is traditionally what is expected by society. Consequently, most children with other LifeColors grow up feeling confused, inadequate and disconnected from the personality they really are.

■ RED

Reds are physical and sexual. They love expressing themselves through their sensuality and their physical bodies. They live their lives in the here-and-now with zest, strength, courage and self-confidence. Reds love to live in physical reality, to manipulate their environment. Reality must be tangible to them. They must be able to see, touch, hear, taste and smell it.

Reds are not abstract thinkers. A wall is a wall and there is no need for further discussion or speculation. Reality is literal, not ethereal or complicated. Reds require proof that something exists. It must have a concrete and tangible substance. Reds remind us that we have bodies, that we are matter — flesh and blood. These robust personalities enjoy the physical aspect of life. They don't try to see life as an illusion or try to escape from it into a fantasy world.

Reds do not focus on spirituality. They will go to churches or join other religious organizations not because they understand the esoteric idea of God, but because they enjoy the physical nature of the events. They enjoy the singing, dancing and physical expression involved in the rituals of worship. Reds are the workers with their religion — moving pews, building churches or setting up the booths for the bazaar. They will help take care of the practical needs of the organization.

This personality is most comfortable and alive when strength and stamina are required. They enjoy the challenges of moving physical objects rather than dealing with mental or emotional problems. They are the workers, able to bring the ideas of others into tangible substance by loading and unloading boxes, moving furniture or building houses, for example. They are not afraid of physical labor or hard work. These personalities are practical, realistic, hard working, action-oriented, and they love seeing the immediate results of their work.

Reds can be refreshingly honest or brutally abrupt in their interactions. They can be very blunt and outspoken with their opinions. In power, they are slow to anger. When they do get angry, they get over it quickly and do not hold grudges.

Reds who are out of power, however, have violent tempers. Once their tempers are set off, Reds can become physically dangerous. Out of power, their rage is often released by punching a hole in a wall, starting a fight, or having intense sexual encounters.

When Reds are in power, they find more appropriate outlets for their anger, such as exercise, sports or therapy. When hurt, Reds respond to pain in much the same way that animals do, by withdrawing emotionally and lashing out physically.

Reds have an almost animalistic instinct for survival. They can sense the physical risk factors and potential dangers involved in a situation. They instinctively know what skills and resources it will take to overcome the challenges. Reds are adept at helping people survive such environmental crises as floods, fires and earthquakes. They exhibit raw courage in the face of danger.

In power, Reds are energetic, courageous, full of stamina and endurance, optimistic, loyal, honest, trustworthy and have a lust for life. Out of power, Reds become angry, easily frustrated, physically explosive and potentially dangerous. Reds can become very closed-minded, believing that the only reality is physical and that their way is the best way. They tend to be protective of their own feelings and thoughts, and they are hard to get to know. It is challenging for Reds to create sensitive, long-lasting relationships with others. They are wary of opening up or trusting others and can often be hurtful with their hard, protective shells.

To stay in power, Reds must find acceptable outlets for their energy and their frustrations. They need to learn when to quit and when to be persistent with their efforts. When no amount of physical strength or endurance will keep the raging waters from flooding a town, for example, Reds continue to fight it. They hate giving up. They can be so stubborn about staying on a certain course that they are not always able to see other options. If the town is flooding, a better attitude might be, "Save what you can, then come back and rebuild." Their never-ending energy and stamina can often wear out others who have been enlisted to help. Reds need to learn the difference between being persistent and being stubborn. They would also do well to learn to temper their frankness and allow others to express their beliefs and points of view.

The life purpose of Reds is to live in the physical world with gusto, courage and energy. They choose to experience life, with all it has to offer, through the bodily sensations of touch, taste, smell, sight and sound. They also love to give substance and tangible reality to ideas and plans. Reds understand action. They want to enjoy life as a physical being.

Relationships

While Reds enjoy the companionship of mates, it is challenging for them to relate to and communicate with their mates on an emotional, intimate level. This can become frustrating to any mate who wants to bond emotionally with a Red. While Reds will be very loyal and hard-working providers, they do not always know how to be available on other levels. Reds are very private individuals. They do not share their inner feelings easily. They usually don't even want to be in touch with their feelings. Reds are not known to be deeply introspective. While Reds enjoy being around people at times, they are very guarded and cautious about getting into relationships. They enjoy being rowdy with their drinking buddies, but then they want their solitude. They tend to go back and forth between being loners and needing camaraderie.

It takes a very strong, independent, self-realized person to be able to handle the fiery personality of a Red. This person must be able to withstand the Red's emotional walls as well as his violent and sometimes dangerous temper. Even though a Red will calm down as quickly as he flared up, a mate can soon become wary and suspicious of his unpredictable outbursts. The Red's personality tends to be very compelling, forceful and potent. Some people enjoy the dynamic energy, strength and invincible power of Reds. They also love the challenge, the drama and the excitement that the unpredictable Reds add to their lives. Most Reds are hard working, down-to-earth realists who offer an honest, practical lifestyle to their mates. Sometimes, however, living with Reds can be compared to running with the bulls.

Sex

Sex for Reds is a lusty, sensual experience. Sexuality is an indispensable part of life for these robust personalities. They consider sex to be one of the animalistic pleasures of life, one of the joys of being in a physical body. Life is to be fully enjoyed with passion, zest and a full appreciation of the physical sensations it has to offer. Sex is one of life's greatest pleasures for Reds. It ranks right up there with hedonistically devouring every imaginable culinary delight at a Roman feast or delicately savoring the very best of fine wines. They relish the sensual experiences of taste, smell and touch.

Sex does not, however, always involve love and compassion for Reds. It is usually about lust, passion and the physicality of being "animal." To Reds, sex is not something that should be taboo. It is a natural, enjoyable bodily experience that should be savored. Reds have a difficult time being members of any society or organization that restricts or denounces sexual activity. Being a member of such a society would eventually cause the Reds anxiety and guilt and make them feel that there was something intrinsically wrong with them. Reds need to feel free to completely experience their sexuality.

Red Parents

Although they are honest, hard workers who will provide for their children, Red parents are not usually emotionally available to them. Reds are not comfortable with their own emotions or with discussing their feelings with their children. It is difficult for them to outwardly share intimate tender moments. Tossing the football around or doing yard work together is their idea of bonding with their children.

Most children can be intimidated by the physical power and explosive temper of their Red parents. The children commonly respond with either respect or fear, or they feel rejected and unloved, depending on their own aura color. This is not to say that Reds are not loving parents. They are very protective and concerned about their children. They just have a hard time communicating or expressing their emotions. What Red parents do offer and teach to their children is an understanding of honesty, the American work ethic and the belief that life is what you make it.

Red Children

Red children are often a handful for parents. While they can be hard workers and are willing to complete a job, they can also be incredibly stubborn and have violent tempers, which can frustrate and upset parents. Red children are most likely the ones who will start fights at school. They understand physical force and brute strength. While they don't want to be leaders, they also don't want to be pushed around. Reds have very independent and strong personalities.

At school, Red children prefer learning about subjects which they can apply to their lives here and now. Auto mechanics, woodshop, cooking and sewing classes are much more interesting to them than a philosophy class. If the class has no practical application to their lives, they find no meaning in it. They are honest workers, as long as they see the practicality in what they are doing.

Red children need to be shown appreciation and recognition for what they have accomplished. Even though *every* child needs and appreciates love, affection, hugs and praise, Red children are embarrassed by an open display of affection. They prefer receiving tangible rewards, such as toys, candy or other gifts. They love to see the immediate results of their hard-earned efforts. Delayed gratification is frustrating and soon intolerable to Red children. If their reward is being able to go to Disneyland, they must go now, not in a month from now. Otherwise, they do not understand the connection between the action and the reward.

The challenge for parents of Red children is to help them find healthy outlets for their frustration, anger and inexhaustible energy. They must also help the Reds understand and learn to express their inner feelings in a sensitive and constructive manner. Teaching a Red child to communicate by having frequent, calm and non-threatening discussions with him about his feelings will help him learn other methods of communicating.

Problem-Solving

The Reds' method of problem-solving is action-oriented — action with power and positive expectations. Reds do not like to sit around and theorize. They leave that job to others. Although they can be very intelligent, they would rather just put the plan into action to see if it works. Reds prefer to work with physical problems as opposed to mental ones. For instance, if the piano doesn't fit through the door, Reds either move it through an open window, widen the door or disassemble the piano. They don't sit around for hours discussing the options. Reds often arrive at solutions by instinct, persistence or pure brute strength.

When in power, Reds have the optimistic outlook that every problem has a solution. They will stick with the problem, trying every possible method to move the piano out of the room. Reds usually find an option that works. They persist even after everyone else has concluded that the situation is hopeless. Reds also have the physical strength and stamina to push the rock up the mountain, enduring beyond everyone else's point of exhaustion. Reds do not like to let their physical environment get the best of them. They can inspire others through their sheer optimism and willingness to continue.

Out of power, Reds can become angry and frustrated. Others can find their never-ending need to persist and conquer intolerable. Reds can wear out their teammates, and in the process accuse them of being weak and useless. The Red's need for conquering the opponent, overcoming the problem, and for victory at any cost can soon alienate him from those who are there to aid and support him in the endeavor.

When solving problems, Reds need to maintain a realistic perspective of the actual importance of the project. While they can usually come up with practical solutions for physical problems, they also need to see that not every problem is best solved on a physical level. Using force, hitting someone or going to war are not always the answers, not even temporarily. (Due to their great courage and dedication, however, Reds can be dauntless heroes during a war.)

Quite often, Reds focus on fixing the symptom rather than the cause. They do not like planning, strategizing or negotiating. They prefer taking action. Just tell them what has to be done and they'll see that it gets done.

Money

Reds do not strive to be rich. Money is not important to them. As long as their basic needs are met and they have some creature comforts, they are content. Reds do like to have nice things — nice clothes, comfortable furniture, quality tools and quality appliances. Their lives, however, are not ruled by material possessions. Reds don't usually worry about money because they know they are self-sufficient. They can always find jobs that can make them enough money to survive. They see money as a real and tangible necessity, but not as something that rules their lives.

Success

Success for Reds is measured tangibly. They look for immediate and concrete results from their labor. They love being able to take action and to bring a plan or idea into physical manifestation. Success is having the courage, energy and stamina to be able to overcome or manipulate their environment.

Occupations

Reds prefer jobs that require physical work, allow them manual dexterity and have immediate tangible results. Reds do not want to wait for something to happen. They want to feel that they have control over the outcome. Reds prefer to be self-employed. This allows them control over their own time and energy. They want jobs where they can see that they have accomplished something physical, real and tangible.

Because they are so powerful and rugged, Reds have a great respect for the power and magnificence of nature, and they often appreciate being able to work outdoors. These personalities enjoy physical strength, stamina and manipulating their physical environment. They also enjoy the challenge of being courageous in dangerous situations.

Reds are frequently drawn to occupations such as:

Firefighter	Repairperson
Rescue worker	Mechanic
Police	Furniture mover
Military personnel	Shop foreman
Football player	Tractor driver and farmer
Boxer	Surgeon
Bodyguard	Bartender
Truck driver	Waitress
Heavy equipment	Butcher
operator	Dancer
Construction worker	

Occasionally, Reds like the singer Madonna show up in the entertainment field.

Health

Health problems for Reds are often work-related. They may suffer from hernias or back aches from lifting too much, cut fingers from a butcher's knife or power saw, burns from a fire, or bullet wounds from an escaping suspect's gun.

To stay physically healthy, Reds need to learn when enough is enough, when not to push things too far. They need to gauge their exuberance when accomplishing a task. They also need to moderate their physical appetites. Because Reds love sensual, animal pleasures, they can tend to love food too much.

■ ORANGE

Oranges are the thrill-seekers and daredevils of the aura spectrum. They love the challenge and excitement of physical danger. They love to challenge their environment and go beyond any accepted physical limits. Oranges put their lives on the line just to feel alive; the stakes must actually be life and death for Oranges to feel a sense of accomplishment and satisfaction. They love the adrenaline rush of excitement in the face of danger. For Oranges, thrills and excitement are the aspects which are essential in life. Everything else is just passive existence. Evil Knievel is a well-known example of an Orange.

Oranges are realists, preferring to challenge and conquer physical reality rather than intellectually discussing abstract philosophies. To these adventurers, life is real and tangible. Spirituality has no meaning to them. They don't want to be bothered by such concepts.

Oranges love to imagine and plan the strategy for the next adventure and then put it into action. They don't like safety devices, however. For Oranges, the greater the risk, the better. They love to "boldly go where no man has gone before." They will plan and review all aspects of the feat until they feel comfortable with it and then proceed to take it to the next dangerous level. Oranges are very good at seeing things through the eyes of their opponent. They strategize what the other driver will do or how the wild prey will react. They plan their actions accordingly. Oranges mentally, physically and emotionally process what it will take to overcome all the elements involved. Their comprehensive mental preparation and planning stages are responsible for their actual survival.

In power, Oranges are incredibly resourceful, with amazing abilities to mentally become their opponents, to calculate every possible maneuver and to boldly take action. In power, Oranges live life at its rawest level, with energy and self-confidence. They awe others with their courage and daring. They are bold enough to go after challenges and live their dreams — even in the face of potential death. Oranges can be found fearlessly risking their lives to save others. They have performed acts of great heroism — firefighters saving people from burning buildings, rescue workers scaling treacherous mountains, police risking their lives to free hostages. Most Oranges do not consider these to be heroic acts. They consider them to be just part of their jobs.

Out of power, Oranges can become very egotistical and self-centered, caring only to live in their own world, regardless of how it affects their families. They do not show affection, caring or compassion easily. Emotional, gentle characteristics do not make much sense to them. Consequently, they can tend to be cold and aloof. Oranges have problems facing the challenge of "knowing themselves," of going inside and learning who they are emotionally, mentally and spiritually. The only risks they appear to be willing to face are those that require physical courage and cunning.

For Oranges to stay in power, they need to realize that life involves balance — a balance of the body, mind and spirit. By staying balanced, risking the challenge of exploring the inner world as well as the outer, Oranges can develop the ability to experience life on all levels. In this way, they may live long enough to attain the wisdom that comes with mature age.

The life purpose of Oranges is to experience physical existence to its fullest extent, to reach the apparent limitations of reality and dare to push past them. What is important to Oranges is the freedom to explore new territories, to face all the elements — man versus nature — and emerge victorious. Oranges do not want to be limited by anyone or anything. They want to challenge life face to face, with daring and courage. They desire to develop physical and mental cunning and the ability to challenge and overcome any physical risks.

Relationships

Oranges are not usually interested in family or marriage. It is challenging for a mate to accept the exploits of the daring Oranges. Most mates would watch helplessly as the Oranges prepared and packed up their gear. The uncertainty of the outcome — never knowing if they would see them again — is usually more than most people could handle. The stress factor involved would be enough to cause the relationship to fail.

Oranges are loners. They are not usually found in relationships at all. Oranges are too interested in their own adventures to be able to commit to the stability of a relationship. Having to be accountable to another feels too restraining to Oranges. They tend to be self-centered in relationships. Facing life threatening risks is for self-satisfaction. They take a challenge to prove something to themselves, not to others. Nor are they willing to put aside their desire for adventure merely to calm the fears or insecurities of loved ones. Living in suburbia with a spouse, children and a nine-to-five job is a slow, torturous death to an Orange.

Being loners, Oranges do not usually need or want emotional bonding with others. Life to them has an almost raw, primitive, animalistic quality to it. Oranges do not relate to sensitivity, compassion and tenderness. Courage, boldness and daring are the aspects which arouse them. They respond to the more primitive level of survival. Surviving their adventures creates more passion and excitement for them than relationships. Accomplishing, succeeding and surviving physical reality is what life is all about.

Because of their physical prowess and skills, Oranges are usually physically fit and trim — features which are attractive to the opposite sex. Oranges do not have problems drawing in partners, just in maintaining and sustaining lasting relationships. To maintain a relationship, an Orange needs to find a mate who is independent, resourceful and emotionally strong enough to handle the Orange's behavior. Perhaps the Orange can find someone who is courageous and daring enough to share in his adventures. However, the mate must respect the Orange's fierce independence and lack of emotional sensitivity.

Sex

Their only goal being the thrill and excitement of their next exploit, sex is not a priority to Oranges. They often use others sexually, then cast them aside or forget about them when it's time to start planning the next trip or adventure. Their attitude is that sex is fun, a nice release, a natural body function, but that real life is out there waiting to be experienced and conquered.

Orange Parents

Oranges are not usually found with children. Children are too cumbersome and restrictive for them. If these independent personalities end up with children, they usually leave the responsibility of raising the children to their mates, causing their mates to become quite resentful of the Oranges' behavior and attitude. Being the risk-takers that they are, Oranges often do not set very good examples for their children. They also tend not to bond affectionately, communicate well or relate emotionally with their children. Oranges are not usually concerned with providing a good standard of living or education for their children.

Orange Children

Even as children, Oranges are adventurers. They will dive from the high board, climb to the tops of trees or jump from roofs. Cuts and bruises do not bother these kids. They enjoy exploring and challenging their environment. Oranges are a handful for their parents, who are concerned for their physical safety. These children are constantly looking for the thrill of the next adventure.

Orange children become quite bored with school. They do not relate to the passive, intellectual, non-physical attributes of school. They are daredevils, and can create discipline problems. They are usually alienated from their peers. Most other students will not take the dangerous risks that Oranges will. Oranges would rather be racing motorcycles down steep mountains or rafting through treacherous rapids.

The challenge for parents of Orange children is to give them the freedom to explore their world without getting ulcers in the process. Since Oranges are determined to live life on the edge, parents can help them learn how to calculate the risks and successfully plan strategies. This is the Oranges' best tool for surviving their exploits. If they can learn to think clearly under the pressure of life-threatening situations, they have a chance of living longer, fuller lives.

Problem-Solving

When problem-solving, Oranges examine all the factors, calculate the risks, go over in their heads all the possible scenarios, make sure they have all the necessary equipment, remove all safety devices to make the challenge as physically exciting and life-threatening as possible, and then they take action. Oranges prefer to work on physical challenges. They see life as a contest. They leave the more mundane challenges and questions of day-to-day living to others. While Oranges are meticulous in their planning and their problem-solving when it comes to potential life and death situations, other types of problem-solving do not interest them.

Money

Because Oranges are such daredevils, they seem to sense that they will probably have a short lifespan, and tend to be irresponsible with money. They look upon money as the tool that affords and allows them to obtain all the necessary products, equipment and instruments for their journeys. Quality is very important to Oranges, so when they go mountain-climbing they take the best equipment money can buy. Money facilitates their adventures. Oranges are not interested in financial security or long-range planning. Most of them do not live long enough to enjoy any retirement benefits. They tend to live more for short term thrills. Working just for the sake of money is far too passive for them.

Success

Oranges succeed every time they overcome the challenge they set up for themselves and survive to tell about it. Success is clearly and simply defined: reaching the top of the mountain, carrying off the stunt as planned, winning the race, getting through the fire unscathed and still alive.

Occupations

Oranges prefer to freelance, getting paid for what they enjoy doing and then having the personal freedom to move on to the next adventure. They do not choose the burdensome responsibility of having employees or being in charge. They also have no desire for administrative duties. Office jobs are too slow, cumbersome and tedious for them. These adventurers like to be as autonomous and free as possible. Being sponsored by a company to race cars, dive for hidden treasure or do promotional stunts out of an airplane are the types of jobs Oranges relish. They prefer to compete individually, rather than with a team. This is the only way their skills can truly be tested. Consequently they do not make great employees or team members. The occupations to which they are drawn include:

Race car driver	Rescue worker
Skydiver	Firefighter
Hang-glider	Police or detective work
Wilderness guide	Deep sea diver
River rafter	Bounty hunter
Wild safari hunter	Private investigator
Stuntman	Guard
Mountaineer	Lion-tamer
Explorer	Trapeze artist

Health

Oranges seem to suffer more from cuts, bruises, scrapes and broken bones than from mental, stress-oriented problems such as ulcers. An Orange's biggest health challenge is staying alive long enough to eventually have the physical problems related to old age. To stay healthy, Oranges only need to consider carefully all aspects of their exploits and plan their feats very thoroughly.

In times past, when raw physical courage and strength were more required, there were more physical colors — specifically more Reds and Oranges — on the planet. Now, however, since humanity seems to have mastered the more *basic* levels of physical survival, mental and emotional colors seem to be more prevalent on the planet.

■ MAGENTA

Magentas are the nonconformists in the aura spectrum. They see life from a different and unusual perspective. They don't choose to abide by society's mores, expectations or standards. These individualistic thinkers consider "following the crowd" to be boring and restrictive. They prefer to live beyond restrictions and limitations. Peer pressure has no effect on them. They follow the beat of their own drummers.

Magentas are very intelligent. They are also innovative and creative, fascinated by the latest gadgets and inventions. Often inventors themselves, Magentas love to figure out new ways of doing things. They enjoy creating bizarre, outrageous and controversial objects which are arty, trendy or even beyond trendy. Their imagination knows no limits. They do, however, deal with the tangibles on the planet. They like taking physical substance and stretching it into new forms which go beyond what people consider "normal." Their art is unique and outlandish — Andy Warhol is a good example of a Magenta.

In power, Magentas have the willingness and the courage to set their own styles. They love change, to go beyond the traditional and the familiar. They love to shock people, to shake them from their ordinary, humdrum existence. For example, Magentas will walk down the street donning purple mohawks and wild clothes. Other people don't usually have the nerve or the desire to live the lifestyle of a Magenta. Magentas act on unusual ideas, trying new things just for the experience.

Because of their outrageous behavior, Magentas prefer to live in large, crowded cities where they don't stand out as much and aren't pressured to conform. These free spirits aren't usually concerned about what others think, but in large cities they are more apt to have the freedom to express themselves.

Spirituality for Magentas is not some philosophical concept or cosmic energy in the sky. Spirituality is more connected with nature. Magentas become more balanced, centered and spiritual when taking walks in nature rather than sitting in a rigid church pew.

These liberal personalities do not usually join groups or organizations. They do not want to be confined or limited by any organization's rules or expectations. These independent souls are not ones for structure. Magentas are not followers, nor do they want the responsibility of being leaders. They set their own pace, create fun for themselves and others and then go their own way. They only lead the way by creating a hole in the wall of accepted limitations and boundaries. By stepping beyond these boundaries, they encourage others to go beyond their self-imposed restrictions as well.

Laughter and the absurd appeal to Magentas. Their strange sense of humor can be interpreted by others as being twisted and eccentric. They are also very outspoken. Magentas love being the center of attention. They love entertaining people, acting, performing and creating outrageous trends. Liking all types of people, they can be comfortable with anyone and they meet people quite easily. Their assortment of friends can be as wild and eclectic as their taste in clothes or home decorating — and the more outrageous, the better. They can have trouble, however, keeping close, intimate friends. They don't like being responsible for or tied down by friends. They prefer their relationships to be fun, free and easy. Being emotionally responsible for anyone is too confining for them.

Although they like people, they are usually loners because most people can't relate to their outrageous way of thinking. While people can be amused and entertained for a while by these free thinkers, most of them eventually become embarrassed by the Magentas' bizarre behavior. The Magentas' biggest challenge is dealing with the loneliness of being misunderstood and socially unaccepted.

Magentas are free spirits. They love to travel, talk with people, explore different cultures and experience life to its fullest. They are always thinking of something new and different to do. However, they will only invest their time in those things which they find interesting.

Since Magentas are not interested in discipline and order, their lives can become very disorganized and confused. They can have trouble remembering to pay the bills — even when they have enough money to do so.

In power, Magentas are creative, self-accepting, self-appreciating and allow others to be themselves. They are generally happy and optimistic, and they prefer to look at life with a sense of humor. These unique personalities tend to be strong-willed and determined to live life exactly the way they want to.

Out of power, Magentas can feel despondent, isolated and lonely. Conforming to the crowd is unbearable to them and can cause severe depression. Yet having friends is usually dependent upon their conforming to a certain degree. When they are out of power, Magentas don't live true to their own curious, innovative style. This creates low self-esteem, boredom and despair. They lose their desire to experience life. Life then seems like a burden or a punishment to the Magentas instead of the joyful experience they know it can be.

To stay in power, Magentas have to love and accept themselves, give themselves permission to be different, see life from their own unusual perspective and allow themselves to act on their creative impulses.

The life purpose of Magentas is to explore the new and to experiment outside of normal, everyday boundaries. They strive to keep life from becoming staid, complacent and common. Magentas love to keep us questioning and pushing beyond our accepted limits, to keep us from being satisfied with the status quo.

Relationships

Magentas like to be around people who have fun and are interested in life. They don't want to be serious or intense for long periods of time. They will eagerly learn about people, laugh, have fun with them and move on. Frequent and short marriages are common for Magentas. They believe in commitment because it is the best way to really get intimate with someone, to *really* learn all about them. Long-term, intense relationships, however, are too much for Magentas. When the relationship turns into a responsibility, they will move on. They only stay married long enough to get to know their mate intimately, to share worlds for a while. Even before the wedding, a Magenta's partner should be well aware that the marriage will probably be temporary.

Magentas also prefer an open marriage. They want the freedom to explore and experiment. They don't want to live with any rules or expectations. After a while, this wears on their partners. Magentas are fun, surprising, quick, and energetic, but after a while, their different way of living becomes tiring for their mates.

Magentas are kind enough not to hurt anyone when they leave. They usually remain very good friends with their mates. Their exits are made with tact and grace.

Sex

For Magentas, sex is a different adventure with each person. It can be an experiment with styles or an experience in getting to know the other person. As long as it doesn't lead to an intense or serious involvement which requires rules or limitations, sex is enjoyable to them. As long as the sex is always different, exciting, fun and unpredictable, Magentas will stay sexually involved with their partners. Magentas, however, are not usually sexually monogamous. Monogamy takes the variety out of life.

Magenta Parents

Magenta parents enjoy the refreshing, clear and unlimited perspectives of children. It is fascinating for Magentas to be around children, to see how they participate in life. But Magentas do not usually cope well with the responsibility of raising children. They are not usually able to provide a stable or secure environment for them. Having no rules or boundaries can be wonderfully freeing and uninhibiting for children, but it can also create chaos and confusion for them, especially once they enter into a more controlled environment such as school. As caring as they are, Magenta parents are more like fun-loving, creative, but rebellious children themselves who would suffocate under the weight of parental responsibilities. Magenta parents can, however, encourage a child to explore his own imagination and creative talents.

Magenta Children

There is not much difference between the child and the adult Magenta. The only difference is that the adults can often have more freedom to express their creative, adventurous side. Magenta children usually have to abide by school rules or parental expectations. This can stifle, frustrate and even inhibit them. Although Magenta children are bright and curious, they only stay interested and involved in the classes they like. When a subject doesn't interest the Magentas, they will look for diversions — especially ones which involve entertaining the rest of the class. School officials consider Magentas "behavior problems" because they don't want to live within rules. Magenta children — like the adults — are bright, innovative, and often social outcasts.

For parents of Magenta children, the challenge is to find suitable and acceptable outlets for them to express their unique, creative talents. Classes such as art, drama, speech or woodshop often provide a more flexible vehicle for Magentas to explore their remarkable styles. While Magenta children can be very independent, they also have short attention spans, so they often need an extraordinary amount of supervision to help them complete projects. Often, the children need to be placed in special classes where they can receive more individual attention. A more unusual or avant-garde approach to education, as opposed to the traditional classroom setting and style of teaching, will keep Magentas more interested. They learn best when they are allowed to be creative with their assignments. Magentas are very bright — bright enough to conceive innovative ideas and approaches to assignments. Their unusual way of thinking originates from a sense of fun and adventure, not from anger or rebellion. They are not malicious people. Hopefully, the educational system will eventually discover that all children do not learn through the same processes, and the system will be readjusted to include meeting the needs of Magenta children.

Problem-Solving

Problem-solving for Magentas is often innovative and outrageous. They can tackle situations from a unique perspective, one which can also seem unrealistic or impractical to others. Typically, Magentas surprise people by actualizing their zany ideas into physical reality. Out of power, Magentas can be so depressed, confused and lost that they have no interest or energy to deal with problems. Magentas can usually be encouraged back to life by someone who reminds them through humor of the absurdity of life.

Money

Magentas can be practical about earning money. They know they need it to pay the bills, though they don't want to be run by it, or work just because society says they must. Magentas prefer to live life in the here and now, not put it off until after they retire. Consequently, Magentas like to work at jobs that pay large sums of money. Then they will quit the job, take the money they have earned, and go on an extended vacation. They will take another job only after they have run out of money.

Magentas always seem to be able to do something to make the money they need. They buy the necessities and play with the rest. They love to buy the unusual. Money allows them to try new things, but it is not essential, because Magentas will always find a way to do what they want.

Success

Magentas judge their success by how much freedom of expression they have, how much joy they are experiencing, and how far they can go beyond society's standards and limits.

Occupations

Occupations to which Magentas are drawn are ones which give them freedom to express themselves and to develop new ideas or products. They prefer to work in unusual situations. They don't like the traditional nine-to-five schedules. Instead, they prefer to work in jobs which make them a lot of money quickly so they can quit and travel. Magentas love to live on the creative edge. They prefer to work on projects that allow them to explore, to be innovative and creative. They are good at imagining something, then producing the physical form.

Magentas have short attention spans, however, so they don't always complete projects. They grow bored and lose interest quickly. They are not always dependable employees. They enjoy jobs that are flexible, inventive, artistic or creative. Magentas are good writers and persuasive sales people. Writing a script for a Monty Python movie would appeal to Magentas, as would selling unusual or creative items. Being an artist, writer, performer, salesperson, photographer or the publisher of an avant-garde magazine would be a good career for a Magenta. Any job that allows them the freedom and ability to be inventive and creative will appeal to Magentas.

Artist	Costume designer
Clown	Photographer
Comedian	Publisher of avant-garde
Actor	publications
Writer	Entrepreneur
Inventor	Salesperson (especially
Set designer	for unusual items)
Art dealer or collector	

Health

Magentas do not have any specific areas that commonly cause them problems, although their unusual, erratic lifestyles and bizarre eating habits can eventually affect their physical bodies. Lack of sleep from attending all night social events or digesting a full dinner at 3:00 a.m. can stress or shock their bodies, causing them to burn out eventually. Because modifying their activities or eating on a "regular" schedule does not appeal to Magentas, they often let their bodies just wear out from abuse.

■ YELLOW

Yellows are the most childlike personalities in the aura spectrum. These playful characters have a great sense of humor. They love to laugh and to make others laugh. Yellows believe life is meant to be enjoyed. They do not like to take life seriously, nor do they like to work. Their work must be play for them. Yellows advocate relaxing, keeping life light and having fun. They like to live life spontaneously. Yellows are wonderful, sensitive, joyful beings, whose life purpose is to help lighten up and heal the energy on the planet. They remind people to not take themselves or their problems too seriously.

These fun-loving, childlike personalities like to please. They want to be liked by everyone. They enjoy giving gifts such as flowers and candy. Yellows are everybody's friends; they are some of the most considerate people on the planet. Being so sensitive, however, they are also easily hurt. The Yellows' feelings are fragile, causing them to cry easily.

Yellows tend to be shy with people they do not know. Once they are in familiar surroundings with people they know, however, they can become the life of the party. People find themselves drawn to Yellows because they feel lighter and happier around them. Yellows like being around people, but they also need time to be alone.

Yellows in their power have abundant energy, as if it is flowing from an unlimited source. With all of this energy flowing through their bodies, Yellows have a hard time sitting still. While they are listening to someone, they will tap their feet, fidget or squirm. This is one of the most recognizable traits of Yellows. It is imperative for them to stay physically active on a regular basis in order to be happy, healthy and centered. "Long-muscle" exercises such as bicycling, swimming, volleyball, tennis, surfing and dancing are great activities for Yellows. Otherwise, the intense, bottled-up energy will create an inner battle, causing the Yellows to become exhausted and, eventually, ill.

When in their power, Yellows like to keep their bodies fit. They can be frequently found doing such things as lifting weights and eating healthy food. Yellows tend to take a lot of risks when they are young, but as they grow older, they tend to avoid physical activities that are risky or dangerous, because of a basic fear of pain. It is especially important for Yellows to release energy through their physical bodies when they are upset, frustrated or angry. When Yellows stay active and fit, they are filled with joy, happiness, a zest for life, and are better able to deal with life.

Southern California is well-known for its Yellows. They love playing outdoors, exercising and eating healthy foods. Many out-of-power Yellows, on the other hand, have gained a reputation for centering their lives on addictions such as sex, drugs and parties.

Yellows are also very creative. (They can even be creative with their excuses as to why they are late. Being late is common for out-of-power Yellows.) While they can be artistic, Yellows can often be insecure about their creative abilities. Yellows especially love to work with their hands — painting, sculpturing, building, fixing appliances or working on cars. (Since Yellows procrastinate, however, the cars they took apart may take months to put back together.) Yellows can also be creative writers. Both physical and creative projects are therapeutic for Yellows.

Dogs are very drawn to Yellows. These childlike Yellows are the perfect, fun-loving playmates for dogs and they often become best friends.

These sensitive, intuitive Yellows can sense when someone is troubled, though they do not like dealing with conflict or problems. If, for example, a Yellow's girlfriend is upset, the Yellow will first attempt to cheer her up. If it is impossible to cheer her up, his next impulse is to run away. He would prefer to help her by physically fixing something for her — her car, her health or her kitchen sink. Yellows do not enjoy becoming involved with heavy, intense emotional problems.

Yellows are also very intuitive through touch. This quality makes them great with massage and healing. When

Yellows give a massage, they instinctively find the areas that need healing. Yellows have the ability to channel energy through their bodies, making them natural healers. When a person receives a hug from a Yellow, she can feel energy coming from the Yellow's body and instantly she feels better.

The fun-loving Yellows have very addictive personalities. The positive addictions for Yellows include exercise, sports and creativity. If Yellows focus on the positive addictions, they remain full of life, joy, energy and creativity. The negative addictions for Yellows include drugs, alcohol, cigarettes, caffeine, sweets (especially chocolate) or overeating. If Yellows indulge in negative addictions, they first become high and full of energy, but then they hit bottom. They lose energy and become depressed, lethargic, apathetic and confused. Yellows' bodies are so sensitive that they will experience the effects of these negative substances for a long time.

It is difficult to convince Yellows to stay away from negative addictions because they enjoy the substances and they do not like being told what to do. If someone tells a Yellow what to do, she will likely do the opposite. They are natural rebels. It has to be their choice. Usually, if Yellows recognize that the consequences of the negative addictions are a loss of energy, joy and creativity, they will choose the positive addictions instead. Yellows are not very self-disciplined, however, so it can be difficult for them to refrain from the negative addictions once they have become involved with them. If Yellows can stay physically active on a regular basis, and maintain their sense of humor, they will naturally tend to veer away from the negative addictions.

Yellows often have a fear of commitment. In their eyes, commitment may take away choices or options; it means they will have to grow up and accept responsibilities. They have a hard time committing to one person or to one career.

Yellows prefer choices and freedom, rather than restrictive responsibilities. While Yellows appreciate being loved, love can also frighten them. Love often involves responsibility. Yellows prefer to be liked. Yellows are the ultimate Peter Pans, actually having a fear of growing up and growing old! Usually, Yellows even look younger than their actual age. Unless they become involved in negative addictions, or there are people making stressful or unreasonable demands on them, they will stay young looking throughout their lives.

The tendency to avoid commitment and hard work often earns Yellows the reputation of being irresponsible and lazy. People with other LifeColors, while enjoying the playfulness of Yellows, can become quite frustrated and judgmental of their easygoing attitude. (See the chapters on relationships with Yellows.)

Yellows need to understand that commitment can help them reach deeper levels of intimacy and self-awareness, and therefore actually add more fun, excitement, and freedom to their lives. Otherwise, Yellows can drift aimlessly, confused and penniless, forever searching for something to bring them joy.

Relationships

In relationships, Yellows can be very sensitive and caring with their mates. Being considerate and wanting to please, it is painful for them to feel they have caused anyone unhappiness, especially those they love. Yellows can have an idealistic picture of what relationships can be. They want playmates who can laugh with them, take care of them (without "over-mothering" them) and, at the same time, not take away their freedom. Yellows still need their time alone.

Yellows like to flirt, but become nervous if the other person wants to explore further than the flirtation. Because they like the excitement of catching someone's attention but don't like to be trapped, Yellows have a tendency to play games. If one chases after a Yellow and comes on too strong, the Yellow will run away. If, however, one then backs away or seems disinterested, the Yellow will come back around to see if that person still likes him. He will be cute, entertaining and bring gifts to assure the person's affection. Once he has accomplished that, he is out the door again.

Often Yellows truly believe they want committed relationships. However, they should look at their patterns to see if they are facing the truth. Fear of commitment can also take the form of desiring mates who are unavailable, unattainable or who have a similar fear of commitment. This type of mate is "safe" for Yellows. To prevent Yellows from playing games, their partners must learn to stand firmly committed to these relationships, and not to react to the Yellows' habitual tendencies to back away. Once Yellows truly fall in love, they are loving, faithful and committed. They will do everything in their power to assure that their mates are happy.

If Yellows are in restrictive or domineering relationships and feel that they are trapped, because of children or other commitments, they can become unhappy and depressed. At this point, the suppressed Yellows will either close down, lose their energy and give up on their lives, or they will develop subversive and rebellious behavior toward their mates. (See Chapter 5 to see the conflict regarding relationships that can arise with Blue/Yellow, Yellow/Violet, Yellow/Green and Yellow/Tan LifeColors.)

Sex

Yellows are very sexual. Their love-making can be very playful. They like to laugh, have fun and make jokes about sex. At the same time, they can also be very sensitive and considerate with their mates. Sex is both a pleasure and a physical release for Yellows. It is at the point of orgasm that they feel a connection with the universe and that the world is beautiful. It is challenging for Yellows to commit to one sexual partner. Monogamy takes away their choices and options. However, once Yellows really fall in love, they are as faithful as puppy dogs. (They also have a fear of being caught or hurting someone's feelings should they stray.)

Yellow Parents

Yellows love to play with children, but they do not necessarily want the responsibilities of raising children. Getting up at 2:00 a.m. to change diapers or feed a baby is not their idea of a good time. Yellows are such children themselves that a woman married to a Yellow man will often complain of having three children, rather than two children and a husband. Children love to be around Yellows because they can be great playmates. Since Yellow parents are more like children themselves, they do not usually want to be disciplinarians with their children. They want to be liked as friends.

If Yellows are in their power, they are great with their children, and can become very attached to them. They find creative ways to teach their children about life.

Out of power, Yellows tend not to be good examples to their children. They tend to be lazy, and often abandon their responsibilities. Sometimes, Yellows out of their power can even become physically abusive parents or develop drug and alcohol problems. When Yellows are upset or frustrated, they tend to react physically. Alcohol and drugs can intensify that reactive behavior.

Yellow Children

Yellow children can either be painfully shy and insecure or they can be exactly the opposite. When shy Yellows are around people they do not know, they run away, hide or quietly withdraw. They seem to be intimidated by people or afraid of not being liked. When the more secure Yellows feel comfortable and familiar with those around them, they become charming little entertainers. Some Yellow children often cause trouble at school by being the "class clowns." They love to make their friends laugh.

Yellow children are very active and curious. Physically, they are constantly on the move, getting up and down and into everything. Because of their physical energy and short attention spans, they have a difficult time sitting still for long periods of time. They fidget, squirm and entertain their classmates. During the long hours of school, it is beneficial to have Yellow children draw, sketch or work creatively with their hands while the teacher is talking. Otherwise, it is difficult for Yellows to sit still and pay attention; their minds wander. As long as there is some form of movement for the children, they can concentrate. (This also applies to Yellow adults.) The physical discipline of Tai Chi is an excellent form of meditation for Yellows because it involves slow movement. Since movement is so meditative for Yellows, they also tend to calm down and develop creative ideas when they are riding in cars. If the ride is too long or restrictive, however, they become restless. Any type of movement relaxes Yellows and allows them to concentrate.

Parents will want to encourage the creativity of Yellow children by supplying them with crayons, paper, building blocks or musical instruments. Directing their physical energy into sports, dance or other positive outlets is also important to their well-being. In addition, parents can enjoy, rather than discourage, the Yellows' ability to make others laugh. Yellow children want to know they are bringing joy to other people.

Yellow children are very sensitive and want to please their parents. Typically, the parents discover that the form of discipline that Yellow children most quickly respond to is physical punishment. Physical contact gets their attention very quickly. This type of punishment, however, can also be very damaging to them. It can be disturbing when a parent realizes how easy it is to rely on physical discipline with their Yellow children. Learning to give the children choices and following up with natural consequences is a much healthier way to discipline Yellow children.

It is not advisable for parents to force Yellow children to sit still, grow up, or to be more serious. Yellows' priorities are to play, have fun, be creative and/or heal people. Forcing goals, standards or priorities upon Yellows will hurt their feelings. They will close down, become depressed and not believe in their own worth. The sensitive Yellows are insecure and afraid people will not like them. Reassuring Yellow children that they are liked and that they bring joy to people helps them open up and live their full potential. It helps them believe in themselves.

Although Yellow children like to please people, they also hate to be told what to do. Parents will frequently hear the word "no" from Yellow children. They can become extremely rebellious. (The "terrible twos" are merely a warm-up for the Yellows' adolescence.) If parents tell Yellow children to clean their room, that is the last thing they will do. They will get better results by giving these children several choices, and explaining the consequences that will follow each choice. For example, when asking a Yellow child to clean her room, the parent can allow her to pick up her toys, make her bed, or put away her clothes first. The choice belongs to the child. Should she choose none of the options, she must also know the consequences of that choice. Parents must learn to follow through with the consequences if they expect a child to learn about making responsible choices.

Yellow children are so sensitive that if their parents argue, they will be the first to sense the unhappiness and try to make everyone happy again. If they feel they cannot improve the situation, they will withdraw and hide, or develop nervous and erratic behavior.

All Yellows need to release anger and frustration physically. This is as true for adults as for children. When Yellows are upset, they want to hit, punch, kick or break something. Parents should encourage Yellow children to release energy positively; to run, swim, ride a bicycle or hit a punching bag. If parents stifle the Yellow child's need to release energy physically, these Yellows will eventually become depressed or self-destructive, turning the energy in on themselves. Yellows can typically turn to drugs or alcohol to numb pain or to avoid problems.

Problem-Solving

When in their power, Yellows are creative problem-solvers. They can create unique, new and innovative solutions. Their solutions are usually designed to make life easier. (It was probably a Yellow who first created the idea of remote control for television.) Yellows would also enjoy reading books with such titles as *A Lazy Man's Guide to Enlightenment*. Often, Yellows' solutions are humorous. Their light-hearted optimism helps them keep their heads clear and therefore problems are not seen as overwhelming or disastrous. Their solutions are easy, direct and innovative.

When Yellows are out of power or living in fear, however, they become insecure about their own abilities and afraid of taking risks. They will ignore or run away from their problems. Running away can include physically leaving, sleeping all the time, getting sick or constantly moving to different places. Yellows do not like conflict, arguing or hurting anyone's feelings. Out of power, they do not like to face responsibilities, hard work or anything uncomfortable. When there are challenges, they prefer to take the easiest route, which is usually either escaping, or doing nothing at all. Once Yellows regain their center, they become relaxed and can once again develop creative solutions.

Money

Money is not a motivating factor for Yellows. It does not take much money to make Yellows happy, nor do they want to work that hard for it. Yellows are not very reliable financially. They tend to play with money or spend it irresponsibly. Yellows are generous to a fault; actually, money seems to disintegrate in their hands. They usually have no idea what has happened to the money they have earned. Yellows often become involved with "get rich quick" schemes because it is easier than working. (This is especially true for a Yellow/Green combination.) To save money, Yellows need to work harder at it than most of the other colors. To manifest more money, Yellows should simply imagine how it would physically feel in their hands. This seems to attract money to them. If Yellows can imagine how something physically feels to them, it will usually manifest for them.

Success

Yellows do not judge their success in terms of money. They judge their success by how much fun they are having, how much freedom and flexibility they have and by how many people like them.

Occupations

Yellows must have fun in their careers. They seldom choose to have only one career in a lifetime (unless they are a Logical Tan/Yellow Combination Color); instead they prefer to move around in a variety of jobs. Yellows are commonly drawn to three basic fields: physical labor or sports, creative and artistic pursuits, or health and healing.

Some occupations which Yellows are drawn to include:

Athlete	Artist
Surfer	Chef (Yellows are very creative
House painter	cooks)
Construction worker	Bartender
Laborer	Waiter/waitress
Lifeguard	Massage therapist
Firefighter	Healer
Gardener	Doctor
Bodybuilder	Nutritionist
Auto mechanic	Veterinarian
Comedian	Court jester for
Musician (especially	the world
drummers)	

For other occupations that Combination Colors are drawn to, for example, Yellow/Logical Tan, Yellow/Violet and Yellow/Green, see Chapter 5.

Health

Yellows in their power are some of the healthiest people on the planet. They are natural healers. Healthy Yellows have very long lifespans. The positive, light-hearted attitude of Yellows, as well as their natural ability to channel Universal energy through their bodies, help them live longer and healthier.

Yellows have an incredibly sensitive sense of smell. They commonly smell everything before eating it, are uncomfortable in strange-smelling places, and are sensitive to body chemistries. They also seem fascinated by normal bodily functions. Physically, Yellows' weak areas are their backs and their knees. When Yellows are out of power, holding back from fear or afraid to move forward, they have injuries predominantly in these areas. The sensitivity of Yellows also makes them prime candidates for colds. Colds are often caused by a suppressed inner hurt and a need to cry. Out-of-power Yellows can also develop drug and alcohol related health problems. Staying physically active and healthy will help them avoid these problems.

Since Yellows channel so much healing energy through their bodies, they can usually heal their bodies quickly. Any time Yellows become ill, it is a sure sign that there are some major fear issues going on inside of them. In order to become healthy again, Yellows must face these issues. It is important for them to move through and beyond their fears.

3. Mental LifeColors

■ LOGICAL TAN

There are four different types of Tans: Logical, Sensitive, Environmental and Abstract. All of the Tans are similar in that they tend to focus on details and they are cautious thinkers. Each of the Tans has a Tan-colored band which encircles the body; they each have variances however in the shades of Tan as well as a different colored second band which accompanies the Tan. Each of the four Tans has a unique emotional make-up that differentiates him from the others.

The Logical Tan has a light tan-colored band that encircles the body and is usually kept tightly drawn to it. This reflects the Logical Tan's tendency to keep his feelings and thoughts to himself. Logical Tans are very logical and analytical. They choose to process every step, from one through ten. Tans do not like to skip or miss anything. Their method of processing cannot be rushed. They need to analyze and comprehend the logic in each step before proceeding to the next. They like to establish a firm foundation, and then slowly build brick by brick, step by step. Otherwise, they are afraid the entire project will collapse on them. Not being risk-takers, these methodical thinkers need to see all the data and all the facts before making any moves. Everything for Logical Tans is done in an orderly and sequential manner. Every detail is meticulously processed.

These security conscious people can get very accustomed to repeating familiar patterns. Moving on to new patterns is not easy or comfortable for the Logical Tan. With familiar patterns, they know what to do, what is expected of them, and what the results will be each time. New patterns pose an entirely different set of problems to deal with. Before leaping into another job or situation, they need to know all the details — *exactly* what they can expect: the salary, the hours, the job duties, the retirement benefits, the health plan and the stability of the company. These Tans prefer each step to follow a consistent pattern.

Logical Tans typically form very habitual patterns. They are more comfortable repeating the same duties day after day. They don't like their routines to be altered. Even rearranging the furniture in their homes can throw them off and cause them to feel awkward until they are able to readjust to the new situation. These Tans are the least flexible and adaptable personalities of the aura spectrum. Their sense of security is attached to sameness, reliability and predictability. They can often get into "ruts." A lifestyle which others may consider boring can be considered by Logical Tans to be stable, secure and comfortable.

Logical Tans will not usually believe in something unless they have been shown the evidence. E.S.P., channeling and psychic phenomena are just "mumbo-jumbo" to them unless they can see the proof themselves, or discover that science has proven their validity. For these Tans, beliefs are based on proof — seeing is believing. They prefer to stay grounded in "reality." These practical personalities want to make sense out of the three-dimensional world. They enjoy analyzing and figuring things out.

Logical Tans have produced such technical achievements as computers, radios, televisions and modern appliances. Very few of the other LifeColors have the patience or persistence to deal with the intricate, detailed components of these inventions. These Tans have the ability to accomplish tasks that others consider mundane or tedious.

Being detail-oriented, Logical Tans also tend to express themselves slowly and methodically. Someone with a Green LifeColor, who prefers to get straight to the point, can become impatient and frustrated listening to a Tan's detailed account of the day's activities. Their stories can seem long and drawn out. Most of the other LifeColors soon stop listening or paying attention. The Green just wants to hear the "punch line." The Blue just wants to know how the Tan felt about the incident.

When Logical Tans are in power they are reliable and responsible. They are also some of the most dependable people in the world. They will accomplish tasks with thoroughness and efficiency, making sure every detail is handled. They can eventually develop the rational and practical proof to support many of the theories produced by others.

Logical Tans can have a very calming and stabilizing effect on people. Their grounded and practical behavior can help others to look at the logic behind a situation. If people are in a hurry to accomplish something, the Tans' slower methods may frustrate and irritate them, causing more stress and panic. But the Tans' behavior can also calm people down by encouraging them to move more slowly and think rationally. "Haste makes waste" is a favorite expression for Logical Tans.

Tans out of power can become stuck, narrow-minded and critical of things they don't understand. Tans can become stubborn when it comes to change, forward movement or discussions involving theoretical ideas. Even with "proof," they can be overly skeptical of scientific methods, or of conclusions based on incomplete data. To regain their power, Tans need only to recognize their skepticism and evaluate whether it is realistic, or perhaps based on a fear of moving forward. After all, most of our scientific facts were once unknown. Exploring other unproven and uncharted areas will keep Logical Tans from becoming stagnant and judgmental. For these Tans to move forward, they must learn to take some risks, jump into the unknown without information, data or guarantees. They need to stay open to the possibility that today's unproven concepts may eventually be validated.

In their conversations Logical Tans prefer to talk about how they think, rather than how they feel. Tans do not choose to talk about their emotions. They keep such information to themselves. They are often not in touch with their feelings. If an emotional incident occurs, the Tans will analyze the situation while keeping control of their feelings. They will emotionally shut down and withdraw, then calmly and rationally discuss the incident.

Relationships

When it comes to choosing a mate, many of the other aura colors are drawn to the stability and reliability of Logical Tans. These Tans are conscientious and consistent providers, who are also willing to be in long-term, committed relationships. However, if one is looking for excitement, thrills, passion and romance, Tans are not the best candidates. Tans are much too practical and logical for such "unnecessary" frills. Many of the emotional aura colors are disappointed when they discover their Tan mates are emotionally unavailable and unresponsive to them. If someone is looking for open, emotional communication and deep bonding, Tans are not the ones for the job. For intellectual conversation, calm and rational thinking, stability, reliable behavior and consistent financial support, Logical Tans are the best choice.

Sex

Logical Tans do not have a very strong sex drive. It's not that they don't enjoy sex, it's just not high on their list of priorities. Frequently, these Tans will put aside sex to take care of practical responsibilities — paying bills, bringing work home from the office or balancing the checkbook.

Being habitual by nature, Logical Tans can also fall into habitual patterns with sex, always having sex on the same day(s) of the week, in the same location and in the same positions. As with other things in their lives, sex can become boring and predictable. Sex is not usually a passionate, lustful, physical experience for them. Rather it can become an obligation or a tradition. This is not to say these Tans are not caring and considerate with their mates. Too often, however, they can become methodical, analytical and concerned more with technique rather than experiencing wild, passionate sexual abandonment. (See Chapter 5 to learn the sexual behavior of Violet/Tans or Yellow/Tans.)

Logical Tan Parents

Logical Tans will usually calculate the costs, consider the timing, evaluate the responsibilities and list all the pros and cons before they will bring a child into the world. After all, children don't always abide by schedules, they are costly and they can disrupt the established system.

These Tan parents are responsible and reliable providers. Their children will be fed and clothed to the best of the Tans' abilities. There will be no excess and no waste. Their children will not usually be spoiled by getting things too easily. Logical Tans believe their children should learn the value of a dollar.

Logical Tan parents are disciplinarians. They want structure and obedience in their homes. They do not typically show their emotions or share openly with their children. (There are some exceptions with Combination Colors. See Chapter 5 to see Tan/Violet and Tan/Yellow characteristics.)

The challenge for Logical Tan parents is allowing their children to be children — to play and be irresponsible. Tans stress responsibility, consistency, accountability, discipline.

Logical Tan Children

Logical Tan children seem to be introspective and often solemn. They, like their adult counterparts, process slowly, cautiously and methodically. These Tans can often be found taking things apart to see how they work. This is especially true for Yellow/Tan Color Combinations. They love to analyze, calculate and see cause and effect relationships.

Because of the Logical Tans' tendency toward detailed and methodical processing, people often interpret these children as being "slow learners." They do not always develop quickly. Often, they do not grasp ideas as cunningly as some of their peers and may have to work longer and harder to complete a task. But the Logical Tan child will develop eventually. Parents should allow Tan children to work at their own pace. These children cannot be rushed; they must be allowed to comprehend each of the steps before they proceed to the next one, otherwise it will not make any sense to them. They must build logically and sequentially upon all of the data in order to come to a conclusion.

At school, these children are usually quiet and withdrawn. They are slow to make friends. This is not always the case, however, if there is another LifeColor in their aura, for example a Violet/Tan or a Yellow/Tan.

Logical Tan children, like their adult counterparts, do not usually show their emotions or share their feelings easily. Most Tans tend to withdraw and then analyze the situation to see what has caused the problem and what the rational solution may be. To the Tan, emotional outbursts are illogical and usually don't accomplish anything. The Tan's habit of closing down can frequently create concern for parents. They commonly have no idea what is truly going on inside their Tan child. Parents will need to be understanding with these children, allowing them to share what they are comfortable sharing, and then letting them figure out the rest for themselves. Parents can sometimes help by reviewing the facts with the children. This gives the Tans more data and tools to come up with a solution.

Logical Tan children do not react to much, although changing their usual and familiar environment by adding a new baby to the home or moving to a new location can cause them stress. These children, like Tan adults, are upset by change.

To keep Tan children from getting stuck in behavior patterns that may feed their fear of change and of taking risks, parents may want to occasionally introduce new ideas or activities into the children's lives. Maintaining a stable and reliable foundation for the children is fine; all Tans need the security of knowing they can count on a few constants in their lives. What can be helpful, though, is adding new concepts, people or objects to their stable foundations, so they get used to the idea that change is a safe and normal part of life. Showing Logical Tan children other possibilities increases their development and creates trust in growth.

Problem-Solving

Logical Tans typically exhibit good problem-solving abilities, provided they can remain open-minded and receptive to many possibilities. Given enough time, they will eventually figure out practical and realistic solutions. When these Tans refuse to see any other choices but their usual, logical answers, they become closed and have difficulty arriving at alternative solutions. Not being risk-takers, they choose solutions which are safe and have proven successful in the past. Logical Tans prefer to preserve the status quo. These thinkers will carefully analyze a problem, incorporate every detail, and conclude with a rational, practical and detailed solution.

Money

Security and stability are important to Logical Tans, who therefore tend to prefer a regular paycheck to the uncertainty and unpredictability of being self-employed.

Logical Tans want money, but they believe they must work long, hard and consistently for it, then safely invest it in long-term, solid, reliable investments, such as T-bills and life insurance policies. The security-minded Tans have the ability to work for the same company for years. Retirement benefits and pension plans are considered major assets to Logical Tans.

These prudent spenders tend to be frugal with their money, buying the least expensive and most practical items. (A Green, who always wants the best, classiest and most expensive items, can become frustrated with the "over-practical" attitude of a Tan. However, the Green, who also tends to spend beyond her means, can learn and benefit from a Tan's practical spending behavior. The Tan can help her stay out of financial debt.)

Success

Success for Logical Tans can be measured tangibly, by how many accounts they have maintained in business, how well they have been able to provide financial security for themselves and their families, and how many of their investments have proven to be profitable. Tans like to see how well they have been able to figure out life, and to what degree they have been able to provide a secure and comfortable niche for themselves and their families.

Occupation

Logical Tans are most often drawn to safe, secure, analytical office jobs. They love to calculate numbers, analyze data and work with details. They prefer secure, long-term positions with stable companies.

Typical Tan occupations include:

Engineer	Office clerk
Architect	Data processor
Bookkeeper	Factory assembly worker
Accountant	Librarian
Computer analyst	Court reporter
Researcher	Appliance or electrical
Scientist	repairperson
Technician	

See Chapter 5 for more information on preferred occupations.

Health

The main health problems for Tans tend to stem from long hours of detailed, mental work. Many Tans have poor vision as a result of straining over computers, financial ledgers or legal papers. Because they usually do sedentary mental work, they often suffer from such maladies as hemorrhoids, headaches, excess weight and weak muscles. Tans also tend to suppress their emotions. This can cause such things as ulcers, stomach or digestive problems, constipation and even impotence.

Logical Tans usually have an additional LifeColor in their aura, which can cause a variety of other illnesses. For example, a Logical Tan/Violet combination is susceptible, more than any other LifeColor, to cancer, heart attacks and strokes. There is a struggle to harmonize the conflict between the grounded, logical Tan and the emotional, visionary Violet. To stay healthy, it is helpful for Tans to worry less about details, rest their eyes occasionally to prevent strain (blinking the eyes frequently also helps with the strain), balance out mental work with physical exercise (this also increases oxygen to the brain so they can think more clearly and effortlessly), and learn to express their feelings more often.

■ ENVIRONMENTAL TAN

The Environmental Tan LifeColor is a deep tan-colored band layered with a forest-green-colored band. Environmental Tans are the bridge between the physical family and the mental family. They experience their reality by physically touching their environment and then mentally analyzing it.

Like their Logical Tan and Sensitive Tan counterparts, Environmental Tans desire security, stability, and logic. They operate best in a world of rules, boundaries, standards, and logical outcomes which follow basic laws of cause and effect. Environmental Tans prefer structure and discipline. They process life in an orderly and sequential manner just as Logical Tans do, but they have the added ability to judge or measure their environment from an inner perception. These amazing personalities can intuitively analyze spatial situations. They can sense the exact distance from one side of a room to the other just by looking at it, hold something in their hands and know exactly how much it weighs or look at a garage full of old junk and know in how many and in what size boxes it will all fit. Environmental Tans relate kinesthetically and mentally to their environment. They physically handle their surroundings, and then internally and methodically process the information.

Environmental Tans demand reliability and dependability from their world — everything must have a logical and rational explanation. Environmental Tans make good scientists or military personnel. These particular fields have a solid foundation of order, cause and effect and predictability. There is a natural hierarchy or chain of command. Environmental Tans are adept at planning strategies based on logic, spatial measurements and the available resources. They meticulously calculate all of the steps and details. Their physical and mental systems can often be overloaded with too much data and information, which can cause them physical and mental stress. They need to absorb information in an orderly manner. Too much happening at once means chaos. These systematic Tans prefer their environment to be neat, clean and orderly. They need quiet time alone to analyze all the information.

Environmental Tans are very intelligent people. However, they frequently have trouble expressing themselves. This personality trait makes them appear to be aloof and unresponsive. They tend to be quiet and shy on the outside while a great deal of information is being calculated and processed on the inside. They carry the belief that their personal lives, thoughts and feelings are not anyone else's business. They relish their privacy and typically withdraw from crowds or social settings.

An unusual characteristic of Environmental Tans is that many of them are fascinated by airplanes, boats, submarines or other vehicles that put them in contact with their environment. They love to sense their physicalness in relation to altitude, velocity and distance. Many Environmental Tans are inspired to own their own airplanes.

Environmental Tans see themselves according to where

they fit into their environment. They are very aware of their physical positioning, even in their offices. They know how far from the wall their desk sits and where everything on their desk needs to be placed to ensure the easiest accessibility.

Life must be tangible, three-dimensional and logical for Environmental Tans to pay much attention to it. They are adept at taking projects, naming and categorizing them and giving them three-dimensional substance.

Environmental Tans have a strong sense of responsibility. They are loyal and competent workers. Having a strong need to complete a task, they often overwork in an endeavor to accomplish a project. They take their agreements and commitments seriously.

Although Environmental Tans are independent and self-sufficient, they are not always secure or trusting of their own abilities or of their environment. They are not always sure that they have taken all the available information into consideration — maybe they miscalculated, or maybe their physical environment isn't as safe and predictable as they have assessed it to be. Environmental Tans want their world to be dependable and reliable. They are not risk-takers, and stepping into the unknown can cause them anxiety. They prefer explainable and probable results.

Out of power, Environmental Tans are not very flexible regarding their understanding of reality. There are basic laws and standards in which they believe. Any changes are thoroughly researched, analyzed and weighed before being given consideration. Needing logical proof at every stage can cause Environmental Tans to become obstinate and slow-moving. Like Logical Tans, they can get stuck in a rut. By accepting only what has been proven in the past, Environmental Tans limit themselves, and can't see broader horizons or other alternatives.

To stay in power, Environmental Tans must be willing to step beyond what their mental and physical senses are showing them and consider other possibilities. They must also be willing to get in touch with their feelings and learn to find a way to express them, at least to themselves. This will keep them from holding in the emotional stress that can eat them up inside.

Environmental Tans are usually serious, self-controlled personalities. Life is not meant to be the playful, spontaneous creation that Yellows believe it to be. Rather it is an orderly, well-planned Universe that needs to be analyzed, categorized and understood logically in order to provide the best opportunities for humankind. Environmental Tans want the planet to be a place where modern technology fits in harmoniously with the physical environment. The Environmental Tans' purpose for being here appears to be to analyze, understand and learn from three-dimensional, physical reality. Many Environmental Tans have an innate desire to help improve or re-balance the physical environments on the planet.

One of the ways Environmental Tans can stay in power is to take long walks in a natural environment, especially one where they can experience the majesty and power of nature. Hiking and experiencing the peaceful strength of unspoiled forests and towering mountains inspires the Environmental Tans to see life from a greater perspective. This seems to broaden their outlook and open their minds to greater possibilities. (Some of the more sensitive and spiritual Environmental Tans actually receive intuitive information by being in the presence of trees.)

Relationships

Environmental Tans are slow to develop relationships. They are very cautious and selective even when they chose friends. When they do develop a significant relationship, Environmental Tans are extremely loyal and committed. Those in relationship with Environmental Tans need to understand their nature in order to maintain harmony. These Tans are very quiet and reserved. They do not openly share their feelings or inner thoughts with anyone, including their mates. The Environmental Tans believe they have an inner understanding and an unspoken agreement with their partners and that their love is obviously known and accepted. They do not need to prove it, test it or discuss it with each other.

This attitude can frustrate those who find themselves in relationships with the mysterious Environmental Tans. These people often feel that they are not receiving the emotional sharing, open verbal communication, or demonstrative and affectionate behavior that they desire from the Environmental Tans. It is also, however, this same strong and quiet Clint Eastwood-style mystique of the Environmental Tans that many find attractive. (Clint Eastwood is, in fact, an Environmental Tan.) Often people will pursue the Environmental Tan for the challenge of capturing and conquering this elusive personality, only to be disappointed when they discover he will not be changed, opened up, or made more emotionally vulnerable.

A person in relationship with an Environmental Tan must have a strong sense of self-esteem. Anyone who needs a lot of emotional reassurance will not do well with this Tan. Environmental Tans frequently withdraw or walk away from uncomfortable encounters. If their mates confront them with emotional issues, their tendency is to shut down or disappear. They are, however, very responsible and reliable providers. Their partners can feel secure in knowing that they will always be financially supported. Environmental Tans will always find a way to pay the bills.

Environmental Tans are not always physically available to their mates. Their work frequently causes them to travel for long periods of time. The archeological site may be miles away in an area that is unsuitable for wives and children, or the environmental research may be taking place at a polar ice station where conditions are too harsh and the location is too remote for their families to join them. Most Environmental Tans are loners, consequently when their work brings them into isolated situations, they are not usually traumatized. They enjoy their privacy and their time alone.

Environmental Tans are very independent mates. They prefer partners who are intelligent and can successfully hold their own in the real world. They do not want mates who are emotionally needy or unable to deal with the responsibility of maintaining a practical, sensible and secure lifestyle. Environmental Tans require mates who have the patience and understanding to allow them to figure out their lives in their own time and in their own way. Environmental Tans require a lot of time, space and freedom.

Sex

Environmental Tans tend to be more sexual than their Logical Tan counterparts because they appreciate and operate more from their physical bodies. They relate more to their surroundings by touching first and then processing the data. However, they must be given ample time to process the information that they have received through their physical senses.

Environmental Tans need to develop a sense of trust and security with their partners before they can totally involve themselves sexually. They tend to be cautious and often inhibited until they learn that their partners are trustworthy and sincere. They frequently remain emotionally distant until a bond of closeness has been established. This can often take a long time for the methodical Environmental Tans. Once security, understanding and trust have developed, the Environmental Tans can be dedicated and committed lovers.

Environmental Tan Parents

Environmental Tans, like Logical Tans, are disciplinarians. They want order, cleanliness and structure in their homes. These practical people think logically and rationally when planning a family. First, a detailed cost analysis is carefully considered. Environmental Tans can be reliable and consistent providers for their children, saving for college educations while also giving their children adequate food, clothing and shelter. Environmental Tans are not lavish spenders; they are prudent and economical. Consequently, they will buy sturdy and durable products and clothes for their children.

Emotionally bonding with their children isn't easy for the reserved Environment Tans. Although they care deeply for their children, it is difficult for them to share their feelings or openly show affection toward their offspring (or toward anyone, for that matter). They often withdraw emotionally, which can cause their children to feel abandoned, rejected or neglected. Environmental Tans believe that providing a secure and stable environment for their children and setting appropriate boundaries for their welfare should be adequate proof of their love.

The challenge for Environmental Tan parents is to open themselves up and be emotionally available to their families, and also to allow their children to be children before they are expected to be adults. Environmental Tan parents need to learn that providing emotional and mental support for their children is just as important as physical and financial support.

Environmental Tan Children

Environmental Tan children are more quiet and reticent than their peers. They are not usually found laughing and playing outside like typical children. Instead, they are more somber and serious. They tend to spend more time by themselves. They do not easily connect with others, but tend to stay withdrawn and removed. They are slow to make friends. However, once they have learned to trust another person, they are dedicated and loyal friends. Having an abundance of friends is not important to Environmental Tans. They prefer instead to have one or two close companions with whom they feel secure and accepted.

Their growth and development are frequently slower than those of other children. To learn, these tactile children need to handle objects, to physically analyze things by touching them. Parents frequently worry about their Environmental Tan children because the children seem so isolated and disconsolate. If the parents can allow their Environmental Tan children to develop at their own rate, and refrain from forcing the children into uncomfortable social situations, these children will eventually grow up to be well-balanced and stable citizens. However, if they are made to feel like social misfits, unacceptable by "normal" standards and misunderstood by their families, they tend to withdraw into themselves even more.

It is beneficial for parents to be loving and supportive of the Environmental Tans' reserved social behavior, and to be patient and understanding toward their slower pace. These children will eventually catch up with their peers. Environmental Tans are actually very intelligent children and will eventually prove their intellectual abilities if given the chance to develop in a safe, secure and non-judgmental environment.

Courses in school which appeal to Environmental Tans are those which allow them to do hands-on experiments and research, measure the environmental impact of technology, study spatial components such as geometric shapes, work with mathematical equations which involve velocity, dimension, volume and weight, or examine minerals, soils and rock formations. These courses can include computer technology, science, geology, botany or any courses which help them analyze and therefore understand their physical environment.

As with all Environmental Tans, it is healing and centering for these children to spend time connecting with the natural environment. Going for walks in the woods can be very therapeutic for most Environmental Tan children. It calms them and gives them a sense of grounded security.

Money

Money has tangible substance for Environmental Tans. Its purpose is to provide security for them and their families. Environmental Tans are loyal, dedicated workers who believe, like their Logical Tan counterparts, that people should work at long-term, stable jobs, earn a decent wage, keep their money in safe and secure money market accounts, and look forward to retirement benefits.

Environmental Tans are practical and cautious when spending or investing their money. They are not gamblers or risk-takers when it comes to deciding the fate of their hard-earned money. These pragmatic personalities believe one needs to work for a long time to build a sturdy financial foundation. Transferring their money into a physical investment such as land appeals to Environmental Tans because land has a real and tangible form which they can touch. They can see their hard work translated into a physical reward which creates a sense of security for them.

Problem-Solving

Since Environmental Tans relate strongly to the physicality of the world, as well as to its mental and logical aspects, they solve problems most effectively by simultaneously collecting and scrutinizing the data, and also physically sensing the solution in their bodies. It's as if they

have a sensing device in their bodies that gives them technical readings and feedback. They can walk the grounds of an
archeological site and not only logically figure out where
another structure may be buried, but they can also locate
the site through sensations in their bodies. Environmental
Tans use a combination of mental and physical senses to
figure out solutions. When planning military strategies,
they move markers on the map to sense whether or not
these maneuvers will be successful.

Environmental Tans are cautious decision-makers,
weighing all the facts and possibilities before committing to
a plan of action. When they are centered, they eventually
are able to analyze enough of the data to draw a conclusion
and recommend a solution. If they are out of power, they
become stuck in their habitual past solutions. When
the same methods are no longer appropriate or useful, this
can cause confusion and mental dilemmas for the
Environmental Tans. To stay in power, they must figure out
ways to introduce new variables into the equation.

Success

Environmental Tans consider themselves successful if
they are able to develop a secure and stable lifestyle for
themselves and their families. They consider themselves
successful if they are able to enhance the quality of life on
the planet by improving the environment through the
combined use of intellect and technology. Environmental
Tan farmers are satisfied when they are able to financially
provide for their families while they physically work with
the soil and provide quality food for people. Environmental
Tan researchers are pleased when they are able to produce a
system which replaces valuable nutrients in the previously
exhausted and abused environment. Environmental Tans
feel successful if they make intelligent, rational and practical decisions which result in profits to their employer.

Occupations

Environmental Tans are often drawn to occupations that allow them to analyze, measure and physically interact with their environment. These types of jobs enable them to sense where and how they fit in to their physical world.

They are drawn to such occupations as:

Archaeologist	Pilot
Geologist	Purchase order clerk
Environmental researcher	City planner
Botanist	Developer
Scientist	Architect
Explorer	Computer operator
Map maker	Lab technician
Forest ranger	Telephone repairman
Military personnel	Aerospace engineer
Shipping and	Electrician
receiving clerk	Farmer

Because Environmental Tans and Yellow/Logical Tan Combination Colors both enjoy physical and mental work, they often share similar career interests.

Health

Even though Environmental Tans frequently work in an outdoor environment, they are careful planners and cautious workers. They analyze situations before undertaking any tasks, so they rarely encounter physical harm. Even if the Environmental Tan is in telephone repair and must climb to the top of a telephone pole, he is careful enough to secure all safety devices first.

Environmental Tans are more likely to experience health problems that are related to mental stress. They are dedicated, hard-working people who push their mental stamina and endurance to the limits. It is important to them to complete their assigned tasks and projects no matter how many long hours they must work.

To stay healthy, it is important for Environmental Tans to maintain a balance between their mental work, physical exercise, nutrition and rest. Frequently, Environmental Tans become so involved in their work they forget about the rest of their lives. Quiet, meditative time in natural surroundings is the most effective rejuvenation process for Environmental Tans.

■ SENSITIVE TAN

Sensitive Tans are the bridge between the mental colors and the emotional colors. Their auras are a combination of a light tan color with a light blue band next to it that encircles the body. Their personalities are a subtle combination of the mental Tan qualities and the emotional Blue qualities.

Sensitive Tans incorporate the characteristics of mental, analytical logic with loving and intuitive compassion. These gentle personalities are quiet, sensitive and supportive. They prefer, like Logical Tans, to maintain a rational, intellectual foundation while they analytically process data. Sensitive Tans are more emotional and intuitive than Logical Tans, but they tend to keep their feelings to themselves. When a problem arises, Sensitive Tans will retreat inside to figure out the most practical solution.

Like their Logical Tan counterparts, Sensitive Tans desire security and stability. Their homes are very important to them. They can become very attached to their possessions, to everything from their furniture to the family pictures on the wall. Sensitive Tans can be very sentimental and nostalgic regarding family memorabilia. While their families are *the* most important element in their lives, Sensitive Tans also love the comfort and security of knowing they have things around them.

These loving personalities, while sensitive and emotional, are not quite as emotional as Blues. In the face of personal conflict, they tend to remain more rational and calm than Blues. While Blues tend to wear their emotions on their sleeves, and can experience strong mood shifts between deep depression and euphoria, the Sensitive Tans are less dramatic with their ups and downs. While Sensitive Tans may lose their center momentarily, they are quick to regain their composure. (Sensitive Tans may want to read the section on Blues, but reduce the intensity and drama by at least fifty percent!)

The "mental-versus-emotional" battle of the Sensitive Tans is not as pronounced or as intense as that of the Blue/Green Combination Colors. The Sensitive Tans' emotional "waves" are more like those in a pond or a lake than those in an ocean.

These serene people can be great secretaries and support personnel because they love to calmly help people while taking care of details. They tend to be withdrawn and shy, so they prefer less conspicuous jobs. They feel the safest and calmest taking care of details in the office — bookkeeping, filing, typing or answering the phone. (Some Sensitive Tans can be overwhelmed by the fast-paced pressure and responsibility of answering a busy switchboard. Other Sensitive Tans, however, can be calm and patient, methodically handling each call without being traumatized.)

Sensitive Tans send quiet nurturing energy out to people. They have a calm sense about them when they are helping people. They can be very efficient therapists because they are sincere and patient listeners. They deduce answers based on data as well as intuition. It is common for Sensitive Tans to put others' needs before their own. They are extraordinarily unselfish. They are delightfully modest hosts and hostesses. They do not overwhelm their guests with hospitality the way Blues frequently can. They are more subtle. Sensitive Tans are so calm, understanding and patient that they are typically compatible with everyone.

Sensitive Tans are very service-oriented humanitarians. They love serving their community, as well as organizations which are dedicated to helping people. Their idea of God or religion is essentially that people should be honest and good, love each other, and treat each other with compassion, patience and understanding. By teaching these concepts, Sensitive Tans help people to create peace and harmony in their homes, their communities and, therefore, the world.

While Sensitive Tans are intuitive, much like Blues, they also want facts and data to support what they feel. Their ability to sometimes support their intuition with common sense and logic helps people trust Sensitive Tans and feel secure with their advice. Together, their logic and intuition create a healthy balance.

However, these two aspects can also create conflict for Sensitive Tans. They may get a feeling or an intuitive sense of something and then proceed to analyze it to the point where they no longer trust their intuition. They can experience persistent arguments in their heads. Their Tan aspect leans toward accepting the apparent physical evidence, while the Blue aspect just feels that something may be true even when there is no data to support the feelings. As an example, a Sensitive Tan may see her employer arranging a business deal with a client. All the facts and figures are checked out. The transaction appears to be running according to the established system, but the Sensitive Tan has an odd feeling that something is wrong. She doesn't have any data or facts to support her feelings, and so just continues typing up the paperwork. Later, when the business deal falls through, the Sensitive Tan feels that if she had just trusted her instincts, she may have been able to search for and uncover the problem.

To stay in power, Sensitive Tans need to learn to trust their intuition and not just depend on the apparent facts. Using both their inner and outer faculties will keep them balanced and enable them to make calm, clear decisions. To live their greatest potential, it is also wise for Sensitive Tans to be in touch with *their* needs, not just the needs of others. Allowing themselves to receive what they need for their well-being will help them maintain their positive energy, as well as keeping them from being abused or taken advantage of by other people.

Relationships

Sensitive Tans value love, commitment, dedication, patience, understanding and good communication in their relationships. (This is exactly what Sensitive Tans give to their mates — therefore, they want the same consideration. They want someone who will listen as well as talk to them.)

These loving souls want mates they can depend upon, who will be secure and stable providers, as well as kind and considerate partners. They don't require partners who are powerful, charismatic or driven to be the best in their fields. Actually, such mates would intimidate them. They prefer practical, reliable and devoted mates who will commit to a long-term relationship. While Sensitive Tans are intelligent, they prefer to work behind the scenes, supporting and nurturing their mates' dreams. But they want to know that in return they will be loved, honored, provided for and appreciated by their mates.

Sensitive Tans will take care of more than their fair share of responsibilities and will be good providers themselves. These thoughtful individuals will also make sure their mates have a comfortable, secure and loving home. Being very loyal, monogamous and committed, they focus on maintaining sincerity and integrity in their relationships.

They are usually calm and sensible when disagreements occur.

Sensitive Tans feel best when they are in secure, stable relationships, but they don't fall apart when this isn't the case. They aren't happy if the comfortable, established structure is upset — for example, in the case of divorce — but Sensitive Tans are too practical and level-headed to let a divorce destroy them.

Sex

Sensitive Tans are usually reserved, loving and affectionate. Sex for them is not a wild, tempestuous, animalistic act. Rather it is to be experienced with sensitivity, sincerity, tenderness and integrity. Sensitive Tans are too gentle and caring to have wild affairs, one-night stands or numerous sexual odysseys. They have more respect for themselves and others than to sexually use people. To them, making love shows that there is mutual affection and admiration between two people. Sex also fulfills the function of procreation.

Sensitive Tan Parents

The Sensitive Tans' greatest priority is the family. Their focus is creating a traditional, stable and loving family unit — mother, father and happy, well-adjusted children. They will, however, be very practical when planning for a family. Taking into account all the potential liabilities, financial circumstances, the quality of schools in the area and the ages of both parents, Sensitive Tans will consider all of the possible consequences involved in their decision before taking action.

Sensitive Tans are usually very calm and rational parents. While they believe there must be a sense of order and discipline in their home, they are usually not unreasonable regarding rules for their children. They believe in setting loving yet fair guidelines.

In power, Sensitive Tan parents can be understanding and supportive toward their children. They allow them room to grow and freedom to experience their childhood, while still setting safe and realistic boundaries for them. Sensitive Tan parents usually have more tolerance and patience for child-rearing than many of the other LifeColors, even preferring to stay home to raise the children. While some of the aura colors feel a strong need to concentrate on a career, Sensitive Tans feel that providing a secure and supportive environment for their family is just as high a priority, if not higher. In power, Sensitive Tans will take an interest in their children's welfare, as well as in the community that affects their children. To support their children, these parents will attend PTA meetings, make decorations for the class Christmas party, or volunteer their help with the carpool if it means supporting and staying involved with their children's lives. They want to make sure their children grow up well-balanced and feeling loved.

Out of power, Sensitive Tans can be weak and ineffective parents. Wanting their children's love, they can frequently become too nice and too lenient. Children learn at an early age how to manipulate the generosity and patient nature of the Sensitive Tans. When these well-meaning individuals are out of power, they can also be too cautious and protective toward their children. None of the Tans are risk-takers, consequently they usually want their children to play it safe, maintain the status quo, stay inside the "normal" boundaries, and perform at least moderately well in school.

To stay in power as parents, Sensitive Tans need to remember to trust their intuition, their "inner knowing," just as much as they analyze the facts. Because Sensitive Tans tend to be cautious, they often take statistics very seriously. If they read that the leading cause of death among teenagers is drinking and driving, they may place unwarranted restrictions on their children because of those statistics. If these parents can trust what they feel, they may see that their children are trustworthy or that their children will be safe. If the Sensitive Tan parents can balance their intuition with their mental deductions, they will survive parenthood very successfully.

Sensitive Tan Children

Sensitive Tan children are usually quiet, polite, practical, sensible and responsible. Since they process information slowly and analytically, they are not always the quickest in the class, but they are some of the most consistent and dependable students. Sensitive Tans seem to understand the value of education. They tend to do well in subjects where analysis and attention to detail is required, like math, bookkeeping, English and grammar.

The Blue aspect in the Sensitive Tan's aura is shown in a desire to help people on some level. They are frequently interested in subjects that relate to people, but that also have a practical application — subjects such as history, sociology, art theory and literature.

Parents need to allow these quiet, reserved children to move at their own pace. School work may be slower for them, but they eventually will get it done. Efficiency and accuracy are important to Sensitive Tans.

Socially, Sensitive Tans tend to stay unnoticed and in the background. They may be late bloomers, if they ever bloom at all. Sensitive Tan children love people and want to be liked, but they are usually shy. They are uncomfortable at parties where a high level of interaction is expected. They prefer instead to be on the party's decorating or refreshment committee. They receive more pleasure from setting up everything in a festive array so that other people can enjoy themselves. On a Saturday night, Sensitive Tans are frequently found studying in the library or reading a book at home. They strive to be nice, well-respected, loving, yet practical people.

Pushing these children out into gregarious social functions will only cause them anxiety. Parents need to be understanding. Sensitive Tan children will eventually find their roles in life. These gentle humanitarians are here to serve their communities by teaching compassion and integrity, not by being football stars, cheerleaders or famous world leaders. They will live life in their own subtle and unassuming way.

Problem-Solving

When solving problems, Sensitive Tans want to calmly review all of the facts, and then take everyone else's feelings and preferences into consideration before making a decision. As much as possible, Sensitive Tans want to make sure everyone is happy with the solution. They do not want to be rushed or forced into making snap decisions, preferring instead to have time to weigh all of the facts and hear all sides of the problem.

Sensitive Tans will never force their opinions, advice or beliefs upon anyone else. They have an inherent trust that good will come of most situations. They believe that people are basically good and loving inside.

When in power, Sensitive Tans calmly and rationally come up with a solution that combines the most practical answer with the one that makes people feel the best. They have the ability to reason with everyone so that discussions don't escalate into emotionally heated fights. Sensitive Tans are natural mediators and peacemakers. They make people around them feel as if they are all winners.

Out of power, Sensitive Tans can get so emotionally caught up in the situation that their common sense is blurred, causing them to be unable to make any decisions at all. Out of power, Sensitive Tans stop trusting their intuitive, inner knowing. Consequently, they are not using all of their abilities to make a decision.

While sometimes frustrated by the slow pace of the Sensitive Tans' decision-making process, people usually trust the Sensitive Tans' decisions and advice because they know everything has been well thought out before coming to a conclusion. Sensitive Tans want things to be fair and loving.

Money

Money is only important to Sensitive Tans because it provides them and their families with security and stability. Sensitive Tans want enough money to pay the bills, buy decent clothes for their children, buy moderately-priced yet comfortable furniture for their home and occasionally go out to dinner.

Sensitive Tans are very cautious with their money. They want savings accounts and safe investments. Not being gamblers or risk-takers, they feel more secure when they know they have a "nest egg." They want money neatly tucked away for the children's college education or for family emergencies.

Sensitive Tans believe that it takes time to build up a financial reserve. They don't usually have the abundant financial assets that Greens have, nor do they have the outrageous number of debts that Greens usually have. Greens "stake" a lot of money in order to make a lot of money. Sensitive Tans prefer the quiet security of building their financial foundation slowly and steadily.

Sensitive Tans are frequently found in occupational positions such as secretaries, bookkeepers, clerks and receptionists where the income can be steady, but not always high paying. It is also common to see Sensitive Tans who have discontinued their education in order to raise a family. When returning to the work force, many of them take jobs that do not require a college education and typically do not pay as well.

Success

Sensitive Tans' priorities are serving their family and their community with love and integrity. They prefer to deal with life in a very calm, rational and sensitive manner. If they feel that they are providing their family with love and security, teaching goodness and compassion to those around them, and contributing positively to society by serving their community, then Sensitive Tans feel they are living successful lives.

Occupations

Sensitive Tans prefer jobs where they have the security of a regular paycheck. They like jobs that can be both helpful and analytical. Sensitive Tans are dedicated employees who work well with others. They prefer low-stress, slow-paced jobs where they can easily know what is expected of them every day. Their list of responsibilities must be well-defined and consistent from day to day. Chaos, last minute deadlines and panic can cause undue stress for Sensitive Tans. They are happier when there are no surprises in the workplace — just a well-planned, efficient and calm environment.

Sensitive Tans enjoy working on details, such as balancing the books or programming a computer, as long as they are also allowed to have interaction with people. They have more patience to deal with repetition and details than most of the other LifeColors.

If they become therapists, Sensitive Tans prefer their clients to be scheduled for long-term, regular visits. They believe the therapeutic healing process has multiple stages and can take a long time. (In addition, Sensitive Tans prefer the economic security of knowing that their clients have committed to a regular, long-term schedule.) Because Sensitive Tans like to be in service for the good of the community, they will take on jobs that require analyzing the community's current situation and making plans to improve it — positions such as city planners or community service developers. Companies would do well to employ the dedicated, hard-working Sensitive Tans, who are more than willing to take care of the mundane details of daily business.

Occupations that appeal to Sensitive Tans are:

Bookkeeper	Therapist
Receptionist	Judge
Secretary	Dentist
Office personnel	Hygienist
Accountant	Welfare/social worker
Arbitrator	Teacher
Counselor	Child care worker
City planner	Community service developer

Health

A common health problem for Sensitive Tans is their eyesight. Like all Tans, they tend to focus on details, which can cause eye strain. Sensitive Tans can take on the same health problems that affect Logical Tans and Blues. These composed individuals tend to stay healthier than the other LifeColors, however, because they have the sense to eat properly and stay calmer and consequently less stressed.

Like the Blues, Sensitive Tans are not exercise fanatics. They do have the common sense, however, to know that the human body needs exercise, and they are more likely to exercise than Blues. There is enough of the Blue aspect in their aura, however, to keep their exercise schedule erratic.

They start out with a schedule, then shift into exercising only when they feel like it.

To remain healthy, Sensitive Tans need only to maintain their common sense, eat healthy foods, stay calm (without suppressing their emotions) and exercise on a regular basis. They can also follow the advice given to Blues and Logical Tans.

■ ABSTRACT TAN

Abstract Tans have a light tan-colored band which is surrounded completely by a brilliant red band. This red is not the same as the Red LifeColor. Their personality traits are entirely different.

The bright and curious Abstract Tans are unique characters in the mental family. They are the most childlike of all the Tans. Abstract Tans are open, friendly and outgoing. They have incredibly optimistic personalities. Though they frequently have high energy, it is also usually scattered. They tend to go in many directions at once. All the other Tan personalities process information in a very logical and sequential manner. They process every step in a linear fashion, from one to ten. While Abstract Tans see all the details and steps which need to be handled, they do not proceed in an orderly fashion. Abstract Tans have random thought processes. Rather than proceeding step by step, they attempt to work on all of the steps simultaneously. They do not sense that any one step is a priority — the first step is just another piece in the project, as is the last one.

Abstract Tans see projects in much the same way as they see jigsaw puzzles. They see all of the pieces laid out simultaneously on the table, but are not sure where to begin to put the puzzle together. They will choose any piece of the puzzle, and then jump over to another section of the puzzle for no apparent reason. Eventually, all of the pieces are put in place and the puzzle is completed; in the process, however, the Abstract Tans have probably driven everyone else around them crazy. Other people, who usually start with one piece of the puzzle and logically build onto it, can see no rhyme or reason behind the Abstract Tans' methods. The Abstract Tans' world looks like an embodiment of confusion and chaos.

Because their thinking is so random and illogical, Abstract Tans have trouble organizing their lives. They don't have any concept of establishing priorities or setting up schedules. They don't do the things first which are the most important or the most timely. Instead, their priority becomes whichever task they happen to be focused upon at that time. When Abstract Tans are preparing for a party, they may decorate the house, then clean the house and then bake the cake, not realizing that the cake could be baking while they clean the house. These scattered individuals are often late for their own parties because they don't schedule their preparation time accordingly. As usual, the Abstract Tans see all steps that need to be taken, but take each step randomly.

Abstract Tans actually don't have a firm understanding of linear time. When they recount stories, the past, present and future all seem to coexist simultaneously. These characters remember all of the facts, but not necessarily the order in which they occurred. People often consider Abstract Tans to be unreliable and flaky because their thought processes — and therefore their behaviors — are so erratic. The Abstract Tans' energy can be exuberant and eager, which often makes them appear to be nervous. When they talk, they frequently go off on tangents and randomly recapitulate the facts. People often have trouble following conversations with the Abstract Tans.

These sensitive individuals often appear to be scatterbrained to others. They are consistently misplacing or losing their possessions and they usually can't remember where they put things last. Their lives seem to be in a constant state of confusion and disorder. Their energy is so unfocused that people around them can become agitated trying to pin them down. Abstract Tans have energy similar to that of fireflies or hummingbirds. Their rapidly vibrating wings move a hundred times a second as they constantly change course in mid-air. People are amazed when the scattered Abstract Tans actually complete projects, because it usually appears that they don't know what they're doing. And yet, while the Abstract Tans' processes seem scrambled, they eventually get all of the pieces together.

Abstract Tans are excited about learning new ideas. They love to immerse themselves in new projects and examine everything about them. They love to research and explore, collecting a multitude of data and information, and then retain only what is important to them. They love to learn from nature, because nature has a sense of order to it. Abstract Tans can learn from nature about chronological events, cause and effect and patterns such as the regular, sequential cycle of the seasons.

These inquisitive personalities love to attend parties or other social gatherings where they are able to talk with a wide variety of people. They are able to gather a lot of information from other people, and store their newly found knowledge in different parts of their mental computers. Abstract Tans also have an unconditional love for humanity. They love people on a very universal and general level. They have a broad acceptance of and a great curiosity about other people's differences. They are interested in learning about other cultures, other languages and other lifestyles.

While Abstract Tans have a great love for people on an abstract level, they also have difficulty experiencing intimate relationships. These Tans are sensitive and childlike personalities who are eager to please and to be liked by others. They can get their feelings hurt very easily, however. Rather than risk being hurt, they tend to stay in their heads and theorize ideas rather than become deeply involved with others. They freely discuss concepts about how and why people feel, think and act the way they do, but won't discuss their own emotions. Having been so misunderstood and unappreciated in childhood, they often have learned not to open up or be vulnerable. They detach themselves from their emotions. Abstract Tans feel safer being around a lot of people, learning and discussing ideas. While they have a general optimistic faith in humanity, it does not translate into a trust of one-on-one, intimate relationships.

When Abstract Tans are in power, they are energetic, optimistic, bright, and friendly. Their accepting nature makes them non-threatening to other people. They have enough energy to handle many different projects simultaneously and can be storehouses of information. Although they prefer the information to be intellectually and factually based, they are not afraid to explore for further information. They enjoy adding to ideas and concepts. Abstract Tans are much more open-minded and flexible than the other three Tan personalities.

Out of power, Abstract Tans can be scattered, forgetful and ineffective. They tend to overcommit themselves and then cannot follow through with their promises. They are easily confused and distracted.

Out of power, these sensitive individuals close themselves off emotionally from others. They slowly retreat inside their heads, which leaves them safe but lonely. While these personalities are usually very sociable, when they are out of power they become more isolated, especially as they get older.

To stay in power, Abstract Tans must learn to give themselves schedules and guidelines. The Abstract Tans, unlike the other Tans, do not operate well within the confines of a rigid, structured system. They need more room to explore and research new ideas. They do need some structure, however, to keep their lives from leaking out in all directions. They need a calendar so they don't commit themselves to too many activities in one day. It is also helpful for Abstract Tans to be associated with people who can help them stay more structured and disciplined. Once they have a well-established and responsible foundation, these lively personalities are free to explore their alternate ideas and projects.

When they are in power, Abstract Tans feel an unconditional love and total acceptance for humanity. With this love and acceptance, they are able to teach people to accept themselves, and to appreciate their differences.

Relationships

Although the friendly Abstract Tans are very liberal with their time, energy and enthusiasm and are very willing to be with other people, they have difficulty opening up to intimate relationships. They are not usually emotionally available to their mates.

Marriage is more like a port in a storm for these disorganized individuals. They want mates who can help to establish order in their chaotic lives. They want partners who are willing to provide a steady foundation and who will understand their theoretical discussions. The Abstract Tans need partners who are stronger, and capable of taking care of their lives. Abstract Tans don't need deep emotional bonds, they prefer caretakers. Frequently, their mates become frustrated, feeling more like parents than partners.

Abstract Tans sometimes have difficulty even finding mates. Their energy is much too scattered and frenzied for most people to handle. Consequently, Abstract Tans tend to flit from person to person, having one encounter after another. They tend to have many casual relationships, but very few intimate, meaningful connections. Their hectic lifestyles also keep them safe from having to be in intimate, committed relationships. They don't focus their energies long enough to be available for serious relationships. In addition, Abstract Tans tend to be attracted to people who are unavailable to them. Actually, what Abstract Tans want are companions. These friendly Tans can become depressed and lonely if they remain single for too long, but they tend to hide their feelings behind cheerful and energetic facades. Their dilemma is staying calm and focused long enough to be accessible to others.

Mates of Abstract Tans soon discover that these frenetic characters are not in one place for long. Abstract Tans are enthusiastic and cheerful, but they are also constantly busy. Their partners have trouble keeping track of them. A person in this relationship must be stable, grounded and patient with the sensitive, childlike Tan. They must be willing to add structure and responsibility to the relationship.

Abstract Tans can bring a great deal of cheerful optimism and enthusiasm to a relationship. With their exuberant energy and wealth of information, a relationship with an Abstract Tan would never be boring.

Sex

Sex must be safe for Abstract Tans. They must feel a sense of security and trust for their partners. It is very challenging for Abstract Tans to completely trust anyone. They tend to live safely in their heads, even during love-making. They rarely abandon themselves to passion. Letting go makes them feel too vulnerable.

All of the Tans tend to be reserved and emotionally cautious with sex. Although they enjoy sex, especially with partners they trust, sex is not a main priority in their lives.

Abstract Tan Parents

As parents, Abstract Tans are very warm, sensitive and caring toward their children. They do not usually provide a disciplined structure for their children, however. Because these Tans are usually so scattered and disorganized, their homes can be disheveled and chaotic. Clothes and possessions are often strewn everywhere. The children are frequently hurriedly hustled from school to baseball practice to music lessons because their Abstract Tan parents have scheduled too many activities on one day. Abstract Tans have very good intentions, but they often fall through on their promises to their children because they overcommit themselves. Abstract Tans experience difficulty organizing their children's lives because they can't even organize their own lives. They are like eager children themselves — children who need looking after.

Abstract Tan Children

These outgoing and cheerful children are usually optimistic and enthusiastic. However, they are often misunderstood because their thought processes are so scattered. They are eager for others to like them, but their chaotic energy often wears on people. These children have very sensitive feelings, and it is at this stage that they begin to lose trust in other people. They fear being hurt and rejected by others who don't understand their erratic behavior. Abstract Tans learn to slowly withdraw their feelings and ideas and retreat into their heads.

Abstract Tans are often chastised for neglecting their possessions. Like their adult counterparts, they leave their clothes and toys strewn everywhere. Possessions are not important to Abstract Tans. They are constantly losing or misplacing things. Parents can become frustrated by the Abstract Tans' apparent carelessness and apathy. Try as they might, it is a struggle for these children to stay organized.

When they see that they are constantly disappointing their parents, and feel their lack of understanding and disapproval, these Abstract Tan children learn to shut down. They learn to see themselves as misfits.

It is helpful for parents to teach these energetic children how to focus their attention. They shouldn't restrict or confine them. They should teach these children instead to learn to follow simple schedules. Parents need to learn patience with these abstract thinkers. Abstract Tan children are not scatterbrained — they are just adept at seeing all of the pieces at once. If they are not forced to follow the traditional, linear ways of accomplishing tasks, and are given the freedom to do the tasks in any order, these children will succeed.

Abstract Tan children function better in non-traditional educational systems. They are curious and eager learners. They are drawn to subjects such as foreign languages or world cultures, but they need time to fully research or experience each subject. Jumping from one topic to another before they have completed the first one causes them to become even more scattered. With help, they can learn to better organize and channel their abundant energy.

Problem-Solving

Abstract Tans, unlike the other Tans, are open to new and fresh ideas. They are willing to learn different approaches. They can see ideas from a myriad of perspectives, and so believe problems can be solved from many different angles. While they are open to exploring various alternatives, and can easily see everyone's point of view, Abstract Tans tend to choose solutions and options that are most closely aligned with their current belief system. They prefer solutions that have an intellectual and rational foundation. They prefer, as do all Tans, to see all the facts and data on the table before making any decisions.

It is easy for Abstract Tans to jump from one solution to another in midstream. Although this tends to confuse and baffle those around them, Abstract Tans can quickly and easily change their directions. But by shifting from one solution to another, and then to still another, Abstract Tans often lose perspective of the original problem. Because they are able to present so many options to the group, however, someone is inevitably able to see at least one solution. Abstract Tans do not solve problems based on which problem is more important, but rather based upon which one happens to be in front of them at the time.

Although Abstract Tans are very unsystematic thinkers, they are capable of finding many unique and feasible solutions to a given problem.

Money

Abstract Tans experience difficulty managing their money. Prioritizing financial obligations is a challenge for them. Their money gets dispersed randomly — the bills that get paid change from month to month. Abstract Tans don't plan well, consequently they don't always spend their money wisely. Frequently they buy items that they already own because their lives are usually in such disarray that they either have misplaced the items, or have forgotten that they already own them.

Abstract Tans have trouble following budgets or financial plans. Their lives operate more smoothly when they employ others to keep track of their financial obligations. They are happier when someone else organizes their money for them.

Success

Abstract Tans are exuberant child-like people who want to be liked. They are happy with their lives when they feel that they are understood and accepted by others. They feel best when they have others around them who can provide a safe and secure foundation for them. They want the freedom to process life in the random and abstract manner which is natural and comfortable for them without being criticized or ostracized. They also do not want strong, invasive emotional demands placed upon them. They are happy when they are able to bring all of the pieces of a project together.

Occupations

Abstract Tans need jobs that involve a variety of tasks, and that allow them to randomly juggle all their skills and talents. They need freedom to create their own schedules, and plenty of room and time to complete the assigned projects. They need free reign to accomplish all the necessary tasks in random order. They cannot feel confined or restricted by stringent boundaries.

Abstract Tans function better when they are employees. They are not organized enough to run their own businesses. However, they also cannot be limited to rigid structures. If they become teachers, for instance, they can be given a list of the school's required topics to be covered, but they must have the freedom to bring the information together in their own random patterns. In a political science class, rather than trace the history and development of politics, they should be free to choose a topic such as "freedom of speech" and randomly discuss events that are related to the topic. They must be given the freedom to get an abstract concept across to the students in their own way.

Although their processes are often chaotic and without logical, sequential reasoning, Abstract Tans eventually put all of the pieces of the puzzle together. They are happiest when they can work on all pieces of the project simultaneously. They prefer their jobs to have an intellectual base, though they are not adept or organized enough to deal with a lot of paper work. They prefer theorizing, reading and discussing ideas.

Occupations that appeal to Abstract Tans include:

Teacher	Gardener
Consultant	Salesperson
City developer	Computer programmer
Landscaper	Designer

Health

Abstract Tans have random patterns of internal illnesses. Health practitioners have difficulty tracking the illnesses of Abstract Tans because nothing stays still long enough to be treated — while treating the Abstract Tan's stomach for viruses, the illness may move to the intestines. Abstract Tans do not follow normal disease patterns. Although practitioners may treat the symptoms which occur in each area, new symptoms can quickly appear in different areas. Abstract Tans commonly have frequent and various health complaints, though most of their illnesses are not serious. Since Abstract Tans do not experience normal illness patterns, health practitioners are more successful at finding cures if they treat the Abstract Tans' mental and emotional conditions rather than the physical conditions.

Being forced to be linear thinkers can cause stress and illness for Abstract Tans. Being forced to fit all the pieces together within tight time frames or within rigid structures can cause illness for Abstract Tans. Illness arises when the scattered Tans become overwhelmingly frustrated by the feeling that they cannot put it all together.

To remain healthy, there are a few steps that Abstract Tans would be well-advised to take. The easily-distracted Abstract Tans must learn to slow down and not take on too many commitments at once. Since they are not efficient at planning their time, they need to find others who can help them plan realistic schedules. Included in their schedules should be a "random" health care plan. They need to include something every day that addresses their health. For example, on some days they can exercise or swim, on other days they can do yoga or stretching exercises. Or they can relax or take a vacation. They can eat a variety of healthy foods every day. The Abstract Tan's health care plan should be a complete package that has a variety of programs.

The most effective way for Abstract Tans to stay healthy is for them to maintain a sense of balance and freedom in their lives. They must be free to process their thoughts randomly. They should stay away from jobs or people who attempt to confine them to linear tasks. Allowing themselves to express their true natures — friendly, optimistic, curious and bright, will also help them to stay healthy.

■ GREEN

Greens are extremely bright, powerful and intelligent. They process quickly, jumping from steps one to ten. They do not like dealing with all the steps and details in between. A project that is too detailed is tedious and boring for Greens. They prefer instead to deal with ideas and concepts. They prefer to develop an idea, organize a plan, and then delegate someone else to take care of the details.

These quick-thinkers are very organized and efficient. They write lists and efficiently check off the items on the list as they are completed. Greens recognize patterns and discover solutions very quickly. When Greens are in their power, they can accomplish anything. They love to set goals and are determined to achieve them. Greens are "movers and shakers" when it comes to taking action.

Greens are highly competitive and enjoy challenges. They thrive on taking risks. Gambling is common for Greens, especially if there is a potential for large winnings.

Being strong-willed, these powerful personalities are determined to have their own way, which they usually feel is the right way. A person is rarely able to win an argument with a Green. Even if her opponent actually wins the argument by proving his point with logic or statistics, a Green will rarely admit defeat. Greens hate to be wrong.

Greens also dislike taking orders from other people. They believe they are more intelligent than most other people. They are quick learners who will listen to the facts and then arrange things their own way. Greens not only *like* to be in control, they seem to *need* to be in control. If situations arise that appear to be out of their control, they become frustrated, worried and stressed. They want to be in control of their emotions, environment, income and relationships. They also have a need to understand everything.

The Greens' life purpose is to experience as much as possible in this lifetime, to accomplish as much as they can, to grow and learn intellectually, and to empower others by example. They love to be challenged mentally. Once they have accomplished something or figured it out, however, they want to move on to another challenge. They are hungry for knowledge and ask a lot of questions. The number one question asked by Greens is "How?" "How did you start your own business?" "How did you become so successful?" "How did you earn your money?" Because they are such avid learners, Greens are typically found seeking further education. They are the perennial students, always obtaining more licenses and degrees. Often they believe that a certificate, degree or specialized training will prove to themselves and to the world that they are qualified for a particular job. Greens are such quick learners that they can simply watch someone else do a job and figure out how to do it themselves, quite often doing it better (at least in their opinion). Despite this ability, however, they still believe that they need the official training and education to prove to the world that they are qualified.

These ambitious personalities are *driven* to accomplish, and become very intense and serious when working toward their goals. They push themselves, always appearing to be in a hurry. Greens are the prime examples of workaholics.

These hard-workers have a tendency to compare themselves to others. They usually compare themselves to people who are more accomplished, rather than to those they have surpassed. Continuously competing and striving for greater accomplishments can keep Greens moving forward. However, their obsessive behavior may also create a constant feeling of unrest and dissatisfaction. They may perpetually judge themselves and their achievements as never being good enough.

Greens often have a fear of failure, although they rarely fail. The self-critical and demanding Greens often judge themselves as failures, but if one were to compare the accomplishments of Greens to those of others, the Greens usually have accomplished more. Greens are their own worst enemies. (No one else would even want the job.)

While some people with other LifeColors are natural counselors, Greens do not usually have the patience to listen to the problems of others. If someone turns to a Green with a problem, the Green will listen, give advice and then expect the other to *act* on the advice. If that person returns to the Green with the same problem, inwardly the Green will judge him as being weak and full of self-pity. She then loses respect for him.

Greens usually have strikingly beautiful features. They take great care and pride in their appearance. They prefer to dress in suave, sophisticated, and usually sexy styles. They cannot tolerate being overweight, looking upon it as a lack of self-discipline and willpower. Should they gain a few extra pounds, they quickly lose respect for themselves. If a

Green has a Combination Color, such as a Blue/Green aura, weight can frequently become a problem. Greens can become so concerned with their appearance that they develop eating disorders such as anorexia. When Greens are out of power, no matter how much weight they may lose, it is never enough.

When Greens are out of power, others have a difficult time being around them. Greens are so aggressive and opinionated that they have a tendency to intimidate others. They can become judgmental, arrogant and impatient. When they want something, they want it *now*. Greens are very demanding of themselves, and often impose their high expectations upon others. They are perfectionists, and their behavior often pushes other people away.

Greens feel they accomplish more when they are alone, and often perform solo. These perfectionists frequently use the word *should* in their conversations. "I should have done it better, sooner or quicker." They tend to believe that life is "hard work." Some of the words most commonly heard from out-of-power Greens are "hard," "struggle," "try," "should," "can't" and "need." Greens want people to know that they have worked hard to accomplish their goals, and therefore deserve respect and admiration. Their lives would be easier if they substituted the words of struggle with the following: "desire to," "easy," "effortless," "will," "can" and "I am." If Greens are not able to say "I desire to do this project" instead of "I have to do this project," they are probably out of harmony with themselves and not enjoying life.

When Greens suppress their power, or when they are blocked from having what they want, they become frustrated, bitter and resentful. They are also quick to blame the cause of their problems on other people or outside circumstances. They frequently blame employees, friends, parents, a lack of time or money. When Greens are upset, they release their frustrations verbally. They say exactly what they think, no matter how it sounds or whom it may affect. They feel that this is the most effective way to change the situation. They can often become hurtful, arrogant and mean. When Greens are out of power, nothing pleases them. (Although, winning ten million in the lottery may placate them for a while.)

The only one who can suppress the incredible power of a Green is the Green himself. Greens block their own power by placing obstacles in their way. By blaming others, Greens give away their power. The quickest method for Greens to regain their center is to take responsibility for their own lives. They must recognize where they are holding themselves back, write a list of everything they want and then take action. By identifying what they want and taking action to obtain their desires, the Greens will feel in control again. Once Greens are back in their power, they become so dynamic and powerful they do not have time to criticize or blame anyone else for the problems in their lives.

Relationships

One of the greatest challenges for Greens, especially Green women, is finding mates. Greens need to find mates they can respect and who can stand up to their incredible power. Their partners must measure up to the Greens' high standards. Greens can quickly outgrow and become bored with mates who are not as ambitious and goal-oriented as they are. They can run over most other LifeColors. Greens also want to make sure that being in a relationship will not deter them from accomplishing their goals. Their high expectations and workaholic behavior often create isolation. Greens frequently build walls around themselves. They are very selective with both friends and mates.

This information is not meant to be discouraging for the Greens. There are LifeColors who can handle the immense power and intelligence of the Greens, provided they stay balanced and in their power. Violets and Reds can both be competent mates for Greens. These colors are awed and inspired, rather than overwhelmed or intimidated, by the power and intelligence of the Greens.

Sex

Before they will be sexually involved with others, Greens must first know that they are admired and respected for their intelligence. They must also be able to respect and admire their partners. Once this has been accomplished, a mate has access to the Green's body. Greens do enjoy sex. When Greens become angry, however, the first thing they withhold from their partners is sex. They will refuse to be touched until the issue is resolved and they know their point of view is respected. A Green's mate can become well-acquainted with the living room sofa or the spare bedroom.

For Greens who are out of power, sex can become an intense power play. They can use it to manipulate, control or overpower their partners. They can become vindictive if hurt. Greens often derive more pleasure from accomplishing goals, negotiating business deals, or making large sums of money than they do from having sex. That can be tough competition for their mates.

Green Parents

The decision to have children is a difficult one for Greens. They do not want to be deterred from their goals and ambitions. Greens do not usually even want pets. (It may have been a Green who invented the "pet rock.") Children and pets can demand a lot of time, energy and money. These are valuable commodities to Greens and they are not always willing to make the sacrifice, even for the sake of having children. If the Greens do have children, they will want nannies or maids to free them up from domestic responsibilities. Greens are not parents who can sit at home for long. They need to be out challenging the business world, accomplishing something and being respected.

Greens are organizational parents. They want the best for their children — the best education, the best training and the best opportunities. They will organize the children as they lead them out the door, giving them lunch money and their schedules for music lessons. (Since time is money, giving the children lunch money is more efficient than spending time making peanut butter and jelly sandwiches.) Greens like their children to keep things well-organized, neat and clean. Everything has its place in their homes. (Any child with Green parents knows that leaving toys scattered around the room will cause the parents to instantly transform into either the Wicked Witch of the West or Rambo.)

It is important for Green parents to pay attention to any overdemanding attitudes they may have toward their children. Green parents can be some of the most impatient and controlling parents. They must remember that they are dealing with growing, developing children, not short adults. Teaching a child to learn responsibility, respect and discipline is admirable, as long as the means do not intimidate or frighten the child, causing him to close down his real potential or unique personality. While Greens like discipline, conformity and control, they may want to remember that they themselves are the first to challenge someone else's attempts to control them.

Green parents operate best when they stay centered and aware. (Not that it is easy for *anyone* to stay centered all the time.) When Greens are centered, they empower and teach their children by *example*. If Greens are frustrated and pushing someone else to change, the truth is that they are probably dissatisfied with their own lives. They need to clear their own fears, blockages and frustrations before they can effectively relate to their children.

Greens, who function well with order and discipline, may want to schedule time with their children. They can use this time to teach them, to learn from them, or just to get to know them better.

If Greens make their relationships with their children as much of a priority as their businesses, they will be successful at both. However, raising children does not *need* to be, nor is it usually the Greens' priority. (See Chapter 5 to see the potential conflict which arises within people with Green/Violet or Green/Blue auras when they are raising children.)

Green Children

Green children are very intelligent. They ask a lot of questions and learn quickly. These strong-willed, determined little people are also the first to challenge their parents' decisions. Greens do not like being told what to do, even as children. Instead, they become accustomed to giving orders. Green children seem more like adults than most adults do.

Green children want to be heard, listened to and respected. They can become frustrated very easily if things don't go their way. They can become very vocal with their protests by screaming, interrupting conversations and demanding attention.

For parents, dealing with obstinate and demanding Green children can be frustrating if they do not understand the priorities of their children. When the children are frustrated, the parents can work with them to develop plans on how they can accomplish their goals. Can the children "earn" the toys they want by doing chores? Can they solve the puzzle another way, rather than persistently and tenaciously putting the piece in the wrong space? Is there a more appropriate way of getting the parent's attention than screaming and interrupting?

These children are quick to understand when their parents discuss situations logically with them. Green children can argue, challenge and resent authority with the best of them. However, they are also inspiring to watch as they develop understanding, strength, determination, self-reliance and independence. Parents of Greens do not usually have to worry about their children being successful. These children will usually come home with high grades, achievement awards and success stories.

The parents should be sure to praise the Green children on their accomplishments. Respect and admiration are extremely important to them. It is beneficial for parents to encourage their Green children to go after any goal they desire and not to fear failure. Since all Greens tend to demand perfection from themselves, if the parents see the Green children being too hard on themselves or emphasizing their own shortcomings, they can instead remind their children of all of their accomplishments. This will help the Green children learn to stay balanced and to appreciate themselves.

Problem-Solving

When solving problems, Greens analyze the situation and develop solutions so quickly that they leave others spinning. They are valuable assets to anyone's business. However, when Greens are off-center or out of power, they can be stubborn and tenacious. They can beat their heads against the wall over and over again, thinking that if they are just persistent enough, they will break through the wall. Often, their persistence eventually pays off. However, clear thinking and exploring other options will usually be the quicker, more efficient ways for the Greens. Since Greens do not like to be wrong or admit that they have made a mistake, it is often difficult for them to change their course or their tactics.

Money

Money is extremely important to Greens. They like wealth, nice clothes, nice furniture, nice homes and nice cars. Having very high standards, they want the best. They are not happy or satisfied when they compromise. If they buy something that was not exactly what they wanted, they will never use it nor appreciate it.

Fortunately, this strong desire for achieving abundance, quality and prosperity has created in them the ability to manifest money very easily and quickly. Greens are traditionally some of the wealthiest people on the planet. (Violets, their wealthy counterparts, also manifest money easily. However, while Greens can work purely for money, Violets cannot. Violets need to believe in what they are doing, enjoy doing it, and know there is a higher purpose involved. Greens, for example, can build oil platforms in places where it may not be beneficial to the environment. Violets would usually protest such actions.)

When Greens do a job, they want to be well-compensated for their efforts. Money represents power, status and security to Greens. (See Chapter 5 to see the potential inner conflicts regarding money.)

Success

Greens judge their success by how much they have accomplished, how many people admire and respect them, and how much money they have.

Occupations

These ambitious entrepreneurs prefer and even need to be self-employed, own their own businesses or at least be in top management. They are very good at delegating authority. Greens like to be in charge and relish telling other people what to do. However, they can also tend to offend people with their controlling and domineering attitudes.

Greens can be found in almost any occupation which enables them to be in charge, challenges their mental skills, and offers a great deal of money. Since Greens can accomplish anything they put their minds to, they can be found in almost any type of occupation. However, if they are not well-compensated, well-respected and mentally challenged, they will be frustrated.

Occupations that appeal to Greens include:

Corporate executive
Business entrepreneur
Banker
Producer
Fundraiser
Organizer
Office manager
Marketing and
  advertising coordinator
Real estate agent

Planning and investment advisor
Salesperson (especially sales
  involving expensive items
  such as cars, gems, insurance
  and homes)
Stockbroker
Business manager and agent
King (or at least "owner"
  of the world)

See Green/Violet, Green/Yellow and Green/Blue for other occupations.

Health

When they are in power, Greens are strong, powerful and healthy. Out of power, however, it is common for Greens to become obsessed and neurotic about their health. The main problem areas for Greens are the stomach and internal organs. They worry so much that they have a tendency to develop ulcers, stomachaches, colitis, and intestinal problems. Because of this it is advisable that Greens stay away from coffee or other stimulating substances. Caffeine can be devastating to their nervous system as well as to their stomach. Greens like the energy stimulation of caffeine. It is usually their only addiction. They can get more work done after a cup of coffee. As the effects wear off, however, Greens become irritable and agitated, causing them to think less clearly. (Greens often enjoy drinking wine or other alcoholic beverages because, at the end of the day, it is the only way that they can shut off their incredibly active minds.)

A major problem for Greens is learning to relax. They do not seem to know how to relax, to take time off or to take vacations. Having a tense body is common for the Green workaholic. With work and stress, they frequently experience a tight neck and shoulders. And Greens often become so worried and anxious that they forget to breathe deeply enough. Another frequent problem area for Greens is the throat. If Greens suppress what they want to say, their throats can become very tight and irritated.

To keep from experiencing health problems, Greens must learn to relax. The only time Greens relax is when they feel that they are in control of their lives. It is recommended that Greens keep a list of things they want to accomplish, so that they feel organized and in control rather than overwhelmed. They should also schedule time to do things that they enjoy rather than work-related tasks (although Greens usually enjoy doing work-related tasks, overworking can cause stress). Greens must learn to appreciate their accomplishments rather than always focusing on their hundreds of uncompleted tasks. Being extremely busy makes Greens feel important, but it also causes stress-related health problems. Greens can ask themselves how important it really is that they have control over every situation. They can evaluate the severity of each situation to see if it really requires worry and concern. They must learn it may not be possible or even necessary to control every aspect of life. If Greens can learn to trust the process of life more often, life can prove to be more cooperative than they had imagined. One of the most important pieces of advice for Greens is to remember to *breathe*. People can think more clearly and rationally (and stay alive longer) when they are breathing more deeply more often.

4. Emotional LifeColors

■ BLUE

Blues are some of the most loving, nurturing and supportive personalities of the LifeColors. They live from their hearts and emotions. Their purpose for being on the planet is to give love, to teach love and to learn that they are loved.

Blues are constantly mothering and taking care of others. They want to make sure that everyone feels loved and accepted. They remember everyone's birthday, take care of the sick and consistently provide a shoulder for others to cry on. People are always turning to Blues for comfort and counsel because Blues will always be there for them. They are the natural counselors, teachers and nurses. The loving Blues always have an abundance of friends. Their friends are a high priority in their lives. They will give up their valuable time and energy to help a friend in need. Blues can become overly-concerned, at times, with everyone else's well-being. They can get so caught up in their friends' dramas that they can frequently end up feeling more distressed and emotionally burdened than the person they have just counseled. It is challenging for Blues not to worry about everyone else's problems. They are the ultimate "rescuers" on the planet.

These sensitive, caring individuals are also the perfect hosts. A Blue will consistently cater to guests' needs, offering food, drink or whatever they need to feel comfortable.

During a conversation, Blues will also check to see if everyone feels included.

Blues are the most emotional personalities in the aura spectrum. They can cry at the drop of a hat. Even watching a sentimental commercial on television can bring on tears. They release most of their emotions through tears, crying when they are happy, hurt, angry or sad. People with other LifeColors may have difficulty understanding the intense emotional personality of Blues. It is their capacity for such emotional depth, however, which makes them so warm, compassionate and caring toward others. They are capable of deeply understanding the feelings of others. Seeing another person cry can often cause a Blue to cry in empathy. (During a group therapy session, if one Blue in the room starts to cry, every other Blue in the room will automatically start to cry with her.)

The Blues' greatest gifts are their ability to give unconditional love and their intuition or "inner knowing." People love being around Blues who are centered and in power because Blues radiate love, acceptance and forgiveness. No matter what mistakes a person makes, Blues will love and forgive them. They look for the good in people. Blues will give everyone a hundred second chances. This behavior frequently earns them the reputation of being "doormats." Blues are often accused of being too nice. People can easily take advantage of the Blues' unselfish and endlessly giving nature. One of the Blues' hardest lessons is learning to say "no." They are afraid that if they do say no, other people will feel unloved and rejected, or will not love them in return. Blues must learn that saying no to people does not mean that they do not love them.

Blues are some of the most intuitive personalities in the aura spectrum. They "know" things. There are often no facts, data or reasons to support what they know, they just feel it to be true. They can "tune into" someone and know if that person is upset. They can feel when something is about to happen. They can think about someone they haven't seen in a long time and that person will call a few minutes later. Any time Blues have a question, whether it is regarding relationships, business, health or other matters, they only need to become quiet and centered, ask themselves the question and they will hear the answer inside every time. The challenge for Blues is learning to trust what they hear inside and not overanalyze it. (While all of us have the capability of receiving intuitive and psychic information, Blues seem to operate through intuition their whole lives.) They operate so much from their feelings that they often speak in those terms, using such phrases as "It just feels right," "I feel that my friend needs help" and "I feel something big is about to happen."

In addition to being helpers, givers and teachers, Blues are highly spiritual. Every Blue believes there is a God, a Higher Power, Universal Intelligence or All That Is. Every Blue had an experience as a child of seeing or talking with God. Blues' lives are often a spiritual quest to learn more about God. They are typically found going from one church or religion to another in search of more spiritual knowledge to explain and validate what they feel inside. Living a good, loving and spiritual life is a strong priority for Blues.

People trust Blues when they are in their power. They know Blues would never do anything to hurt anyone and that their intentions are always loving. When out of power, Blues seeking love can become overly dramatic, consumed with self-pity, manipulative, and not as trustworthy. When the Blues regain their balance and become centered, people once again believe and trust them.

Because of their loving integrity and dedication to high moral standards, Blues can only do something they believe in. When Blues believe in something, they are some of the world's greatest promoters. If they discover something they enjoy or that has helped them, whether it be a movie, a book, a restaurant or a religion, they want to share their discovery with all of their friends.

Blues want to be loved more than anything in the world, though they often doubt that they are loved. They doubt their self-worth. Blues can hear a hundred times that they are beautiful and loved, and yet if one bad thing is said, it is the negative they will remember. Blues often "test" people (especially their mates) to see if they "really" love them. "If he really loved me, he would run after me if I left him." "He would remember my birthday since I did so many wonderful things for him on his birthday." "He would worry about me if I didn't answer the phone for two days." One of the Blues' greatest lessons is to learn that they are loved just the way they are, not for what they *do*. Blues are the ultimate "doers" — they feel people love them because they buy them gifts or work hard for them, rather than because they are themselves lovable people. Blues are good "givers," but not good "receivers." They even have trouble receiving compliments. Because they do not want to bother or inconvenience anyone, they feel guilty asking for or receiving help. They also have trouble delegating authority. Consequently, Blues can get incredibly over-worked and overwhelmed with responsibilities, and with volunteering all of their time.

Blues hold onto the past and onto guilt more than any of the other colors. Far into their adult lives, they continue to feel guilty about things they did as children. Blues usually blame themselves when things go wrong. They habitually defend themselves and apologize for their behavior. "I'm sorry" could be the Blue's theme song. If a person steps on a Blue's foot, the Blue will apologize for being in the way. Blues also tend to take things personally. It's difficult for them to be around angry people. They see others' anger as a personal rejection.

When Blues are out of power, they get into victimhood, martyrdom and self-pity. It looks as if life has treated them unkindly "after all they have done for everyone." Blues need to realize they have made choices to serve and to give to others. No one has forced them to make sacrifices. When out of power, Blues use their giving as a subtle form of manipulation. Blues struggle with wanting to be loved, and not knowing how to ask for it. It is when they don't receive the love they want, or when they don't *recognize* or *accept* the love given to them, that Blues create their dramas of their victimhood and martyrdom.

Because Blues are "rescuers," they want to be rescued when they get depressed. Because Blues "know" when someone else is upset and needs love, they expect that others "know" when they are upset. However, not all of the other LifeColors are as intuitive as the Blues. Nor do they all feel a need to rescue people. While the Blue retreats into the bedroom and waits for someone to rescue her, others do not understand, and can even resent being manipulated by the Blue's behavior. Out-of-power Blues can search endlessly for love, all the while pushing away the help that *does* come their way.

Blues can become so depressed and emotional that they contemplate suicide, though they will not usually go through with it for fear of hurting the people they love. They then imagine being at their own funeral to see how many people would attend. (Just another test by Blues to see if they are loved.) Out-of-power Blues will "hit bottom" in this way before they will accept help from others. They will become over-worked, overwhelmed, ill or devastated over relationship problems. Hitting bottom is also the only time Blues give themselves permission to stop rescuing everyone else, and take care of themselves.

To become centered again, Blues must learn to love themselves, which is their hardest lesson. Blues need to understand that all of their actions are always based on one of two motives — to give love or to be loved. If they can learn that both of these are legitimate motives, then they can begin to be more gentle and understanding with themselves. Blues are typically afraid that if they love themselves, no one else will. Their greatest fear is being alone and unloved.

To regain their power, they also need to calm down and get in touch with their inner knowing again, to hear the answers inside. They need to trust that they are loved. If Blues really become depressed, their quickest cure is to do something nice for someone else. As soon as the Blues focus their attention on helping someone else, they forget about their own problems and become less depressed. (Helping others can only be a temporary solution, because Blues often become overly involved in helping others to avoid facing their own problems.)

Relationships

The two most important priorities in a Blue's life are spirituality and relationships. Blues want to be married. (See Chapter 5 to see the conflict that frequently arises with Blue Combination Colors.) The sentimental Blues want more than anything else in the world to be in bonded, loving, committed relationships with their mates. Blues are happiest when they are in good relationships. They are the most devastated and depressed when they are alone or in bad relationships.

Because relationships are so important to them, Blues tend to give themselves away or change who they are just to be loved. They often feel that they are not good enough as they are. They will change their hair style, the way they dress or their own behavior in an attempt to become the person they think their mates want them to be.

Out of power, Blues tend to choose mates who need rescuing or who emotionally abuse them. In addition, because Blues are very loyal, committed and monogamous, they will hold on to unhealthy relationships, feeling that if they just love their partner enough, the relationship will work out. Despite everyone else's opinions and advice, Blues will hold onto their relationships. They have a difficult time letting go of anything or anyone. They do not even like the words "let go." To Blues, to let go of someone means to stop loving them. Because love is a necessary element in their lives, it devastates Blues to feel they must stop loving anyone. Blues do not deal well with the guilt, sadness, loss and pain of ending a relationship. When ending relationships, they need instead to continue to love that person and expand outward to love another.

Blues have so much love to give that they can often overwhelm people who have other aura colors. When Blues love someone, especially their mates, they want to be around them all the time. When someone of another LifeColor (i.e., a Yellow) needs time alone, a Blue will take it personally, believing the other person doesn't love her as much. (See the chapters on "Relationships" to see specifically how Blues relate to each of the other LifeColors.)

Sex

To Blues, love and affection are more important than sex. They love to be hugged, held and cuddled. Being very moral, Blues grow up being the "good girl," only sleeping with someone they love. Meaningless sex is difficult for Blues. Sex is often looked upon by Blues as being "bad" or "unclean." (Someone with a Blue/Yellow aura can experience conflict with her morality, since a Yellow likes sex so much.) Blues can have difficulty experiencing sexual satisfaction unless they completely trust their partners and feel devoted love from them. While making love, it is common for Blues to cry in moments of passion (which can thoroughly confuse their carefree Yellow partners, who are usually laughing and joking while making love). Making love is a deeply emotional experience for Blues. It expresses their love and commitment to their partners.

Blue Parents

Being "natural mothers," most Blues want children (unless the Blue is "burnt out" because she has mothered everyone else). Blues want to bond emotionally with their children. They love to read them stories, hug them, and be involved with their lives. While they are some of the most loving and compassionate parents, Blues can often "smother" their children in the name of love. They tend to sacrifice their own lives, goals and ambitions by living their lives for their children.

When their child is learning to ride a bike, Blue parents want to hold onto the handlebars so he doesn't fall and hurt himself. They believe this is the best way to show that they care. Through such actions, however, they are telling the child that they do not believe in him, that he is incapable of succeeding without them. The child becomes insecure regarding his own abilities and then becomes dependent upon his protective parents. Blue parents need to realize that the most loving attitude is to believe in their children and help them believe in themselves. They need to "release the handlebars," and show their children love by inspiring and empowering them, not by creating dependency.

Children often feel guilty "abandoning" their Blue parents when it is time for them to leave the nest. Blue parents can be good at tying apron strings to their children. Blues love to feel needed by their family. They should remember, however, that there are plenty of other people on the planet for Blues to help. They do not need to channel all of their energy and attention into their children.

Children need to realize that their Blue parents only want to know that they are loved and appreciated. When Blues are in power, they intuitively know how much their children love them. They are truly giving and nurturing parents, who are devoted to caring for their children.

Blue Children

Blue children are very loving and emotional. They try very hard to please their parents so that they will be loved. Blue children want to be good helpers. Not wanting to upset or disappoint anyone, Blue children are usually well-behaved and well-mannered. Being emotional and sensitive, they are similar to Yellow children. Blue children will sit indoors, however, calmly combing their doll's hair or playing with blocks, while Yellow children run around outdoors, climbing trees and playing sports. At a young age, the sensitive Blue children want to help and take care of everyone. They are very aware of and compassionate toward the "underdog" at school. They feel sorry for anyone who seems lonely. They want everyone to feel loved and accepted.

Blues usually develop an early interest in having relationships. Every Blue has an early romantic picture of being in a loving and fulfilling marriage. They always want to buy their partners gifts or bake them cookies. Because of their lack of self-worth, Blues can experience many traumatic experiences of unrequited love. Usually, Blue children are actually very loved by their peers. A Blue/Yellow or Blue/Violet combination can be one of the most popular cheerleaders or class leaders in school. Even though Blue children have an abundance of friends who care about them, when they are out of power they often feel unloved, unworthy and lonely. Blue children, like their adult counterparts, do not always comprehend what it means to be loved by others. They often have a low self-worth.

(Note: Yellow and Violet children are quite similar to Blues. They are all sensitive and emotional. However, Blues are the most emotional of the three, Yellows are the most energetic and active, Violets are the most powerful, authoritative and independent. If dance, music, creativity, sports, freedom and independence are important to the child, chances are the child is a Yellow/Violet, a Yellow/Blue or a Blue/Violet combination aura.)

Problem-Solving

When Blues are centered, they solve problems by asking their inner selves. They must learn to listen and *trust* the answers they receive, however. Any time Blues have questions, whether about relationships, business or even what to eat, they only need to become quiet and centered, ask themselves the questions and they will hear the answers inside every time. Their only challenge is trusting what they hear.

When Blues are out of power, their method of solving problems involves sitting in a corner, crying to be rescued. They often "pray for help," but aren't always listening inside when the answers come. The Blues' quiet knowingness will give them the answers they need and solve their problems every time.

Money

People and relationships are more important to Blues than money, so they often struggle financially. Since Blues are very good givers, but not very good receivers, one of the common challenges for them is learning to receive money. They usually feel that their services should come from the heart, not from a desire for money. Blues commonly feel that being spiritual means being opposed to having material wealth.

Because money is not a priority, Blues are usually fearful of not having enough, especially when they have families to support. It is common for them to choose low-paying, service-oriented jobs. In addition, it is easier for them to complain, suffer and dramatize their hard work and sacrifices than it is for them to ask for a raise. (Refer to Chapter 5 to see a Blue/Green's conflict regarding money.)

Blues are happy being givers. But by never learning to receive, they are cheating others out of the joy of giving, and are, to a certain extent, looking down on them. Blues are saying by this action, "I am prosperous, abundant and powerful enough to give to you. You, however, are not prosperous, abundant and powerful enough to give to me." The most loving and empowering thing a Blue can do is to allow others to be prosperous, abundant, generous and capable of giving. This empowers the other person to feel good about himself.

Blues also feel guilty having more than their friends or family. They subconsciously feel they must stay down in the "pit," suffering with everyone else, not being prosperous, abundantly wealthy or in harmonious, satisfying relationships. If friends are suffering financially, Blues will either empathize and complain about their similar financial situations, or give them money to help them out. Blues will usually try to help everyone out of the pit first before they will help themselves. They feel that sacrificing their needs and putting others first shows how loving they are. Blues can have a fear of success, of being unloved and alone or of being seen as selfish if they succeed.

As long as Blues feel that they must help everyone else first, they are destined to be stuck in the pit forever. The Blue's most loving action is to get out of the pit first themselves. By showing people that they can live their dreams of abundance, health and happiness all the time, they will actually be helping people more. (The only motivation for Blues to get out of the pit is knowing that it will help others.) They must be brave enough and loving enough to lead the way, to inspire others to live their full potential by living their *own* potential. Blues need to learn that love, happiness, prosperity and spirituality can all be connected.

Success

Blues define their success by how many people love them, and by how many people they have been able to help. The quantity and quality of friends, the length and quality of their marriages, the depth of their compassion and loyalty to those they love, and their dedication to their spirituality are what Blues consider to be most important.

Occupations

Because Blues are here to be in service, they are usually drawn to the helping professions, such as teaching, counseling and nursing. They work best one-on-one with people. (While Violets are also oriented toward helping people, they work more often with groups rather than with individuals.) Because Blues feel that love and money do not mix, Blues have created these professions as some of the lowest paid positions in the professional field. (Most "service" organizations are also "nonprofit" organizations.) Blues do not believe that they should profit from helping others. Learning that prosperity and spirituality can co-exist harmoniously is a major lesson for them.

Any occupation that allows them to help other people appeals to Blues. Such occupations include:

Teacher	Volunteer
Counselor	Religious or church helper
Nurse	Nun
Child care worker	Housewife
Assistant or Director	Mother
at nonprofit	Maid
organizations	Waitress
Secretary	Social worker

See Chapter 5 regarding occupations for Blue/Yellow, Blue/Green and Blue/Violet auras.

Health

Blues do not focus much energy on their physical bodies, and they are not motivated to exercise. Walking to the mailbox and back is usually the extent of the Blues' exercise program. They rationalize and create a thousand reasons why they cannot or do not have time to exercise. Because they rarely send energy to their bodies, most Blues often have cold hands and feet.

When Blues are depressed, they prefer to escape from their bodies, and therefore don't send healing energy to their bodies. (See Chapter 5 to see the inner conflict that is created with a Blue/Yellow aura.)

Physical weak spots for Blues include the throat area, from choking back hurt and swallowing tears. Blue women can experience problems with the breasts and uterus. They create problems such as vaginal infections, cramps and breast cancer, because they typically carry feelings of guilt, shame and inadequacy regarding sex. Obesity is also found most frequently among Blue women, who often doubt that they are pretty or sexy. When they fear not being loved, Blues will often put on layers of fat for protection, particularly below the waist to protect their sexuality. Extra weight also keeps Blues "grounded" and in their bodies.

Walking, breathing and meditating are healthy activities for Blues. Releasing past guilt and the fear of not being loved will also keep them healthy. When Blues learn to give themselves as much love as they give to everyone else, it will be easier and more pleasant for them to stay focused in their bodies, and therefore allow their life energy to keep them healthy.

■ VIOLET

Violets are the dynamic, charismatic personalities who are leading us into the New Age. All Violets are developing their skills and taking on their roles as leaders on the planet. While some are showing up as leaders, others are joining together in groups to work for common causes, such as Greenpeace, Comic Relief for the Homeless, Farm-Aid, and International Wildlife Coalition — the list, of course, is nearly endless.

Violets are here to save the planet and change it for the better. Violets have an inner sense that they are here to do something important, that their destiny is greater than that of the average person. Because this is a Violet Age, any Violets who are not accomplishing what they came here to do are experiencing an inner "push" — even an inner "earthquake." Inner forces seem to be shaking them up and pushing them to move into action, to fulfill their life purpose.

The Violet Age began in the mid-sixties, definitely a time of social change and upheaval, and will continue until approximately the years 2000-2014, at which time the planet will begin its transition into the Indigo Age. Violets will lead us into the Indigo Age, into an era of peace and harmony.

Violets have extraordinary emotional depth and compassion. Their compassion tends to extend to a world-wide scale. Watching a program about starving children in Africa can overwhelm them emotionally, often inspiring them to get involved and to make changes. Violets in their power are very passionate about the causes they believe in.

Violets are also passionate about music. The vibrational qualities of music can fill Violets and move them to ecstasy or to tears. It is best for these musical connoisseurs to listen to either positive, empowering and inspiring music or calming and centering music. If they listen to angry and negative lyrics or nerve-shattering music, they will become irritable, fragmented and confused. The Violet's energy and mood is greatly affected by music. For them, music is the universal language.

These visionaries also love to travel. (Since Violets are here to save the planet, they have to see and understand what they need to save.) Violets' careers and lifestyles must afford them the freedom to travel or they will become frustrated and feel limited and unfulfilled. They need to travel the world, explore other cultures and expand their horizons.

Violets are visionaries. They can literally "see" the future in their mind's eye. Violets process life through their "third eye" or "inner vision." They have the ability to see the future, the trends or the outcome of situations. They can see a work of art completed before they begin creating it, a house built before they design it, and the results of a project before they start working on it. They can see the future results of anything they focus their attention upon — from fashion trends to music trends to the fate of the world. Violets who are in their power and in touch with their vision can see what must happen to ensure the survival of the planet. They can see that the planet will survive, and have a message to pass along to humanity. When Violets are not yet in touch with what that message is, it is because they are not centered or quiet enough inside to hear it.

While some of the LifeColors process mentally and analytically, needing to understand every step in the process as they go, Violets see the bigger picture. They jump from step one to step fifty without necessarily seeing all of the steps in between. If they trust their vision, Violets know that step fifty will occur, though they don't always know what it will take to accomplish it. It is common for Violets to speak in "vision" terms, using such words as "I see," "I picture," "I envision" or "my dream is."

Violets believe that what they "see" is common sense. They do not understand why everyone can't see what they see. To most of the other LifeColors, what Violets see is way beyond their comprehension or limited sight. To those who need to understand all of the facts and data in order to calculate an outcome, Violets' visions can seem unrealistic and impractical. Violets are often accused of being idealistic dreamers. If Violets can stay focused and in their power, however, they will inspire and earn the respect of those around them when their dream actually manifests itself.

Violets have very charismatic and magnetic energy, and people are drawn to them. Violets also love to be the center of attention. They are natural performers. (If they also have Yellow, Blue or Tan in their aura, they may have a conflict regarding being the center of attention. Yellows, Blues and Tans tend to stay in the background.) When Violets perform to audiences, energy and information literally channel through them. The information seems to come from a higher source, touching and inspiring anyone who hears it. After speaking or performing for an audience, Violets feel larger than life, full of energy and power.

When Violets are out of power, they can become narcissistic, arrogant and pompous, thinking that they are better than everyone else. It is difficult for people to be in the presence of self-important Violets. Out-of-power Violets can also develop dictator-like personalities. They love to be idolized by their "subjects."

When Violets are in their power, they are much more accepting and compassionate toward others. They allow others to follow their own paths, while they follow theirs, knowing that everyone has their own direction. (While Greens tend to "control," Violets in their power tend to "allow." Out of power, Violets have dictatorial qualities which are similar to those of Greens who are out of power.)

To stay centered, Violets need to keep a clear perspective as to how they fit in with the larger universal scheme. They need to remember that they are only a part of the whole, and that they are here to help the planet. If Violets can be aware that everyone is a part of the same greatness, they can stay humble and secure enough not to become arrogant and self-obsessed.

If the visionary Violets can stay focused, their energy will propel them forward. Out of power, Violets become scattered and overwhelmed. When they don't trust their vision, they see too many possibilities. They will then either attempt to accomplish all of them at once, taking on ten projects simultaneously — or they become mentally paralyzed, unable to do any of them. Violets cannot be told to limit their visions, but they can be encouraged to focus on no more than two or three projects at a time. This focus enables them to be more effective with their energy. Focused Violets are inspiring. When Violets do not trust their vision, they can lose touch with it and become lost and confused.

It is important for Violets to take time to center, focus and meditate. This helps them to get in touch with their vision. Listening to empowering or beautiful music, mentally surrounding themselves with the color violet, and meditating are valuable tools for keeping Violets in their power. The most imperative of these tools for Violets is meditation, which can be as simple as quiet, reflective time that allows them to get in touch with their visions and their higher selves.

The Universe will support Violets on their path by almost magically and effortlessly opening all the doors before them. Violets know that this is the way the Universe naturally operates. While many of the other LifeColors cling to the belief that life is hard work and struggle, Violets can teach us to trust the universal flow.

Relationships

Violets want relationships, but their lives will not be put on hold for them. They want partners who will live their vision with them, share a similar path and be an inspiration to them. They want mates who are willing to travel with them.

Violets are passionate with their relationships. They are willing to bond emotionally with their mates. In their power, Violets tend to be very accepting in their relationships, and can usually get along with most of the other colors. Blues feel free to cry with the compassionate Violets. Greens are allowed to be strong-willed, temperamental and even controlling. Violets will listen to and respect the Greens, and then choose what they (the Violets) want anyway.

With the strong sexual appetite of Violets and their desire to be the center of attention, they are prime candidates for extramarital affairs. They see that there are many options available to them. Violets have a charismatic and sexual chemistry, and are strongly attractive to others. Violets who do not keep a loving and focused perspective can hurt their relationships by needing too much attention for their ego satisfaction.

Sex

Violets, Yellows and Reds are the most sexual colors in the aura spectrum. Violets love sex and are extremely passionate. During love-making, Violets often sense the universal connection of everything. Making love can be a cosmic experience for them. While Yellows are sensitive to their partners, once they have finished making love they are ready to jump up and go play. Violets can stay next to their partners in a bonding embrace until the encounter has naturally and fully concluded.

If Violets go too long without sex, they become increasingly frustrated. This is often the point at which affairs occur. Affairs can also occur when a Violet is afraid to move forward to his next stage of development or on to his greater visionary project. Channeling his energy into sex or relationships can be a strong and seductive diversion.

Violet Parents

Violets love children and will bond with them emotionally. They see the potential in children and willingly share in the responsibility of raising them.

In power, Violet parents can be very accepting, seeing the bigger picture and knowing that the child will probably outgrow any immature behavior patterns. These loving parents usually teach best by leading the way and being examples.

Out of power, Violet parents can become dictators, insisting that their rules must be obeyed. They will not listen to opposing arguments or other viewpoints. They can also become so scattered and busy that they don't have time for their children.

Occasionally, Violets will stay at home with the children during their early formative years, but they soon feel the need to become involved again in the "real" world. Violets cannot just sit at home and be parents. As much as they love their children, they have too much to do in this lifetime. They need to have a positive impact upon the planet.

Violet Children

Violet children, like their adult counterparts, are natural leaders. Other children are drawn to follow them. Violets can appear to be "taken with themselves" at times. In their power, however, these children will have compassion toward others and not abuse their power.

Violet children tend to be more sexually oriented at a younger age, often experimenting with sex and their bodies. This seems natural to Violets, and so parents need to deal with the topic in a mature and non-judgmental way. Otherwise the children grow up believing that there is something wrong with expressing their natural passion through sex.

These visual Violet children usually love artwork and reading, putting their own visual pictures to the stories that they hear.

Because Violet children have such a unique visual perception, they are often able to see energies that others have long since learned not to see. Violets are the first to actually see auras, spirits, angels, other dimensions, or energy waves. If Violet children say that they see something, it is better for the parents to encourage them to describe what they see than to belittle their "active imaginations." By denying or demeaning their visual experiences, parents will teach the children to mistrust their own vision. This will cause them to become scattered and unclear of their direction later in life.

Violet children see a lot of options and want to explore all of them. Violet children will have several different piles of toys out at the same time. (This could irritate the Green parents who want order, cleanliness and discipline.) Parents of Violet children need to teach them to *focus* (not limit) their attention.

Problem-Solving

When solving problems, Violets in their power have the ability to visually lift themselves up and see past the problem to the solution. They see the future and therefore know how the problem will be solved. Violets out of their power cannot see past the four walls of a room. They are confused as to which way to turn to get out of the room, causing them to become disoriented and overwhelmed. Violets must learn to trust their visions and to act on what they see.

Money

The wealthiest people on the planet are Greens and Violets. The difference between them is that Greens can take jobs just for the money, while Violets cannot. Violets must believe in what they are doing, enjoy it and know that there is a higher purpose involved. When Violets are in their power, the money flows in. While Greens want money for the things it will buy — clothes, cars and furniture — Violets want money for the *freedom* it gives them to do what they really want.

Success

Violets judge their success by the quality of their performances, and by their ability to effectively reach their audience. Violets have a statement to make. They feel fulfilled when they know that they have reached the world with their message and have inspired change. Violets need to know that they have done their part in making the planet a better place in which to live.

Occupations

Violets are most fulfilled when they are self-employed, or as independent as possible. Violets have difficulty working for anyone else because they see too far ahead of others to be limited by the short-sightedness of others. Occasionally Violets can work for an organization, but they need to feel they are a team member and able to be part of the decision-making process, not just an employee.

Because Violets are here to inspire change on the planet, and are charismatic in front of audiences, they are usually drawn to one (or all three) of the following categories:

The first area is communications or the media. Violets are the performers and the "communicators" on the planet. The media is a perfect vehicle for Violets to reach the masses. Violets can do this through such vehicles as performing on stage or in front of a camera, singing, dancing, acting, playing music or modeling. Violets can also reach large numbers of people through performances off-camera such as directing, producing, writing, painting, designing or photography. Paul McCartney, Cher, Elvis Presley and Rick Springfield are examples of Violet performers. (George Lucas, Steven Spielberg, Bruce Springsteen and Barbra Streisand are some examples of Violet/Green Combination Colors.)

Another area of interest to Violets is teaching and psychology. Violets enjoy teaching workshops, seminars or classes. Since they are spiritual leaders, they may also teach and inspire as ministers. Violets seem to have an intuitive understanding of human behavior, which makes them natural counselors. The only way Violets can tolerate being psychologists or therapists, however, is if they lead frequent group sessions, write books, or interface with the media. Focusing on individual clients day after day is too small, tedious and limiting for Violets. They need to feel that they are effectively reaching the world on a greater scale.

The third area to which Violets are often drawn is law, politics or "causes." (Since Yellows and Blues do not like politics and Greens usually have no patience for politicians, Violets with these Combination Colors tend to pull away from law and politics. Blue/Violet and Yellow/Violet Combination Colors will frequently become involved in causes, however. They will usually choose environmental causes such as saving the whales and the rain forests, or humanitarian causes such as helping starving children and the homeless.)

Violets are natural mediators. They want people to

listen to one another, communicate openly and discuss matters in a calm and fair manner. Abraham Lincoln, Martin Luther King Jr., John and Robert Kennedy, Mikhail Gorbachev, Nelson Mandela, Ronald Reagan, Gary Hart are all examples of Violet political leaders. (Note what happened to some of the Violets who showed up as leaders before the Violet Age. Some of their ideas were too far ahead of their times and, out of fear, they were eliminated from their leadership positions. Now that it is a Violet Age, the "radical" ideas of Violets are becoming accepted.)

Other areas to which Violets are drawn include philosophy, religious studies, world travel, music, literature, art, the humanities, futuristic space development, fashion design, interior decorating, investments and architecture.

Typical Violet occupations include:

Performer	Psychologist
Actor	Social worker
Singer	Activist
Musician	Consultant
Artist	Lecturer
Writer	Politician
Designer	Lawyer
Producer	Corporate president
Director	Business owner
Camera operator	Developer
Photographer	Investment broker
Teacher	Leader
Minister	Astronaut

See Chapter 5 for occupations preferred by Violet/ Logical Tan, Violet/Yellow and Violet/Green.

Health

With the scattered tendencies of out-of-power Violets, health problems take on a similar "shotgun" effect. Health problems for Violets are varied and unpredictable. To maintain good health, Violets need to focus their attention on a few projects, not scatter their energies by becoming too busy. Meditation has a calming influence and can help Violets stay centered, which in turn keeps them healthy.

■ LAVENDER

Fantasy, enchantment, dreams, myths, spiritual beings, angels, fairies are all concepts which fill the Lavenders' mind.

Lavenders live in a fantasy world. They prefer to spend their time out of their bodies, where life is pretty and enchanting. It is challenging for these airy beings to live in three-dimensional reality. They prefer imaginary pictures of the world, seeing butterflies, flowers and wood nymphs rather than dirt, concrete and large cities. Physical reality seems cold and harsh to them.

These sensitive creatures are fragile and frail, and their physical appearance is often weak and pale. Their skin is often alabaster white because they don't like being outdoors, unless it is to be gently surrounded by beautiful gardens and flowers. These child-like personalities are sensitive and simple. They would rather spend time watching clouds float by or daydreaming. They prefer to escape this reality with all of its demands and responsibilities.

The Lavenders' behavior tends to frustrate others who may expect them to be dependable and responsible. Lavenders have no understanding of what it means to hold a responsible job or to earn money. They are more familiar with other dimensions and imagined realities. Lavenders even have a difficult time relating to or connecting with the concepts of time, space and physical matter. They tend to experience events in their imaginations, but they are not usually grounded enough in physical reality to actually accomplish anything tangible. Because they have a hard time differentiating fantasy from "reality," they tend to be spacey and forgetful. They are not sure if they actually told someone they would attend a party or if they just imagined it. The Lavenders' innate ability to use their imagination makes them extraordinarily creative. They are also highly intuitive. Using common sense, logic and reason, however, are not as easy for these gifted spirits.

At first, people are fascinated by the Lavenders' creative imagination, but after talking with them for a while, people wonder if anyone is "at home." The Lavenders' eyes can appear glazed, almost as if they are under the influence of mind-altering substances. Lavenders have a tendency to leave their bodies during conversations with other people. Their concentration tends to drift into other worlds. Their seemingly uninterested behavior can irritate and insult other people.

At the same time, Lavenders can be very entertaining and educational. They can take us beyond our limited and perceived reality into a world filled with possibilities. Lavenders believe that other worlds exist. They enjoy playing in other dimensions and other realities. While they can fully experience these other worlds, they often have difficulty explaining their experiences to others. They can become lost, agitated, or even angry if they are expected to translate what they have seen to others. Their experiences do not necessarily make sense in three-dimensional reality.

The visions and ideas of Lavenders seem unrealistic and illusionary to others. (While Violets are also accused of being unrealistic dreamers, their visions have at least the potential to be actualized. In addition, Violets are dynamic and powerful enough to fulfill their visions.) Most Lavenders dream and fantasize, but don't usually follow through with their ideas. Lavenders need to be with people who can see the potential in their ideas, and are capable of forming plans and taking action.

Once Lavenders experience something in their imagination, they feel it is too much effort to recreate their vision into tangible form. If they create stories, they do not necessarily feel drawn to write down the stories in a book. They have already received the emotional effects and feelings from the experience, and that's all that matters to them. Lavenders don't feel obligated to share their experiences with the world. They can experience all they need in their own inner world. They prefer to live in their inner fantasy world, because the outside world often can't compare.

Because of their creative talents, Lavenders make excellent artists and writers. They are especially adept at writing poetry or children's fiction. Painting pictures of fairytale castles in the sky or mythological characters appeals to these whimsical beings. Through their visual and imaginative styles, they have a unique ability to take people into a fantasy world that is alive with feelings, sensations and sounds.

Lavenders can perceive energies through their unique inner senses. Frequently, they are able to "see" other dimensions, hear colors, feel sounds and experience other realities. Being forced to stay in their bodies can be physically painful for Lavenders. They need to escape into their dream worlds for the same reason that people need to sleep. It helps them relax and recuperate from the stress of the world.

In power, Lavenders can use their creative talents to show people the possibilities of other realms. In power, Lavenders have the ability to transform their visions into works of art, thereby enhancing the lives of others. Lewis Carroll, the author of *Alice in Wonderland,* is a perfect example of a Lavender who has inspired the imaginations of people around the world.

Out of power, Lavenders have difficulty functioning in the real world. They cannot hold jobs or pay their bills, and frequently require others to support them. Out of power, Lavenders can be much like timid rabbits who, when frightened, run down the rabbit hole and into another dimension.

To stay in power, Lavenders need to be brave enough to face the real world, and to stay in their bodies long enough to be a useful and functioning part of society. They can allow themselves to explore their imaginations, but they also need to learn to be responsible adults. Escaping into other realities is fine, but Lavenders need to remember to come back. They need to be willing to apply the information that they have learned in these experiences in the three-dimensional world.

Lavenders are gentle and free spirits who are not attached to following rules, limits or systems that dictate how they should live. They live by their feelings and intuition, rather than by their intellect. They want to be free to move in whatever direction feels right at the time, and their directions change as often as the clouds do. Lavenders are not here to make a social statement, change the planet or rescue others. They just want to be free to explore their imaginations and experience other realities.

Even their spirituality is not easily defined. Lavenders have the feeling of a "Presence," but not the limited description of the typical anthropomorphic "God." These fantasy-oriented personalities enjoy soft music, wind chimes, candles, incense, meditation and the rhythmic sounds of chanting. They enjoy any sound, color or texture that can inspire their imaginations, help them leave their bodies, or take them into an etheric state of mind.

Lavenders see life as a magical world of adventure filled with fairies, spirits and angels. They are here to explore other realities and then describe them to us. They are here to stimulate our imaginations, to inspire our sense of wonder and to keep the idea of magic alive in us all.

Relationships

Lavenders are often not available for relationships because they live so much in their own inner worlds. They are not always willing to be an equal partner in a relationship which requires communication or the sharing of responsibilities. Lavenders do not like commitment because it carries with it a sense of responsibility and a requirement to focus on physical reality. They don't need relationships the way some of the other LifeColors do. They are content to be loners. If Lavenders want companions, they simply use their imagination to create some.

At first, their mates are attracted to and fascinated by the imaginative Lavenders. They soon learn, however, that they are living with fragile butterflies who are sometimes present and sometimes not. While these sensitive personalities are gentle and good-natured, they are not always reliable or responsible partners. Because Lavenders are not grounded, they have a hard time offering any sort of stability to a relationship. Usually, their mates will need to financially support the bewildered Lavenders, unless some of the Lavenders' creative ideas pay off and make money. Otherwise, they cannot be bothered with, nor can they even comprehend the concepts of jobs, budgets, bills or even household chores. Their mates quickly learn not to depend on the unreliable Lavenders.

While Lavenders want to be loving and supportive mates, and their intentions are good, their follow-through is poor. Because they don't usually act on their intentions, they can appear to be inconsiderate and uncaring toward their mates. Seeing disappointment in their loved ones' eyes can devastate the sensitive Lavenders. They have a fear of disappointing others and of not being loved. If Lavenders feel that they have failed, they withdraw more and more into a fantasy world. They do not know how to deal with rejection. Their tendency to withdraw when situations become uncomfortable usually irritates their mates even more. Their mates feel abandoned, left to solve the dilemma by themselves.

It takes very loving and patient people to be able to understand and maintain relationships with Lavenders. Since Lavenders are so naive and childlike, their mates may feel more like parents than spouses at times. However, if treated with gentleness and kindness, these loving Lavenders will be gracious, sensitive, appreciative and dedicated mates. Their loved ones can eventually find the Lavenders' innocence and creative imaginations endearing and lovable.

Sex

Lavenders love to fantasize during sex. They love to be experimental and creative, allowing their imaginations to take them anywhere. As long as they remain physically safe in their explorations, Lavenders will play. Sex can be both gentle, or an exotic experience for them. During love-making Lavenders commonly leave their bodies to drift in and out of other dimensions. This can add a level of excite-ment and fascination for the Lavenders' partners, or it can leave them wondering if they are even a necessary element in the experience.

Lavenders do not enjoy sex as much if it leads to serious attachments and commitments. At the same time, they must feel safe and trusting of their partners if they are to lose themselves in the experience at all. Lavenders don't want any demands placed upon them. They do best with partners who are sensitive, caring, playful, trustworthy and free.

Lavender Parents

Lavenders are fascinated by children. They relate wonderfully to the child's free imagination. Together,

Lavender parents and their children enjoy reading stories, going to movies, decorating their rooms, designing art projects, or writing stories. Having parents who will help them design Halloween costumes or create birthday party decorations can be fun for children. However, Lavender parents are not always there for their children. They can be irresponsible and unreliable parents. Lavenders are frequently scattered and forgetful, and they don't always follow through on their promises.

If their children need serious help or require counseling, Lavenders typically withdraw or "float away." They do not feel capable of dealing with intense emotional situations. Their guidance usually comes in the form of stories in which the children take imaginary journeys. The stories can often include morals or lessons that the children can find if they are aware enough to listen for them. The Lavenders will talk of helpful fairies and protective angels to calm the children and show them that they have nothing to fear. While there is no reason to doubt the existence of such helpful entities, this information doesn't always help these children prepare for the realities of school, peers and adults in positions of authority.

Usually, Lavender parents will not be the disciplinarians or the providers in the family. However, they will teach their children to believe in magic, dreams, spirits, creativity and the possibility of other realities. Children of Lavender parents learn not to expect much from these fragile adults. They learn to turn to the other parent for answers, or grow up quickly on their own.

Lavender Children

Lavender children, like Lavender adults, spend most of their time in fantasy worlds. They are very fragile children who often seem afraid of the "real" world. These gentle and sensitive souls often have difficulty relating to other children, preferring instead to play with imaginary friends.

They spend quite a bit of their time daydreaming and often experience trouble in school because they do not pay attention. These children are not troublemakers looking for attention, it's just that they are usually not aware of where they are. They drift easily in and out of other realities.

Lavender children are very creative, and relate best to subjects that allow them to explore their imagination and creativity. Courses such as art, creative writing and design help them exercise their natural skills. Subjects that involve mental calculations, logic, memorization or communication skills intimidate Lavenders. Usually they become lost in excessive data. Once they are overwhelmed, they withdraw into their own worlds and hesitate to return to the real world.

Parents can become easily frustrated by the Lavenders' irresponsible behavior. No matter how much the parents talk to a Lavender, it is useless. Lavender children aren't listening — they have drifted off into another world. They can be adept at making it look like they're listening when in fact they're not. (Just because a child doesn't listen to his parents doesn't mean he is a Lavender, however. Every child stops listening at one time or another.) Parents must learn how to gently coax these escape artists back into physical reality. Anytime a Lavender sees an angry or disapproving look on his parent's face, his first response is to withdraw and hide. Yelling at him only increases his fear of being in this reality. But if Lavenders feel this world is a safe and pleasant place to be, they are more willing to spend time here.

All Lavenders, children included, just want to be free to use their imagination. They don't cope well with responsibilities, which can be quite a challenge for parents. It is helpful for parents of these unique personalities to calmly teach these children a basic sense of responsibility, and how to be productive with their creativity. Parents must be patient, sensitive and not overly demanding. Otherwise, the timid Lavender children will retreat into their inner worlds, possibly never to emerge again.

Problem-Solving

Typically, these ungrounded personalities don't like problems. Dealing with controversy or conflict forces them to pay attention to physical reality. It also makes them see the unpleasant side of life. Lavenders are not usually practical enough to be efficient problem-solvers. In power, however, they can be very creative and inventive. Although their solutions aren't always rational, they occasionally are so creative or innovative that someone else is able to find a practical solution in the midst of their ideas.

Being highly imaginative, Lavenders can create games or stories that enable people to solve problems, overcome management conflicts, or solve personnel difficulties. Their inventive style of turning problems into games can be less threatening for people who tend to become emotionally attached to the problem. However, since Lavenders are so illogical and ungrounded, people often have trouble trusting the Lavenders' solutions. They rarely appear to be realistic. Lavenders are also quiet and unassuming, so most of the time people don't pay any attention to them or their ideas.

When Lavenders are out of power, they don't want to face problems. They have trouble coping with reality in the first place. They are easily distracted by their imagination and their daydreams. Analyzing problems can overload the Lavenders' sensitive systems very quickly. It is beneficial for Lavenders to find friends and loved ones who can gently and patiently help them find rational solutions to their problems.

Money

Lavenders have a difficult time understanding money. Financial obligations are not only burdensome, they are too much a part of physical reality. Money is also physically dirty and unappealing to them. These childish personalities prefer to escape into other realities where everything that they want is easily manifested.

Lavenders feel that if money is to exist at all, it should be used to obtain pretty clothes, crystals, ornamental jewelry or other fanciful items. These creative creatures resent having to put their energy into working hard at jobs they dislike, just to pay for such basics as rent, bills and car payments. The type of life in which people must struggle just to have money is not worth living for Lavenders.

Because Lavenders don't understand such complicated concepts as budgets, investments and financial planning, they can easily get into financial trouble. They spend money as fast as they get it, consequently they can become overwhelmed with debts. It is helpful for Lavenders to either learn how to effectively manage their money or find someone who can manage it for them.

Success

Lavenders want the freedom to live the way they want and where they want, whether it be in or out of their bodies, in physical reality or in other dimensions. They prefer to live out of the reach of critical, unaccepting "realists" who try to force them to live in a three-dimensional world.

They prefer to live in a simple and fanciful world where they can freely roam with their imaginations. Their ultimate joy is to be financially supported, so they have the freedom to be creative dreamers. (While others such as Greens prefer to work, to be mentally challenged and to accomplish, Lavenders prefer the opposite. They enjoy relaxing so that they are free to dream.)

Occupations

Lavenders are pleasant and friendly, but they work best in quiet, low-stress environments that allow them plenty of time to daydream, fantasize and create. Working regular office jobs is painful for them because too much mental concentration is required. Lavenders do not do well calculating or analyzing details, nor can they be expected to organize anything. They are too forgetful and scattered. They have trouble even remembering their customers' orders in a restaurant. Lavenders don't like to be burdened by too many responsibilities. They won't be rushed or pressured.

Careers in art or theater appeal to Lavenders because they allow them to explore their imagination and creativity. These free spirits will frequently create through many art forms.

Occupations that are attractive to Lavenders include:

Storyteller	Dancer
Artist (especially fantasy art)	Actor
	Costume designer
Writer (especially children's books)	Interior decorator
	Set designer
Mime	Teacher

Health

Since Lavenders spend very little time in their bodies, they can have frequent and varied health problems. Because they don't always send their Life Energy through their bodies, everything from their skeletal structures to their organs can suffer. Lavenders are just not very attached to their physical bodies. If they feel pain or discomfort, they merely leave their bodies, rather than deal with whatever warning signs they are receiving. This is similar to a person turning up his car radio when the car begins to make strange noises. Lavenders are not always aware of the benefits of good nutrition, exercise or preventative medicine.

There are not any specific areas in which Lavenders commonly experience health problems. But a lack of life energy can cause the entire body to slowly deteriorate. However, if the Lavenders stay in power and spend more time focused in their bodies, they have a remarkable ability to heal their bodies by using their imagination. Lavenders are adept at imagining the "dragons" (cancer cells) being killed by the "white knights" (white blood cells) in their bodies. By focusing their imagination on healing, Lavenders can effectively cure themselves. To stay healthy, it is wise for Lavenders to remember that they *have* bodies, and to take realistic, tangible steps to take care of them. Eating healthy foods and exercising are good beginning steps.

Floating in and out of their bodies can actually be beneficial for Lavenders. Leaving their bodies relaxes them and reduces stress. Spending too much time in physical reality can actually create stress-related problems. Lavenders need to occasionally focus on their bodies in order to take care of them. Balance is important for Lavenders.

■ CRYSTAL

Crystals are a clear conduit or channel for healing energy. Being natural healers, Crystals help their clients clear blockages to enable their own natural healing process to take place. While healing, Crystals are able to keep their thoughts and emotions out of the way, and this makes the healing pure. Crystals do not always understand their healing abilities. It can often frighten and confuse them and cause them to feel overwhelmed.

Since their own LifeColor is clear, Crystals tend to take on other people's colors when they are in their presence. They can be "auric chameleons," taking on the characteristics, behavior patterns, emotions and thoughts of that color.

Consequently, in-power Crystals can get along quite well with others. A Yellow, for example, feels he can relate to a Crystal who, when she is with him, acts and thinks like a Yellow. However, inconsistencies are created with Crystals that can also confuse people. One minute they think and behave like Greens. A short while later, they can act like Blues. The intensity of the characteristics taken on are in proportion to the amount of time the Crystal spends with the other person. Because Crystals tend to absorb the colors of the other person's aura, that other person can, at times, feel an energy drain when he is in the Crystal's presence.

Crystals are physically fragile and delicate. They like everything to be pretty, clean and gentle — like a fairytale. Because they like simplicity and cleanliness, their environments tend to be uncluttered, quiet and orderly. Crystals require a lot of time and space alone to meditate, reflect, nurture and balance themselves. It is healing for Crystals to surround themselves with nature. Growing flowers or planting gardens is very therapeutic. It gives them a chance to commune with God in peace and serenity. Crystals tend to avoid environments or people who are harsh. The world often seems cold, heartless, rough, insensitive and dirty to Crystals. They can become disillusioned easily, and this can cause them severe distress.

Though they tend to be very quiet, Crystals are also quick thinkers and learners. They love to read books, watch movies, attend the theater — anything of social significance or that inspires them to ponder the meaning of life. They prefer spending time alone rather than with others. Crystals love to spend time contemplating life and spirituality. They live their lives by intuition. If they don't follow what they know and feel inside, Crystals become depressed and confused. They lose touch with themselves and their purpose. A Crystal's life purpose is to be a clear and willing channel for healing energy. The Crystal seeks to learn to be quiet inside so that a pure understanding and a true connection with God can be made.

In power, Crystals are the gentle and serene healers on the planet. When they allow themselves to do this work, they have a sense of inner peace and harmony. Even if the Crystal is not working in the healing arts, his peaceful energy can heal those around him. The Crystal's quiet and sensitive nature can appeal to everyone at sometime or another. Crystals are quiet, well-meaning souls. They vibrate at a very high spiritual level, and this creates a very clear channel for healing energy.

Out of power, Crystals can become confused, disoriented, and depressed. They feel no purpose in living and tend to shut themselves off from life and others. Crystals often lack self-confidence and are constantly looking for reassurance and approval from others. Being sensitive and easily hurt, they retreat inside with their emotions. They are often insecure about making their own decisions, becoming dependent on others to run their lives.

Unsure of their own self-worth, Crystals' low self-esteem makes them uncomfortable in large crowds. They retreat inside where it is safe, and watch others to see what is socially acceptable and appropriate. Crystals who are off balance don't act from what they know to be true, but from *learning* certain behaviors and responses from others. When they are out of power, Crystals seem to forget why they came to the planet. They have no idea what they are supposed to do or what is expected of them. This frightens them, and they look to others for answers and protection. Because of their identity problem, Crystals tend to overly involve themselves in other people's affairs. This distracts them from having to dealing with their own lives.

To stay in power, Crystals must learn to go within. They need to learn to commune with God on a regular basis.

They must constantly retreat to their own environment to "clean" their auras of the chaotic influences from other people. This will help them stay centered, clear and remain open channels for the healing work they came here to do.

Relationships

Those in relationships with Crystals must understand their quiet nature and allow for their need for solitude. The Crystals' tendency to withdraw does not mean they are cold or conceited. Rather, peace and quiet are necessities in order for them to remain balanced and unfragmented. Crystals can too easily pick up the frustrations, attitudes and behaviors of their mates, and this can cause these fragile personalities to become overwhelmed. Giving themselves time for quiet meditation allows them to clear their auras and cleanse their energies.

In power, Crystals can have a calming, healing effect on their mates, and this keeps their relationships loving and harmonious. Out-of-power Crystals may have such low self-images that they withdraw inside themselves for protection, leaving their relationships empty and disconnected.

Crystals are not aggressive, ambitious, driven personalities. They do not like to be the center of attention; they prefer instead to remain in the background where it is safe. These simple children do not strive to be leaders or decision-makers. They are too easily confused by information, emotions and opinions. Therefore, Crystals need mates who are willing to be leaders, decision-makers and powerful protectors. Their partners must also be patient, allowing and quiet, so that the Crystals are not intimidated by them. Crystals need safety, peace and calm from their relationships.

Sex

Crystals enjoy sex, but it can frequently be a traumatic experience for them. Because they interact with the other's aura so intensely during love-making, it is often painful for them to disconnect emotionally afterwards. Fear of the resulting pain can cause them either to withdraw physically and emotionally from the other person or to remain distant for protection, which makes them appear unfeeling and frigid. Crystals can remain single and/or celibate for long periods of time because of the potential emotional trauma involved in intimacy. They may end up preferring to live alone because it is easier and quieter. Their behavior is not a result of childhood problems; it is, by nature, their choice.

Crystal Parents

Crystals can relate to children because of their simple, unfettered natures. Crystals are like children in many ways. Both are naive and fragile. Both prefer a simple existence. However, Crystals can easily become overwhelmed by the frantic and exuberant pace of energetic children. A Crystal mother needs to retreat to the quiet solitude of the bedroom or the bathtub much more often than any of the other colors. Crystals are loving, gentle and sensitive parents who have a low threshold for confusion, disorder and noise. They are not disciplinarians nor do they take charge of most situations. They usually depend on their mates to raise the children.

Crystal Children

Crystal children are much like their adult counterparts. They need a lot of time alone to retreat into their bedrooms for solitude and quiet. Crystal children are incredibly fragile, easily fragmented and frequently display low self-esteem. They are overwhelmed by the confusion at school. They are often uncomfortable with their peers. They tend to be shy and withdrawn, although they are also very loving and gentle. Parents of Crystal children need to allow them a lot of time to retreat, and to spend time alone. Parents need to be very gentle, accepting, understanding and patient with their Crystal children. Crystals will never outgrow their need for solitude, but by understanding this need and allowing themselves to stay quiet and balanced, they can at least maintain their self-esteem and self-appreciation.

In power, Crystal children are intelligent and can excel in most of their courses. Communication, drama or speech classes can frighten them, however. Crystals do not like expressing themselves in public or being the center of attention. Instead, they enjoy classes which help them explore the beauty or the meaning of life, classes such as art, philosophy or music appreciation. (Yellow and Tan children can also be quiet and withdrawn. Read the list of occupations to see which seems to fit most closely with the personality of your child.)

Problem-Solving

Crystals are cautious when solving problems, leaning toward the solutions that have been proven successful in the past. They are very good at summing up the thoughts and feelings of everyone involved and giving an objective, detached summary, but are not usually brave enough to make suggestions as to the solutions. They do not volunteer their ideas; they wait until they are asked. Crystals prefer solutions that are simple, clear, uncomplicated and low-risk. They are definitely not executive decision-makers.

Money

Money provides security for Crystals and is handled with care. Money is a complicated concept for Crystals, but they are very conscientious and responsible with it. They would never think of shirking their responsibilities or not paying their bills. Crystals do not like taking risks or getting into trouble. They keep their lives as easy, clean and simple as possible. They can make enough money to pay their bills, but have no concept of how to invest it. Crystals prefer to let someone else handle the financial responsibilities, while they tend to the peaceful and spiritual aspects of life.

Success

Crystals judge their success by how calm and peaceful they feel, and by how clear and effective their healings are. Having a sense of inner serenity and a connectedness to God/Universal Life/All That Is, is life itself for Crystals.

Occupations

Crystals are at their best in clean, quiet, low-key environments such as libraries, doctors' and church offices. They are dedicated, efficient and hard-working employees. They do particularly well in situations where there is structure and where details are important. No matter how repetitious a job may be, Crystals are patient and calm enough to take care of the details. They prefer the security of working for others. They are not usually powerful or ambitious enough to start their own businesses, and they prefer jobs where they can work quietly and alone.

Because they love beauty, Crystals are drawn to the arts. Because they have an ability to intensify energy in their bodies and create an outward flow, they are also drawn to the healing professions, such as massage, physical therapy and medicine (especially holistic medicine). Healing is the field in which Crystals experience their greatest power. When clear and centered, they have an unusual and powerful ability to amplify healing energies from the Universe, as well to transfer that energy to those who need it. Crystals are drawn to occupations that are healing, artistic, creative, natural, quiet, simple or reflective, such as:

Librarian	Interior decorator
Secretary	Florist
Receptionist	Herb grower
Massage therapist	Physical therapist
Healer/doctor	Nun
Dental assistant	Monk
Artist	

Health

Because Crystals are emotionally sensitive and easily shattered, their physical bodies are fragile as well. Health problems can become a major concern for these gentle personalities. Almost anything can go wrong with Crystals. They can even take on the health problems of their companions. For example, if a Crystal spends time with a Green, she can end up with the same health problems as a Green, in areas such as the stomach, the internal organs or the neck and shoulders. The Crystals' vibration resonates at such a high frequency, and is so sensitive and vulnerable that it is important for Crystals to spend time in solitude and quiet meditation to clear out any negative energy influences they may have absorbed.

■ INDIGO

Indigos are the New Age children. They are very spiritual with an inner awareness of the real truth about life. Mankind seems to be only now uncovering evidence regarding the true nature of reality and information known by the ancient mystics. Indigos already possess that knowledge.

Indigos are the LifeColor which will be predominant on the planet during the New Age, which is predicted to begin shortly after the year 2000. The New Age is the era during which humanity will experience peace and harmony on the planet. Indigos know that in the future, we will be living in cooperation with the environment and with each other. There will no longer be disrespect for life. There are many Indigo children being born on the planet at this time, which is an indication that we are preparing for the New Age.

Indigos are so advanced spiritually, people tend to see them as bizarre or eccentric. They can appear to be androgynous. It's difficult to tell if they are male or female, heterosexual or homosexual. Indigos appear to have incorporated both the male and female aspects within themselves.

These sensitive souls have an inner sense that we are all actually divine beings, not merely physical beings, and that who we really are goes beyond what we see. Indigos believe that matter and physical reality are illusions, that Life is really composed of "God-force," energy or living consciousness. They know that everything in the universe is somehow connected — that time, space, distance and form are not the separate entities that they have been made out to be. There is no separation except in the human mind.

In power, Indigos are aware, bright, creative and independent individuals. They live life from higher principles. These advanced souls feel that all life should be honored and treated with integrity, compassion and love. They follow their own inner knowing and abide by higher truths. They understand spiritual concepts more easily than physical concepts. However, they are highly inquisitive and curious about life in a three-dimensional world, and they need room and time to explore it.

These incredibly gifted and sensitive individuals are constantly questioning and searching for verification to support their inner knowingness. Indigos are more interested in understanding the truth and higher life principles rather than in learning about society's rules, beliefs or limited versions of reality. Indigos will not be limited by antiquated ideals or short-sighted beliefs.

Indigos cannot be coerced into doing anything they do not believe in. They will not accept direction from others unless they feel that they share the same ethical beliefs and the same inherent understanding of the truth. No amount of social pressure will force them to compromise or follow rules they do not agree with. They do not believe in the concepts of guilt or punishment, so neither can be used effectively to persuade the Indigos to go against their basic beliefs.

With their clarity and innocence, Indigos are extraordinarily truthful. Much to the dismay of society, Indigos are honest, forthright and unwilling to be cajoled or forced into any kind of mold. They cannot be manipulated by peer pressure or by promises of acceptance and love from others. Indigos must live their lives in accordance with the highest principles that they understand. "Selling out" causes them to become depressed, anxious and self-destructive; it goes against their basic nature.

While Indigos are very honest and independent, they are also very compassionate and accepting. In power, they will not be caught up in the illusion of physical appearances. They understand that people sometimes create dramas in their lives, and can be very compassionate toward these people. However, they are also aware that there is a greater picture and a higher purpose to life. They see that people are divine beings who can become lost in the "movies" and "dramas" of their own creations. They feel that people will eventually "wake up" from their dramas, and comprehend the true meaning of life. They believe everyone must be allowed to grow and awaken at his own pace.

Many Indigos have difficulty adjusting to their bodies, because they don't seem to totally comprehend living in a physical world. Their bodies often feel to them like foreign space suits. Indigos are not always sure how to operate their bodies. In addition, their inner senses seem to be attuned to very high frequencies. Even their five physical senses seem to be more refined, similar to a dog's sensitive sense of hearing. This sensitivity can cause them to be easily overwhelmed and overloaded. Indigos can even be highly sensitive to foods, able to incorporate into their diet only foods that are naturally and organically grown.

With this highly developed system, Indigos seem to be able to see or detect other energies, spirits, auras or other dimensions. They have the ability, on an inner level, to commune with animals, children, plants and nature in general. Because Indigos can often be found talking with imaginary friends, they are accused of having very active imaginations or even of being psychologically imbalanced.

People frequently have trouble understanding the Indigos' unique ability to comprehend other realities — for example, the idea that trees have souls, that the earth can literally cry in pain and that we are all connected in consciousness.

Indigos also have a knowledge at a very young age of life cycles. They know that life is a continuous process and that death is a part of that process.

These gentle souls feel connected to everything, and anything they own becomes a part of them, like an appendage. The object takes on the Indigos' energy. It can be painful for Indigos to lose something that they own. It is not that they are concerned with physical possessions. They see these objects as having a living energy they are able to connect with, just like most people connect with their pets.

Indigos have difficulty putting the concepts that they intrinsically understand as truths into words. There is not always the vocabulary to explain what they know. In addition, Indigos feel that putting such expansive ideas and concepts into linear language limits the holographic picture of what life truly is. They do not separate their lives into categories of work, play, relationships and education. Rather they see that all of these aspects fit together as a whole experience.

Indigos can be very fragile and sensitive beings, much like children. Out of power, they can become frightened and disoriented. They lose touch with their inner knowing and then do not understand life. Because the current state of the planet is not in harmony with the Indigos' belief system, many of them are having difficulty understanding what's happening here. The world doesn't look or behave the way they feel it should. War, conflict, violence, poverty and starvation are alien concepts to Indigos. They don't understand how human beings could create such aberrations. Since we are all one, how can we commit such atrocities toward ourselves?

Because Indigos are just now starting to show up on the planet, they do not have much reinforcement or many teachers who can explain to them what's really happening here. There is very little physical evidence at this time to support what Indigos feel to be the truth.

To hide from their confusion and quiet their inner voices, Indigos often turn to drugs or alcohol. This causes them to sink even further into confusion and despair. Because Indigos do not always have the words to express their feelings, communication becomes difficult and sometimes impossible when they are in this bewildered state. These sensitive and misunderstood souls will often end up in institutions, where professionals will analyze, "reform," and mold them into socially acceptable people with traditional values and perceptions. Many people do not understand the advanced and unusual perceptions of Indigos, so traditional therapy can intensify the Indigos' inner conflict.

To stay in power, Indigos must trust what they feel inside to be the truth. They must remember that they came to the planet with all the knowledge they need to live life with joy, fulfillment and harmony. They need to stay committed to and stand firm with their beliefs that love and truth will ultimately show life for what it really is — a beautiful and creative expression of "All That Is." By being a living example of these principles, Indigos will eventually show people how to create a peaceful and harmonious world.

Out-of-power Indigos can sometimes feel isolated and misunderstood, but they also seem to be aware that Life surrounds and encompasses them, and this gives them an inner knowledge that they are never really alone. Although Indigos are very sensitive, they are also very independent. While they love people, they don't seem to need that much interaction with others.

Meditation and prayer are useful tools to help Indigos stay in touch with their spiritual understanding and to stay in balance. Indigos are fully actualized human beings who believe that there is more to us as beings than is physically apparent. They understand energy and consciousness. In power, they live from high principles, from conscious love and a greater "knowing." They are aware that all of life is connected.

Indigos are here to usher in the New Age, to teach us to live from higher consciousness and higher principles so that we can create peace, love and harmony on the planet. Indigos are the new spirit, the new energy, and the new consciousness on the planet. What they intuitively know, all humanity will know in the coming New Age.

Relationships

Indigos are selective. They need to be with mates they can trust, mates who will allow them to operate from their unique belief system. Indigos need mates who can support their New Age, spiritually advanced way of thinking. Indigos are very gentle and committed partners who prefer their spouses to be best friends and companions first and foremost, and secondly lovers. These unique beings relate more on a soul-to-soul basis with their partners. They need mates who will be nurturing, dedicated and understanding, while allowing them their independence and curiosity.

Indigos are very loyal and monogamous partners. Their principles do not allow them to be unfaithful. Indigos are, however, very sensitive souls who can be hurt quite easily if their loved ones show anger or disappointment toward them. They understand the essence of commitment, and this allows for deeper levels of bonding.

Sex

Sex for an Indigo is a deeply spiritual, bonding experience between two souls, not merely a physical function. Indigos do not have sex unless they feel a deep sense of love for the other person. They do not comprehend, for example, a Red's attitude and belief that sex is for purely animalistic, lustful, physical pleasure. Since Indigos have incorporated the male and female aspects within themselves they do not *need* sex to feel a sense of completion or wholeness. Sex is cosmic union. Indigos become emotionally and spiritually absorbed in the experience, not even aware that there are physical bodies involved.

Indigo Parents

Since Indigos are fairly new on the planet, there are not very many Indigo parents at this time. Indigos, while being powerful, are also much like sensitive children themselves. Indigos believe that we are souls experiencing creative physical reality on the planet. They also have a sense that, through their physical bodies, other souls are allowed passage onto the planet. Indigos don't feel a sense of ownership toward their children. They have a sense that they are here to teach and guide the young souls until they are able to develop an understanding and life of their own.

Since Indigos have a natural, intrinsic understanding of right and wrong, they expect the same of their children. They are shocked if their children don't behave with these standards in mind. At this time, they have a difficult time teaching their children how to adapt to the ways of the world. Their teaching comes from a higher awareness of the way the world should be. Indigo parents do not relate to disciplinary acts of physical punishment. When teaching their children, they tend to emphasize love, compassion, and honoring people as divine beings.

Indigo Children

Even as babies, Indigos are unusually bright, aware and inquisitive toward their surroundings. They are also extremely sensitive, and tend to cry easily. Their senses are highly developed, so they can be easily disturbed, frightened or overwhelmed. These advanced souls require very little sleep, even as infants. They need only enough sleep to rejuvenate the physical body and then they are ready to explore this physical, three-dimensional creation we call earth.

Indigo children tend to be loners, because they are rarely understood or accepted by their peers. These children also cannot be forced to do something that they don't understand or that doesn't feel right to them. Threats of punishment, pleading, rationalizing or physical force cannot make Indigo children go against their inner beliefs. If parents or teachers attempt to force these children to operate against their values — for example, by asking them to pick flowers when they believe that flowers are living entities with souls of their own — this will create confusion and anxiety for them. They have such an inner awareness of the difference between right and wrong that they do not need discipline. It is when parents and teachers don't allow Indigo children to act according to their beliefs that they create resistance in these children.

Indigo children are very inquisitive. They will not accept simple answers just because those have been the traditional answers in the past. The answers must *feel* like the truth to the children or they will reject them and continue to search. This can frustrate parents as well as teachers. Indigo children have difficulty relating to most of the traditional subjects taught in school. They don't understand the relationship between these subjects and the spiritual life. Indigo children are not rebellious or angry children, they are merely hungry for truth. When they finally do get answers which resonate with higher principles, there is no further conflict.

Problem-Solving

When in power, Indigos solve problems according to higher principles. The answers must be ethical, loving and humanitarian. They will not accept answers that lack integrity just because they are quick or convenient. Indigos will never cheat, lie or steal, so friends and employers can always count on these loving souls. When in their power, Indigos trust their inner sense to tell them the right thing to do.

Out-of-power Indigos can become fearful and lost in a world alien to their beliefs and what they know to be true. They lose touch with their inner knowing. These sensitive individuals can become confused, disoriented and mistrustful of their own solutions. When out of power, Indigos don't understand how their cosmic awareness fits into worldly reality. With their unusually sensitive physical and emotional systems, they can become very withdrawn, causing them to feel isolated and misunderstood. They have a hard time explaining their belief systems to others, so they feel out of place.

Money

With most of the traditional concepts and beliefs on the planet being foreign to Indigos, it is no surprise that they do not relate easily to the concept of money. Indigos do understand energy exchanges, however, and they can be taught that money is an energy form that is exchanged for goods or services. Sacrificing life, love, health or freedom, however, for bits of silver or pieces of paper is not something Indigos comprehend.

Having such an understanding of integrity, Indigos are not irresponsible. They will support themselves. But they see money as an energy form that facilitates experiences and provides the necessities in a three-dimensional, physical world. They do not need a lot of money to survive on the planet. They seem to know other methods of manifesting what they want in life. Money is only one form of created energy.

Like their other spiritual counterparts, Blues and Violets, Indigos cannot work just for the money. They will not do anything that exploits people, harms the environment, endangers animals or goes against their belief that life is sacred. Making money is not a reason to forsake principles.

Success

Indigos are happiest when they are able to live their lives in harmony with their beliefs. They feel successful when they have been able to find an answer that explains physical reality, and that resonates with their inner knowing. They also feel happy and fulfilled when they are able to help other souls on the planet.

These advanced souls feel joy when they see the world moving toward peace and aligning itself with higher spiritual principles. They feel successful when they know they are being aware and living the highest Truth that they know.

Occupations

Indigos are very sensitive and creative individuals. They prefer occupations that allow them the freedom to create, to travel, or to connect with life in its various forms. They have the sensitivity and patience to work with children, the ability to understand and communicate with animals, the creative talent to be artistic, and the love and compassion to work with people.

Indigos don't actually relate to the concept of "work." At birth, Indigos have a belief that life is energy and should manifest into whatever form we ask it to take. However, many Indigos are re-trained and re-educated at a young age to believe in the traditional and limited laws of manifestation, which is that people work for a living.

Indigos need space and freedom to be able to question and explore physical reality. Working for others can be restrictive and limiting if there are too many rules. Starting their own business and being responsible to employees, however, can be too much of a burden for Indigos. Jobs which allow them to be independent yet secure are ideal for these advanced souls. Although they are faithful and trustworthy employees, they are too sensitive to be in the typical business world. They enjoy jobs that enable them to love or support others.

Usually, Indigos remain quietly in the background. They do not need the attention of the masses. However, occasionally a creative Indigo such as Michael Jackson is brought by his exceptional talents into the spotlight.

Occupations that interest Indigos include the following:

Artist	Animal caretaker
Designer	Child care worker
Writer	Social worker
Musician	

Health

When they are in their power, Indigos understand that the body is just energy. Consequently, they know how to heal themselves by using the power of their minds. When these fragile personalities become afraid and disoriented, however, they forget these principles. Their health can deteriorate because they don't feel connected to their bodies.

Indigos' biggest health problems can involve their mental health. They can feel like aliens in a strange land with no one to communicate with or to share their feelings with. Emotional depression can cause physical maladies which range from the common cold to liver failure. They have sensitive physical systems and can be easily over-loaded, so they are vulnerable to whatever virus is in the air at the time.

When Indigos regain their center and reconnect with their inner knowing, they can heal their bodies quickly through the use of will and consciousness. The best way for Indigos to stay healthy is to stay connected to their "source" through regular prayer and meditation.

5. Combination Colors

We all have either one LifeColor or two LifeColors, which I call Combination Colors. These combinations can complement each other or they can create inner conflict. People choose their LifeColors before they are born. They often choose two LifeColors because of the extra power, creativity, compassion, intelligence or patience it gives them. For example, a Violet may add a Green aspect to help her take action and accomplish what she envisions for the planet.

Occasionally these two colors work in harmony with each other, providing an effective and harmonious balance. However, it is more common for people to experience conflict between the two colors or to live more from one color than the other.

The following sections describe both the inner conflict that can occur within a person who has a combination aura, and ways to overcome the conflict. There are many different possible combinations of the LifeColors. The following describes some of the most common combinations. Some of the LifeColors are rarely found in combination. For example, an Orange/Crystal combination would be rare, if one exists at all. It is more common for a Lavender to be a part of a Combination Color rather than purely a Lavender (for example a Violet/Lavender). This seems to give the person more capability in dealing with the "real" world.

■ VIOLET/YELLOW

Violet/Yellow Color Combinations are creative visionaries and/or healers for the world. When in power, those with this Color Combination have an energetic charisma. Many artists and performers are Violet/Yellow combinations. (An example of a Violet/Yellow combination is Kenny Loggins, Singer/musician.) This Color Combination also enters into the healing fields. Violet/Yellows are here to inspire humanity or save the environment, but they often choose to use creative or "behind-the-scenes" vehicles to do so. Violet/Yellows are usually more shy and sensitive than those with pure Violet auras.

For the most part, people with these two colors do not experience much conflict. Yellows and Violets can be quite compatible — as long as the Yellow is taking creative action to fulfill the Violet's vision.

These colors both love to be artistic, help people, listen to music and travel (although Yellows also love to stay home, so this combination needs a balance of both). Yellows love to travel to escape or to have fun. Violets travel to learn about other cultures and situations on the planet. When people with this Color Combination enter into the healing fields, they frequently want to travel with their work so they can reach more people.

People are drawn to Violet/Yellows. They love the joy, lightness and energy that radiates from the Yellow and the powerful charisma that flows from the Violet. The innocent charm of the Yellow keeps the potential arrogance of the Violet in balance.

Usually, those who choose this Color Combination have done so because they want to help the planet, but they want to do so through their creativity, humor or their healing abilities. Violet/Yellows also want to make sure they have fun while they help, inspire or "lighten up" humanity. Their methods are usually sensitive and non-threatening to people. This Color Combination frequently becomes involved in environmental causes because the Yellow aspect is connected with the earth and the Violet is drawn to "causes." In power, Violet/Yellows have the physical energy and the creative ideas to help the planet.

Regarding relationships, this personality usually prefers a mate who can be both a playful friend and an inspirational partner who shares the same vision. The Violet/Yellow wants someone who has a sense of humor, shares the same physical interests and hobbies (sailing, tennis, bicycling, hiking, etc.) and allows him the freedom to pursue his dream.

Problems can arise with a Violet/Yellow when the flirtatious Yellow aspect gets the charismatic Violet aspect into sticky situations. Both of these colors are sexually attractive. They both are very sexual and enjoy having choices. The Yellow aspect traditionally has a fear of commitment. Therefore, it is common for a Violet/Yellow to draw in a lot of lovers at once and be unable to choose between them or commit to any of them. An in-power Violet/Yellow can be a very sensitive, committed partner once she has found a compatible mate. Usually, the most compatible combinations are Blue/Yellow, Violet/Yellow or, sometimes, Green/Yellow.

There are a few areas where the individual with this combination may experience conflict. The Violet's visions and purpose on the planet can overwhelm and frighten the Yellow, who prefers to stay low-key and in the background. The Violet's visions can be so enormous that the Yellow fears his performance will be inadequate. He often becomes too shy and insecure to take on the Violet's grandiose dreams. Also, the Yellow fears the amount of work that may be required. When the Yellow aspect of a person doesn't want to work that hard, or procrastinates due to fear, his Violet aspect can become frustrated and impatient. Violets want to live their visions *now*. To hide out, the Yellow aspect may become entangled in negative addictions, such as alcohol and drugs. This not only delays the Violet's dream, it blurs his vision. A person's own Yellow aspect may sabotage the Violet's vision out of fear and insecurity. The Yellow aspect will support the Violet's vision if he believes it will be fun or creative. The Yellow aspect must learn to trust the Violet in order to create a way to manifest the visions.

Another potential conflict involves money and jobs. The Violet aspect will want to be independent and self-employed. The Yellow aspect is often insecure about his ability to commit to a business and do the amount of work required. Yellows are not usually good with money — it disappears rather quickly in their hands, which frustrates the Violet aspect. Violets want money so they have the freedom to do what they really want to do. This person may want to hire someone else to keep the books, so that the Yellow aspect doesn't have to worry about keeping track of finances. In this way, the Violet aspect has a chance of maintaining financial stability in his business. It is challenging for the Yellow aspect not to spend the money as soon as the Violet aspect has earned it. The Yellow wants to spend it on toys, parties or drugs. Here again the Yellow with its addictive and playful personality can cause trouble for the Violet. This problem appears frequently in the entertainment business, which is where many Violet/Yellow personalities are found.

If the Yellow aspect can stay physically active, healthy and away from negative addictions, this Color Combination can be dynamic, energetic and charismatic.

The occupations that most are attractive to Violet/Yellows include:

Performer	Healer
Actor	Physical therapist
Musician	Chiropractor
Artist	Doctor
Dancer	Acupuncturist
Writer	Massage therapist

Comedian	Magician
Fashion designer	Pilot
Interior decorator	Teacher (especially of art,
Graphic artist	dance or sports)
Environmentalist	

■ VIOLET/TAN

The Violet/Tan combines the Violets' vision to help the planet with the Tans' practical and logical abilities to bring these visions into reality. These people also have the ability to explain visionary ideas to those who need facts and data. They can describe the bigger picture in linear terms that make sense to other people.

Of all the Combination Colors, Violet/Tans and Yellow/Greens have the most potential for inner conflict. These two combinations have totally opposite characteristics within them. While a person's Violet aspect is seeing great visions, jumping from step one to step fifty, the Tan aspect is telling him he must remain safe and practical by staying at steps one through ten. If the individual is balanced and centered, his Tan aspect may be persuaded to proceed toward step fifty; however, the Tan aspect will insist on processing every step along the way. Therefore, it may take a long time for the Violet aspect to reach his dream.

It is common for these two colors to be constantly battling each other. The Tan personality is the one that most frequently judges the Violet personality. Tans accuse Violets of being "unrealistic dreamers." A person with this combination can have a difficult time understanding his own feelings, visions and emotions. If this combination does not proceed (even if cautiously) toward the Violet vision, serious health problems can develop. This Color Combination has the highest incidence of heart attacks, strokes and cancer. It is not easy for Violet/Tans to live with the kind of conflict that arises when these two colors are out of power or at odds with each other. Violets have intense emotional feelings. Tans do not like to express their emotions. Suppressing such deep emotions can cause health problems.

If the Violet/Tan can proceed toward the Violet's vision, the person will have a healthy constitution and no illnesses. It is very important for both aspects of this combination to win. The Violet's vision must be accomplished, but the Tan must be able to process each step of the way.

The Violet aspect wants to be independent and self-employed. The Tan aspect, however, wants the security of a regular paycheck along with health and retirement benefits. A Violet/Tan combination can be content working for a well-established organization that allows a certain sense of autonomy — being a corporate executive, for example, or a lawyer in a law firm, or a college professor. Violets want to earn enough money to enable them to do what they really want to do on the planet. The Tan believes that only patience, hard work and wise investments will enable him (after retirement) to experience the Violet dreams. Waiting to fulfill his dream can be tough on the Violet — it is more fulfilling if his current career involves doing something important. This combination must feel that he is accomplishing a greater purpose, while also providing financial security for him and his family.

This Color Combination may attempt to change the judicial or educational system in an orderly and legal manner. He does this by working through all the proper channels and established systems. The Violet aspect wants to travel. The Tan assesses that travel is not practical or economically feasible at this time. The Violet must then wait until a vacation is practical and the financial situation is secure. The Violet wants freedom and the Tan wants security. The Violet dreams and envisions great projects. The Tan remains logical, practical and analytical. While the

Violet desires to be a musician, the Tan aspect convinces him to stay at his stable, secure and well-paying job.

When the Violet speaks in front of an audience, inspired words and ideas can flow from him. The Tan aspect, however, wants to know that he is basing his information on researched facts and data. Violet/Tans make excellent mediators because they have not only the ability to see the bigger picture, but the intellect to review all the facts and details. Violets also have the ability to help people communicate with each other. Therefore, people feel confidence in Violet/Tans being fair and impartial arbitrators. If this combination can stay centered and balanced, he can earn the respect and admiration of those around him.

In relationships, this combination can be a very traditional, reliable, yet compassionate partner. Violet/Tans can exude sophisticated charm, radiate subtle and powerful sexuality, and have a quiet stability that many are drawn to. Since these colors have such opposite characteristics, however, the person can also be a Dr. Jekyll and Mr. Hyde. He can be open, communicative, passionate, warm, and loving one day, and then closed, practical and cautious the next. He can tell wonderfully vivid and picturesque stories, then suddenly switch into reciting facts and details, leaving his audience baffled as to where the charismatic speaker went. People are drawn to his calm charisma, but they are not allowed to get too close. Although the Violet aspect wants to be the center of attention, the Tan aspect is very quiet and private.

Careers that Violet/Tans are drawn to include:

Lawyer	Station manager
Computer technician	Psychologist
Politician	Printer
Physicist	Publisher
Mediator	Editor
Scientist	Writer

Government personnel	Land developer
Space scientist/researcher	Businessperson
Astronomer	Investor
Film and television personnel	Social worker
Musician	Public speaker
News broadcaster	Minister
Journalist	Teacher

■ VIOLET/GREEN

This Color Combination is one of the most powerful in the spectrum. With the Violet's vision and the Green's ability to accomplish projects, there is little these two aspects cannot achieve when they work together. When this combination is balanced and in power, the Violet/Green can write, produce and direct an entire movie almost single-handedly. He can build a financial empire that surpasses most others. This combination, in power, is virtually unconquerable.

But because Green and Violet are two of the most dynamic and powerful LifeColors, they also create some of the fiercest battles when out of power. A Green is one of the only LifeColors who can successfully sabotage or hold back the charismatic Violet. The Green aspect doesn't usually trust, and therefore judges the Violet's vision. The Green aspect wants to know *how* the Violet aspect plans on accomplishing his project. If the Violet is out of power, he can't see the steps or describe the plan. He can only see the final picture. The Green challenges the dream, declaring it to be impractical, unrealistic and full of pitfalls. He then lists all of the reasons why it *can't* work out: the timing isn't right; there isn't enough money, training, or education; people won't respond to it, they'll think it's foolish; it's far too grandiose.

If the Green aspect is allowed to talk the Violet aspect out of his dream, the person will become discouraged, depressed and ultimately lose respect for himself and his "foolish" visions. When the Violet aspect has a vision, he can't allow the Green to reduce it to rubble. He must inspire the Green to come up with the plan to achieve the dream. A scattered Violet often sees too many potential visions, which can drive the Green crazy. The Green aspect wants order, discipline and control. The Violet/Green would be wise to make a list of priorities, so that the Green feels that things are under control.

A Violet/Green is frequently afraid of his own power. He is afraid of his Green aspect becoming insensitive and controlling and his Violet aspect becoming arrogant. These two aspects can have a deep mistrust of each other's negative capacities, and therefore usually end up suppressing the positive qualities as well. The Violet distrusts the Green's aggressive, powerful nature, fearing it will scare away other people. The Green distrusts the Violet's vision, fearing that failure to manifest the vision will cause him to lose the respect of his peers.

In power, these two lead by example. They earn the respect of those around them by accomplishing and fulfilling their dreams. In power, they have no need or desire to abuse or hurt other people. George Lucas, Barbra Streisand, Bruce Springsteen, and Tony Robbins are some examples of Violet/Greens in their power who have accomplished great projects that have inspired and empowered the world. Violet/Greens are multi-talented individuals.

There are other Violet/Green personality traits that can cause inner conflict. Violets love to travel, for example, and Greens don't want to be bothered by the inconvenience of traveling. If Violet/Greens do travel, they travel first-class. They prefer nice hotels, fine restaurants and efficient travel arrangements.

There are also conflicts regarding relationships. The charismatic Violets attract people to them like magnets, while the Greens' protective shield usually pushes people away. Greens have high standards when choosing friends. Violets enjoy socializing with people, while Greens prefer to spend time alone. A balance is necessary for this combination, otherwise they will never be in agreement or in harmony.

A Violet prefers the companionship of a loving, supportive and inspiring mate. However, the Green has such high standards and is such an intense workaholic that few mates are able to keep up with this strong combination. The passion, energy and desire to accomplish are so strong with a Violet/Green that it can be a challenge to satisfy his hunger. This desire to expand, to explore new territories, and to reach new heights can affect every area of his life — career, relationships, finances and even sex. While the Violet/Green is driven to fulfill his visions and high ideals, he may also be unable to find a special mate to match his power and energy.

Money can create an interesting dilemma for this combination. While both of these LifeColors want money, Greens desire it for the power and possessions it can buy, and Violets want it for the freedom it gives. Violets can only work on projects that they believe in. If the Green aspect wants to take on a job or project just for financial gain, this combination will experience conflict. The Violet/Green may sabotage the project, or punish himself for becoming involved in something that he really didn't want to do. Both these colors are able to manifest money easily. Greens and Violets are often among the wealthiest individuals on the planet. This Color Combination should never experience financial difficulties, unless he holds back on his powerful capabilities or he overspends because the Violet aspect feels unfulfilled. Occasionally the Violet/Green will create a lot of money and use it to benefit others.

Family situations can also be challenging for a Violet/Green. The Violet aspect loves his family and wants to spend quality time with them. He sees the value in being emotionally available to his children and spouse. However, he also feels he has valuable work to accomplish on the planet. The Green is usually a workaholic and rarely at home, and a problem can develop for the Violet/ Green personality.

Violets are usually affectionate and compassionate parents. Greens, who want discipline and control in the home, have a hard time showing their emotions. If the Green aspect — who is never at home because of work — snaps at his children, then the Violet aspect feels guilt-ridden and torn. Parenting can be quite a challenge for the Violet/Green. However, if he can create a balanced schedule that includes time for business as well as family, he will lead a happier and more fulfilling life.

Deciding upon his life purpose and goals is one of the strongest conflicts for the Violet/Green. Violets have a strong desire to help save the planet, to inspire humanity, or to benefit it somehow. Greens are more concerned with learning, accomplishing and financially providing for themselves and their families. Greens feel that trying to change the world is not only impractical, but improbable as well. If the Violet/Green successfully creates huge financial empires but does nothing to help improve conditions on the planet, he will feel empty and unfulfilled. The Violet's dreams and desires cannot be ignored. Both the Green and Violet aspects need to be fulfilled.

The Green aspect often bargains with the Violet by promising to pursue the Violet's vision "as soon as I am financially established and successful." However, no matter how much money the Green acquires, it is never enough. The Violet/Green becomes more and more frustrated, caught between the desire to make more and more money and the urge to live his Violet vision.

This combination must definitely be self-employed. He has too much vision and power to be limited by anyone. The Violet/Green must either create a profession that allows for financial success while accomplishing the vision of helping people, or he must allow the two aspects to take turns. For example, the Green can run a bank or sell real estate, but the Violet must be able to get involved in causes and "Violet activities" after business hours.

People have usually chosen Violet/Green auras because they intend to have an impact on the planet in a powerful way. The Violet visionary wants to make sure that he has enough intelligence, ambition and drive to accomplish his goals, and so adds the Green abilities and characteristics.

Careers that appeal to Violet/Greens are:

Producer	Financial broker
Director	Stockmarket investor or advisor
Manager	Corporation president and owner
Radio or television station owner	Entrepreneur
Performer	Political backer
Writer	Politician
Seminar & workshop coordinator	Business owner
Speaker	Business consultant
Publisher	Real estate agent
	Advertising and marketing agent
	Bank owner or manager

■ BLUE/VIOLET

A Blue/Violet Combination Color doesn't experience as many conflicts as some of the other combinations. Because Blue and Violet are both in the emotional family, they are both very loving and compassionate. Violets tend to be stronger personalities than most Blues. They don't cry as easily and do not react to situations as personally as Blues do, but both colors care deeply for people and have strong, intense feelings.

An interesting phenomenon commonly occurs with this Color Combination. This is a personality that appears to be living two different lives in one lifetime. The Blue/Violet may begin her life predominantly as a Blue, her main priorities being marriage and family. She may begin her career as a counselor, a teacher or a nurse. The Blue's life revolves around helping others. Sometime during her life, she shifts into her Violet aspect. Her home, marriage and family are no longer her main priorities. She still loves them dearly, but feels drawn toward helping people on a greater scale. She longs to travel or become involved in planetary causes.

This transition can cause the Blue/Violet considerable guilt and confusion. During this time she may even feel she no longer desires to be married. (Just because someone doesn't want to be married anymore, it does not mean she is necessarily a Blue/Violet Color Combination. Blue/Yellow combinations can also experience a shift in their desire to be married, but these colors do so because they want to have more fun and freedom.) The Blue/Violets develop a strong desire to do something more meaningful and fulfilling on the planet. They also want more freedom to grow and evolve. The Blue/Violets need to know that they don't necessarily have to abandon their families to follow their dreams. They just need to readjust their lives to incorporate their new desires.

There are a few conflicts which can occur within this combination. The Blue aspect often fears the power and potential arrogance of the Violet aspect. The Violet's visions seem too grand and overwhelming for the sensitive Blue. She wonders: If she's that "great," will people still love her? If she actually becomes a powerful leader, will she outgrow her friends and family? She may fear that if she actually becomes independent and powerful, she may never need a significant relationship partner again. The Blue aspect will suppress the power of the Violet if she fears that she will be alone and unloved as a result.

An example of a Blue/Violet transition is the loving Blue counselor suddenly deciding she wants to start teaching group workshops, write a book or produce a video so that she can help more people on a larger scale. Another example is a Blue/Violet teacher deciding to quit her job to travel the world, learn about other cultures and become a journalist. In addition, the unassuming and charitable Blue starts becoming more interested in money so that she can have more freedom to travel or to pursue greater dreams.

Many other personality traits begin shifting from the Blue to the Violet. For example, the moral, monogamous and committed Blue begins to become increasingly interested in sex and passion. All of a sudden, the loyal Blue finds herself considering extramarital affairs for the first time in her life. The horror and confusion this can create for her is overwhelming. To balance out the increased sexual drive, the Blue/Violet can instead channel her energy into her new Violet vision. Often, affairs occur because the Blue is afraid to pursue the Violet dream. She subconsciously hopes that focusing her attention on another relationship will fulfill this strange new impulse for change. After all, the Blue aspect always felt a relationship would fulfill all her needs. An affair accomplishes very little but to delay the feeling that she needs to do more with her life.

For both aspects of this Color Combination to be happy, the individual needs a loving, secure and yet inspiring mate who will share her same dream. The Blue/Violet also needs a career that allows her the freedom to travel and the ability to help humanity. While money will never be her first priority, she needs enough to give her the freedom to pursue her visions.

While her family will always be important to her, the Blue/Violet will never be content to just sit at home and be a housewife. She must feel that she is contributing something of value to the planet. This can include exploring her creativity through art, music, photography or writing as well as through joining organizations which benefit humanity or the environment.

For this combination to stay balanced, the Blue/Violet must learn to love, support and trust her own dreams and visions. (A Blue usually loves and supports everyone but herself. She must learn to support her own Violet aspect.)

This combination is initially interested in the Blue careers, and then switches to the Violet careers. These careers include:

Teacher	Writer
Psychologist	Artist
Therapist	Travel agent
Minister	Flight attendant
Missionary	Tour guide
Musician	Foreign language interpreter
Actress	Speech therapist
Public speaker	Social agency director
Volunteer for political environmental causes	Photographer

See the individual chapters on "Blues" and "Violets" for a more complete list of occupations.

■ YELLOW/GREEN

When in power and balanced, this Color Combination has the capability of being a creative genius. Out of power, however, this personality can have the most severe inner conflicts of all the Combination Colors. Being highly intelligent when the Green aspect is in power, and abundantly creative when the Yellow is in power, this combination can create almost anything. Yellow/Greens are some of the best writers or inventors on the planet. They can also have a sharp and witty sense of humor.

This combination usually prefers to be self-employed, since both Greens and Yellows hate being told what to do. Greens operate better when they are in charge, and Yellows prefer the flexibility of having their own schedules. However, business is an area where conflicts can arise. Greens are usually workaholics, believing people must dedicate themselves to long hours of hard work in order to be successful. Greens don't know how to relax. Yellows do not like to work hard, preferring instead to play and enjoy their lives. Yellows must see their work as play. It must be fun and/or creative or they quickly lose interest. It is easy for Yellows to change careers in mid-stream. Greens believe people must commit themselves to a certain course until they have accomplished their goals. The Yellow and Green aspects can wage quite a war over completing projects. If the Yellow/Green procrastinates or doesn't reach his goal, he loses respect for himself, believing he is irresponsible and incapable of success.

Greens consider financial wealth and prosperity major priorities. Yellows are usually overly generous and irresponsible with money — they spend it almost before they get it. Yellow/Green combinations typically love to spend money on toys — fast cars, expensive sports equipment, computerized games, expensive jewelry or anything that is fun and flashy. While these toys are great once the Yellow/Greens have an abundance of money, the desire for these toys can frequently cause them trouble. It is common for these individuals to struggle with money until they are centered and in power. Frustrated, unfulfilled Greens compensate by spending a lot of money, while the Yellows allow money to slip like water through their hands.

Yellow/Greens can also experience conflict when it comes to making friends. Yellows are very friendly and easygoing. They like people and people are easily attracted to them. Greens, however, tend to put protective walls around themselves, allowing only a few select people inside. The Yellow/Greens can appear moody to others. One day they are laughing and playing, the next day they are serious and closed down. Yellows like to hug people. Greens respectfully shake hands and allow others their space. Yellows want people to like them. Greens, who don't much care whether or not people like them, frequently overpower and intimidate people. People with this combination can one day feel isolated and friendless, then the next day enjoy being by themselves. Commonly, Yellow/Greens will yell in frustration at people, and then feel bad and try to make jokes to cheer them up. The friendly yet abrasive behavior of Yellow/Greens can be confusing to people.

The Green aspect likes to make plans and act quickly. The Yellow aspect likes to be spontaneous and easygoing. The compulsive Green writes a list of things to do, but the Yellow, who rebels against lists, soon loses it. The Greens take life very seriously and can worry about everything, especially money. Yellows don't take anything seriously and believe everything will work out just fine.

The Yellow aspect is sensitive and can cry easily, while the Green aspect feels it must stay in control of emotions. People with this Color Combination often feel that they have two different people inside them who are fighting for dominion.

For Yellow/Greens to achieve inner harmony, both aspects must have what's important to them. The Yellow aspect must have time to relax, play, exercise and take vacations. Though the workaholic Green is afraid that the Yellow won't ever want to work again, the Yellow aspect usually does return with increased energy and renewed creativity. The only way the Yellow will fully cooperate with the Green is if the Yellow enjoys the work that has been chosen. Work must either be fun, creative, healing or allow the Yellow/Green to have a flexible schedule. This combination must learn to achieve a balance between having free time and being mentally stimulated, between being creative and making money, and between having friends and spending time alone.

The Green needs to accomplish things and occasionally take risks. The Yellow usually procrastinates and fears taking risks. Yellow/Greens want to have a lot of money, but they don't want to work hard for it. Winning the lottery, gambling or inheriting large sums of money appeal to Yellow/Greens.

For a Yellow/Green to be happy and balanced, both aspects must learn to support each other. The Yellow aspect can assist the Green aspect by supporting the Green's risky ideas with creative Yellow solutions; trusting the Green's ability to accomplish anything he puts his mind to; helping the Green take action by not procrastinating; keeping the Green from excessive worry and anxiety by bringing in the Yellow sense of humor; not fearing commitment so that the Green can accomplish a goal and allowing money to be the Green's priority.

The Green needs to support the Yellow aspect by allowing the Yellow quality time to play and relax without making demands on his free time; allowing the Yellow time to exercise; allowing the Yellow to have fears and insecurities, but empowering and inspiring him to move through them; not pushing or criticizing the Yellow so hard that he develops back problems ("get off his back"); listening to the Yellow's creative ideas and keeping the Yellow away from negative addictions through self-discipline.

Without cooperation and balance between the two aspects, a Yellow/Green will be in constant inner conflict, and will stop himself from accomplishing or enjoying his life. A Yellow/Green who is centered, balanced and in power not only enjoys his work and play, but makes the desired amount of money. He accomplishes goals while not taking life too seriously. The balanced Yellow/Green is a dynamic, powerful, energetic and creative force. Many extraordinary inventors, scientists and composers have had this LifeColor combination.

Interesting occupations for Yellow/Greens include:

Writer	Car salesperson
Producer	Professional athlete (especially
Inventor	individual competition — golf,
Doctor	tennis, etc.)
Pilot	Owner or manager of:
Chiropractor	Restaurants
Entrepreneur	Sports teams
Musician/composer	Health clubs
Jeweler	Auto repair garages
Real estate agent	Construction companies
Attorney/teacher	

People choose to come to the planet as a Yellow/Green combination for many reasons. They usually want to be powerful and accomplished creators, artists, healers, athletes or business people, yet they also want to have fun and enjoy life.

■ YELLOW/GREEN/VIOLET

A common phenomenon which occurs with a person who has a Yellow/Green Combination Color is that she adds Violet around the two colors to calm down their conflict. Adding the Violet qualities along with the new purpose of helping the planet elevates the person's goals and visions beyond the Yellow/Green conflict. It is similar to two brothers disagreeing over what they want. Each one is set on winning. Yet when they both envision a dream that is greater than either of them, they tend to set aside their differences and work together to achieve the dream.

Often a Yellow/Green who has experienced inner conflict in many areas of life — career, relationships or health — suddenly discovers after adding the Violet aspect that she has an inspired desire to use her talents to help humanity. This new goal creates a new happiness. A Yellow/Green songwriter who has been enjoying a creative and successful career, and has made a lot of money, decides she wants to write songs which make political statements which inspire people to change the world. Perhaps another Yellow/Green, who has been experiencing stressful health problems, is so happy and fulfilled by realizing her new visions that she stops worrying about her health, and it miraculously improves.

Another Yellow/Green, whose inner conflict has been reflected in his relationships, suddenly finds self-satisfaction and inner harmony by seeing a goal which is greater than himself. His relationships then reflect the new balance.

If a Yellow/Green doesn't stay in power with the new Violet aspect and stay focused on the Violet visions, he simply adds to his confusion by bringing in another set of desires. But if a Yellow/Green can stay balanced with this new Violet layer in his aura, he can become a creative and talented humanitarian, who takes action to fulfill his dreams.

■ TAN/GREEN

This Combination Color can conceptualize and plan a project, and also be patient enough to accomplish the details of the project. While a Green usually needs to hire someone else to take care of the tedious details, a Tan/Green combination can do the entire job. This Color Combination is rare. People do not usually have two LifeColors in the same physical, mental or emotional family. This usually signifies that a person is living two lives in one lifetime. (See the "Introduction" for further information.)

Conflict can arise within this combination when the Green impatiently insists that he jump to step ten of a project as quickly as possible, while the Tan aspect wants to slowly and cautiously process each step, one through ten, without skipping or missing any details. A Green can become frustrated by the Tan's need to be so methodical. There is often an ongoing mental push-pull, "hurry up but be careful" inner dialogue with a Tan/Green.

While a Green is a risk-taker, a Tan fears risk, choosing security and stability instead. Preferring to be self-employed, a Green quickly becomes impatient with his own Tan's need to have a regular paycheck. The ambitious Green needs ongoing challenges. Once he has accomplished something, he wants to move on to the next project. A Tan, on the other hand, dislikes change, preferring instead to maintain the status quo. The Green will want to quit his job and move on, but the Tan will be afraid of giving up the security.

Focusing time and energy on a career rather than on a relationship is more important to a Tan/Green. He has difficulty relating intimately with anyone. A Tan/Green definitely operates mentally. There is very little emotional expression with this personality. Even the Green's occasional frustrated outbursts are subdued by the reserved Tan.

To achieve compatibility between these two aspects, the Tan must learn to trust the quickness, intelligence and strength of his Green. The Tan must learn to take risks and not hold the Green back. At the same time, the Green aspect needs to learn to be patient with the Tan, not to push so hard or worry so much. The Tan will provide the Green with a secure and stable lifestyle if the Green can just relax a little and not be so demanding.

This combination prefers occupations that are mentally stimulating, yet practical and secure. A Tan/Green often chooses desk jobs, especially those which involve working with money, setting up financial systems or analyzing budgets.

Tan/Greens are often found in the following occupations:

Accountant	Executive
Insurance agent	Tax analyst
Banker	Civil servant
Investment consultant	Governmental and county
Employee in a large	office worker
business firm	Researcher

There are a few different reasons why a person may have chosen to be a Tan/Green. Often, a person with these LifeColors has added the Tan to enable himself to experience the process of completing his projects. He receives satisfaction from developing an idea as well as taking all the steps to complete the task.

Another reason may be that this combination Tan has added the Green aspect to speed himself up and to keep from becoming stuck. A Tan/Green may find himself becoming more of a risk-taker when he reaches middle age — it's as if the Green aspect becomes weary of the Tan's caution and finally becomes the dominant force. A balance between ambition and practicality is always important for this personality.

■ TAN/YELLOW

A person with this Color Combination typically loves to take things apart, analyze them and see how they work.

With both Tan and Yellow in the LifeColor bands of the aura, there is either a calm inner balance, or there is much conflict between them. Because a Tan wants to stay reliable, grounded and responsible, he is not always happy with the carefree, irresponsible attitude of a Yellow. The Yellow aspect may lure the Tan away from his duties, causing him to feel lazy, non-productive and weak. Or perhaps the Tan will suppress the Yellow by making him sit inside and work, not allowing him to play, relax or have a good time. The Yellow aspect may rebel by suppressing his creative talents, becoming depressed and causing his body to become overweight or ill.

The Tan and Yellow aspects of the personality need to learn to work in balance and harmony with each other. When the Tan allows the Yellow time to exercise, play and relax, the Yellow will respond with good health, joy and creativity. When the Yellow cooperates with the Tan to help him accomplish a job, the Tan will feel more financially secure, stable and relaxed. Physical exercise, relaxation time, and play are just as vital to this Tan/Yellow comb-ination as financial security, meaningful work and a stable lifestyle.

Since both Tans and Yellows fear taking risks, the progress of this combination will usually be slow, steady and methodical. Moving too slowly and analytically, however, can often frustrate the Yellow aspect, who prefers to be spontaneous and playful. While a Tan needs to see facts and data for proof, a Yellow is at least curious about new ideas. Consequently, this combination usually stays open-minded enough to check something out before passing judgment or making an evaluation.

In his power a Tan/Yellow is a creative, reliable and responsible thinker, who is also sensitive, considerate and fun-loving. Though he can be shy, people usually like him. A Tan/Yellow out of power can be critical, narrow-minded (usually out of fear), lazy, irresponsible, lifeless and generally unhappy.

A Yellow is very sensitive and can cry easily. A Tan, on the other hand, prefers to keep his feelings to himself. These opposing characteristics can create inner conflict because of suppressed emotions. These traits can also give a person the ability to stay calm, and to balance his sensitivity with logic and understanding. A Tan usually wants a stable, committed relationship, while a Yellow traditionally avoids commitment. Frequently, a Tan/Yellow will get married at a young age, but later will experience a "mid-life crisis," and want to go out and play. Not all marriages with a Tan/Yellow need to fall apart at this stage, however. The Tan aspect is often rational enough to work through the crisis.

This combination needs to enjoy his work. His job can be either creative or physical, but it must always be fun. If the Tan/Yellow does not enjoy his work, the Yellow aspect will eventually rebel. Measuring, drawing, designing, fixing, playing, creating or healing are the activities which a Yellow/Tan usually enjoys.

A Tan/Yellow may have chosen this Color Combination because he wanted to be creative, be a healer or be playful, but he also wanted to be reliable and responsible. A Tan/Yellow may have also chosen these colors because he was curious about three-dimensional, physical reality. The Tan typically takes apart and analyzes the physical objects which exist in the curious Yellow's physical world.

Careers for a Yellow/Tan include:

Architect	Pilot
Engineer	Postal worker
Draftsman	Graphic artist
Designer	Writer
Doctor	Musician
Massage therapist	Actor
Dentist	Mechanic

Chef (Yellows often love   Technician
   to cook and to eat)   Electrician
Medical technician

■ BLUE/GREEN

The Blue/Green Color Combination embodies the yin/yang or male/female characteristics more than most other combinations. The Blue aspect embodies many of the qualities which are considered to be "female" — loving, nurturing, emotional and receptive. The Green aspect personifies the more "male" characteristics — intellectual, assertive, aggressive and action-oriented. When the Blue/ Green is balanced, and has achieved a harmonious "marriage" between the two aspects, these personalities are powerful helpers and humanitarians. They take action to help people.

People who have chosen this Color Combination love and help people with their Blue aspect. They have brought the Green aspect in to make sure they accomplished something with all of their love and compassion. Blue/ Greens want to "put their money where their mouth is," not just talk about loving and helping people.

These powerful yet loving individuals are proficient at managing non-profit organizations or other agencies that help people. Blue/Greens are skilled managers and directors. They enjoy the balance between working with people, organizing plans and developing ideas. They are usually found in positions of authority because they don't like others to tell them what to do. They are motivated self-starters. When these Blue/Greens are in power and centered, they are dynamic, motivated and concerned individuals.

Intense conflict can also arise between the Blue and Green aspects. Blues and Greens are often critical toward one another. They have different goals and priorities. The three areas in which Blue/Greens experience the greatest inner conflict are relationships, career, and money. There are consistent and irritating inner dialogues that occur within the Blue/Green personality.

Relationships are their greatest challenge. This includes relationships with spouses and family, as well as with friends and co-workers. Blues want to be in loving, committed relationships with their mates. They tend to give themselves away in relationships, and will do anything to be loved. Greens, on the other hand, usually put careers and business ahead of relationships. They don't "need" relationships and are usually unsympathetic toward the Blues' relationship dramas. When the Blue aspect feels she wants a mate, the Green argues that she shouldn't "need" someone else to complete her life. The Green aspect believes that she can be satisfied by succeeding in her career. The Blue aspect longs for the ideal loving companion, but the Green aspect, having very high standards for a mate, usually pushes away potential candidates. She claims that they are boring and inadequate. The frustrated and lonely Blue/Green wonders if she will ever find a mate who will fulfill both the Blue's and the Green's needs. When she finally does find a mate, she will be loving and supportive in one moment, then impatient and demanding in the next. This can cause guilt and frustration for the Blue/Green, as her conflicting behavior pulls her mate in and then pushes him away.

Blue/Greens can be very loving, but also very demanding of their friends and co-workers. While they enjoy people, Blue/Greens also feel that they accomplish more when they are by themselves. People are often drawn to the loving and considerate Blue aspect; however, they frequently feel "blocked" by the invisible wall that often surrounds the Green. Greens are particular about choosing friends, while Blues open their doors to everyone. The

Blue/Greens' contrasting natures can confuse the people around them. Only by accepting and balancing both aspects will they avoid feeling schizophrenic.

Raising children can also create dilemmas for the Blue/Greens. The loving Blue aspect feels that she should stay home to nurture and "mother" her children. The ambitious Green aspect, however, wants and needs to be active in the business world. Blue/Greens need interaction with intelligent and motivated people. Unless they work out of their homes, they become frustrated by having to stay at home. Eventually they will drive their children crazy by attempting to teach and organize them all the time.

Blues are very intuitive, while Greens are very logical and analytical. The Blue aspect will frequently receive intuitive information that the Green aspect questions and challenges because of lack of supporting evidence. If Blue/Greens can learn to trust the Blue's intuition and use the Green's intellect to plan accordingly, these individuals can experience less conflict and greater, more fulfilling life experiences.

Although Blues are natural counselors, Greens become impatient with people's problems. Blue/Greens work better in counseling positions that allow them to give advice and direction — for example, as career counselors or personnel directors. (While Blue/Greens are drawn to helping people on a personal, one-to-one basis, the Violet/Greens usually help large groups of people through the media.)

When choosing careers, Blue/Greens want to know that they are helping others, but they want to be paid well to do it. Money can create a conflict for these individuals because Blues and Greens have different attitudes about money. Blues are in service from the heart and have difficulty receiving money. Greens, on the other hand, are insulted if they are not well-compensated for their services. Jobs that offer both can be a challenge to find, since most "Blue" jobs don't pay well. The Blue/Greens are usually not the full-time volunteers (unless they are independently wealthy and do not need an income). The Green aspect wants to be compensated for services rendered.

Occupations that are attractive to Blue/Greens include:

Director for nonprofit	Office manager
or service organization	Loan officer
Fund raiser	Event coordinator
Personnel director	Public relations director
Career counselor	Business consultant
Hospital administrator	Store owner (clothing,
Real estate agent	antiques, jewelry, etc.)

■ BLUE/YELLOW

A person with a Blue/Yellow Combination Color is usually loving, carefree, cheerful and energetic. This personality definitely loves people. She is caring and nurturing toward other people, but also wants them to "lighten up," laugh and have fun. This combination is usually a high-energy person. The loving nature of the Blue combined with the sparkling, creative and energetic nature of the Yellow make this combination a fun-loving and artistic teacher or a gentle healer.

The Blue and the Yellow personalities are similar in many ways, so this Color Combination doesn't experience many traumatic inner conflicts. Both Blues and Yellows are loving, caring and generous people who like to help others. They are both sensitive to the needs of others. Although Yellows can be rebellious individuals, both Blues and Yellows are people-pleasers — it is important to them both that people like them.

There are a few areas in which conflict can occur for the fun-loving Blue/Yellow. The Blue aspect of the person is typically more emotionally serious, while feeling that she must help people. The Yellow aspect rebels against the Blue's intensity, believing that the most effective way to heal people is to teach them to have fun. The Blue aspect considers becoming a nurse. The Yellow aspect doesn't want to be around sick and depressed people all day. If this person does become a nurse, she will be the playful spirit who always wears a smile, and bounces into everyone's room to cheer them up.

Since neither Blues nor Yellows make money a priority, this combination frequently experiences financial difficulties. Blues have a hard time receiving money for services, and money disintegrates in the Yellow's hands. However, this combination tends to be happy regardless of the financial situation.

The four areas in which an out-of-power Blue/Yellow can experience the most inner conflict are relationships, sex, exercise and children. The Blue aspect wants an emotionally fulfilling, monogamous and committed relationship. Although the Yellow aspect wants a playmate, she has a fear of commitment. A Blue/Yellow can sabotage her relationships and not even be aware that she is doing it. The Blue aspect will find a mate, but the Yellow aspect will run away to be free of the commitment. She frequently makes it appear that the other person has chosen to leave her, when in reality she is the one who has pushed him away through her fear of commitment. The Blue has a hard time letting go of relationships, while the Yellow is ready to move on because things aren't fun anymore. This personality frequently has multiple marriages. It is helpful for a Blue/Yellow to choose a mate who can laugh, play and yet emotionally commit to her. A Yellow/Violet is an excellent match for a Blue/Yellow.

Sex can be another problem for this Color Combination. The Blue is very moral and monogamous. In order to sleep with someone, she must love him. The Yellow believes that sex is a fun, playful experience that doesn't need to involve serious commitment. Even if she is in a relationship, the Yellow aspect can entertain the idea of having a playful, sexual interlude with someone else. This can cause waves of horror and guilt for the loyal Blue aspect. If the Blue/Yellow can stay balanced and channel her energy into physical exercise or creative projects, extramarital affairs can be avoided.

Exercise is another challenge for a Blue/Yellow combination. The Yellow needs to stay physically active to maintain a sense of well-being and harmony. However, the Blue's idea of exercise is walking to the end of the driveway. She is not motivated to exercise. When the Yellow aspect feels a need to exercise, the Blue aspect creates a hundred excuses why she can't. A Blue/Yellow who doesn't exercise will experience low energy, depression, stiff muscles and backaches. Once she drags herself out to exercise, she feels better. Setting up a regular exercise schedule is highly recommended for this Color Combination. (Gardening is also a very therapeutic form of meditation for her.)

The Blue/Yellow combination commonly experiences weight problems. The emotionally vulnerable Blue puts on weight for protection. The sensitive Yellow also adds weight for protection. In addition, when she is insecure and experiencing low self-esteem, her addiction to food, sweets or alcohol compounds the problem. When the Blue/Yellow feels good about herself and stays physically active, weight is not a problem.

The question regarding whether or not to have children can be a complicated issue for a Blue/Yellow. Most Blues have a desire to have children. Yellows, while they enjoy playing with children, are not always sure they want the responsibility of raising children. Having her own children may force the youthful Yellow to grow up too quickly. This person can fluctuate back and forth between being the child's parent and being their playmate. If parenthood becomes an overwhelming responsibility, the Yellow aspect is suffocated and it will gradually disappear.

To stay balanced, a Blue/Yellow combination must, first of all, stay physically active. Dance or exercise is imperative to her creativity, health and joy. She must also keep a light and healthy perspective on her relationships. Becoming emotionally heavy or overly-concerned can crush her spirit and destroy relationships. Disgusted with the intensity and the pain, the Yellow will cause the relationship to disappear. The childlike Yellow aspect can add lightness to the emotional and moody Blue aspect and keep the Yellow/Blue from becoming depressed too often.

The Blue/Yellow can frequently experience dilemmas regarding her choice of careers. The Yellow, who really prefers not to work at all, changes jobs constantly. Committing to one career is boring and restrictive to her. The Blue/Yellow must allow herself to have a career that she enjoys. The Blue/Yellow wants a variety of careers that allow her to have fun while she is being creative, physically active or helping people. Frequently, the Blue/Yellow holds two or three jobs simultaneously, which allows her to have choices, be spontaneous and not get bored.

Occupations which are attractive to a Blue/Yellow include:

Artist	Aerobics instructor
Dancer	Flight attendant
Actor	Elementary or pre-school
Hair dresser	teacher
Manicurist	Physical therapist
Facialist	Massage therapist
Florist	Art teacher
Waitress	Writer
Ski instructor	

In power, this delightful creature is loving, playful, cheerful, creative and energetic. She helps people by bringing warmth and joy into their lives.

■ THE RED OVERLAY

People who have added red in the outer bands of their auras have done so because they feel a need for protection. These individuals were not born with this red in their auras, but added it sometime after birth. The color red vibrates at a slower rate, therefore it is denser and stronger, making it a suitable protective barrier. This red band is not the same as a Red LifeColor, which someone is born with and which is located in the band closest to the body.

Intense anger and rage are the hallmarks of people with red in the outer bands of their auras. If these people don't eventually remove the red from their aura, their protective shield will eventually become their prison. While the red protects them from others, it also shuts them off from life and all life has to offer.

Usually people are unaware of the red in their aura. There are obvious signs when red exists in the aura, the most dramatic being an explosive, intense anger that can flare up over minor incidents. People with red overlays have short fuses. They tend to see life as a battleground. They also have a tendency to be self-destructive, and to sabotage their lives. These people will sabotage their health, their relationships and their careers. Often, they will suppress their strong feelings of anger, which only causes more complications and self-inflicted pain.

People usually add red to their aura for one or more of the following reasons: They have had a *life-threatening situation* at birth or at a young age, which caused them to perceive that they may die, or that the world was not a safe place. Examples of life-threatening situations can include birth complications, severe illness, choking, drowning or suffocating. Many people do not remember these incidents, and so the source of their anger remains a mystery to them. They frequently have feelings of dread or of impending disaster for reasons unknown to them.

People may also add red if they have been *physically, emotionally or mentally abandoned or rejected*. Red bands frequently appear in people who were unwanted children, adopted or separated from a parent at a young age. Frequently, as children, these people blamed themselves for their parents' behavior or attitudes. They felt unloved and inadequate. The fear of abandonment and rejection caused them to add red in their auras.

The most obvious and traceable causes for red in the aura are those cases in which people have been *physically, emotionally or mentally abused*. Children who have been sexually abused, physically beaten, or raised by alcoholic parents usually feel that the world is an unsafe and undependable place and that protection is necessary for survival. They feel betrayed by the adults who were supposed to love, nurture and protect them as children.

There are three basic methods for removing the red in the outer bands of the aura. One method is to visualize the red disappearing or changing into another color. (This is only effective if you truly have faith in the power of visualization.)

Another method is to re-live the past in your imagination, but re-write or re-interpret the circumstances. For example, if a person was physically abused, he should "see" himself as the adult he is now, protecting the child he was then. He can visualize himself preventing the abusive behavior by standing between the child (himself) and the abusive adult. If he felt abandoned and rejected as a child, a person can visualize going back and playing with the child (himself), comforting him, and telling the child that he loves him. Imagination and visualization techniques are important when working to re-write the past. The emotional, mental and physical body will respond by feeling safer, more secure and more loved, thereby lessening the need for the protective red in the aura. These visualizations can be very powerful and effective tools for releasing red in the aura.

The third method is therapy. A person can work out his anger by discussing, re-living and understanding what happened, and by forgiving the people who caused him to feel unsafe and unloved. Therapy can help the individual to make new, healthier decisions as an adult and release past traumatic experiences. Until true understanding, forgiveness and release are experienced, and it feels safe to let go of the protective red shield, the person will usually hold onto his anger and self-destructive behavior. People with red in their auras run the highest risk of heart attacks, cancer and other life-threatening situations. They have a hard time living with their internal fear, anger, guilt and doubt. It is important to release the red overlay in order to live full, healthy lives.

6. Relationships with the Physical Colors

The following chapters are meant to serve as guidelines for relationships, not to create judgments or limitations. By identifying your LifeColors and those of your mate, you can use the tools included here to help you relate to one another with more understanding.

Anything is possible — even in relationships. With enough love, commitment and determination from both partners, any relationship can succeed — although not everyone wants to work that hard.

Even though any relationship combination is *possible*, not all of them are common or probable. For example, it is rare to find the Physical colors, specifically Reds, Oranges and Magentas, married to any of the Emotional colors. They don't seem to have much in common. Because some of these relationships are so rare, the sections involving these combinations will be brief.

If you have a Combination Color, you will need to read the individual relationship sections that deal with your particular LifeColors. For example, if you have a Blue/Green Combination Color, read how Blues relate to each of the different LifeColors, and then read how Greens relate to each LifeColor. If you suspect that your partner also has a Combination Color, reading each of the relationship sections that apply will enable you to identify the potential strengths and weaknesses of your relationship.

The use of "he" or "she" in the following descriptions is purely *arbitrary*. What is true for a Yellow male/Green female relationship will also be true for a Yellow female/ Green male relationship, and so on.

■ RED

Red and Red Relationship

Although they have the same needs, two Reds are so stubborn, strong-willed and potentially volatile that they probably wouldn't be able to be in relationship together for long. Neither is usually able to communicate feelings in an intimate or sensitive way. Both tend to be direct and brutally honest, which may result in hurt feelings and create walls between them. Both would be willing to put plans into action, but neither has the patience to figure out the details. If they were able to come up with a plan, both would have strong opposing ideas as to how the plan should be implemented. If this couple could allow each other the required individual space and time, and if they could work together with the same direction and goal in mind, they could make a very powerful, working team.

Sex with this couple would be a wonderful, passionate experience. Both love lustful sex. Because these two are so much alike, they have the ability to understand each other's needs. At parties, Reds seem to stay outside the circle of activity. These two could stay on the outside and be loners together. Hopefully, a desire for rowdy revelry with friends would hit them both at the same time. In the Red-Red relationship, neither would feel an overwhelming need for philosophical or theoretical discussions. A mate having that need would feel unfulfilled in a relationship with a Red.

Reds would most likely find this relationship quite a challenge to maintain. They could each benefit more from a relationship with someone who is patient and willing to take care of the details in their home and business.

Red and Orange Relationship

Both Reds and Oranges prefer to see reality as physical and tangible. They both love dealing with their environment. Although they both like raw courage and stamina, a Red prefers physical power and strength, while an Orange prefers mental cunning and wit. Reds and Oranges both tend to be loners — finding them in a relationship together would be uncommon. They are both incredibly independent and require a lot of time alone.

In some ways these two are compatible. They share a common belief that reality is tangible, that life is to be experienced with zest and vigor and that nature is to be respected for her power. However, neither one of them is a great communicator. They don't express their emotions well.

The powerful Red can be very domineering and volatile, although the anger passes just as quickly as it arises. An Orange doesn't like to be dominated, controlled or told what to do. He is very independent and adventurous. Chances are, he wouldn't stay around the strong-willed Red too long.

Their activities, desires, and needs are different. An Orange is in constant need of physical challenges and adventures. He wants to test his mental skills and physical prowess. He is away exploring more than he is at home. An Orange likes to scale cliffs, race cars or jump from planes. He wants to challenge and outwit an opponent, even if his opponent is a mountain. He thrives on physical danger. A Red prefers physical strength and endurance, working with her environment to accomplish something. Each insists his way is the appropriate or superior one. A Red woman prefers sensuality, sexuality and power to thrill-seeking in a race car. A Red man prefers strength, muscles and driving heavy equipment to risking his life jumping out of a plane. A Red loves to manifest ideas and plans in physical form. She enjoys staying home with her simple creature comforts. A Red and an Orange would not have the same interests or hobbies.

The Red loves sex. The Orange doesn't care very much about sex. The Orange will use sex as a physical release and then leave. A Red wants passion, lust, and the ongoing satisfaction of a physical relationship. An Orange prefers the excitement of climbing a mountain or skydiving.

If these two were found in a relationship, they would each need a lot of space and time to be alone. This couple would need to find physical activities to share together, since neither of them is adept at verbal communication. They will most likely not discuss emotions, feelings, philosophies, religions, relationships or family. These two are probably better off as friends than marriage partners. There would be little, if any, emotional intimacy between them. Neither is proficient at opening up, communicating or being sensitive.

Another reason that this couple may not be compatible is that a Red likes to be practical, logical and down to earth. She is not afraid of commitment or hard work. An Orange is just the opposite. He prefers challenges that look impractical and impossible. The daring and impractical Orange would eventually frustrate the Red. The Orange is usually more concerned with his own needs and desires, caring little how it affects his mate. He is not interested in being a team player. The loyal and trustworthy Red is interested in working out matters as a team. Even though she also tends to be a loner, she occasionally needs camaraderie.

Both Reds and Oranges prefer to be the masters of their own careers. Although they have this interest in common, neither would be able to work with or for the other. While they both prefer to be self-employed, neither of them wants to handle the practical affairs of the business. Neither enjoys doing paperwork. Although these two are not usually compatible mates, with an Orange's ability to calculate, strategize and figure out plans, and a Red's ability to carry them out, this pair could manage to pull off projects together as business partners.

Red and Magenta Relationship
See Magenta and Red Relationship.

Red and Yellow Relationship
See Yellow and Red Relationship.

Red and Logical Tan Relationship
A relationship between a Logical Tan and a Red could be very challenging. If a Logical Tan communicates at all, he prefers to speak with someone who can discuss intellectual ideas. He wants facts, information and data. A Red is not too concerned with communicating at all. Both of these personalities tend to withhold their thoughts and feelings. The Red, who has a volatile temper, would confuse the logical, sensible, and always-in-control Logical Tan. A Tan does not appreciate or see the logic behind emotional outbursts. A Red is not usually able to explain why she loses her temper.

When the Red loses her temper, the Tan tends to withdraw, shutting off any means of communication. The Red's anger does not intimidate the Tan. His protective walls shield him from the Red's emotional display.

The relationship between a Red and a Logical Tan could be an interesting one if both remained in their power. They could provide balance and stability for each other. Logical Tans can provide ideas and plans, and Reds have the energy to put them into action. Therefore, as business partners, they could work very well together.

However, in a personal relationship, these two would not have a lot in common. Both colors tend to keep their thoughts and emotions to themselves, so intimacy would be lacking. A Red is very sexual. A Tan does not have a high sex drive. A Red expresses herself sexually and physically. A Tan prefers mental stimulation. These differences can cause conflict in the relationship.

A Red prefers getting involved in physical activities, while the Logical Tan chooses to sit behind a computer or explore mental challenges. A Tan tends to be more inter- ested in taking things apart, analyzing them, figuring out how they work and what their purpose is. A Red has no interest in analyzing anything. She does not choose to question what makes something work, but prefers to work with physical substance.

These two have very little in common. They rarely share the same interests, the same types of friends. The activities of a Logical Tan are not usually enough to stimulate the Red. The Red would probably, therefore, have to spend evenings or free time out with her friends. A Logical Tan prefers the company of intellectual people. A Red would want to get together with her friends to drink and have a rowdy, good time. The Logical Tan would find the Red's attitudes and behaviors mentally unstimulating. The Red, who loves to live life with zest and a lusty vigor, would find the Logical Tan's sedentary ways slow, stiff and analytical.

On the other hand, these two could offer an interesting balance to one another. A Red could stimulate the emotional and physical sides of the typically mentally calculating Logical Tan. The Red could also take action on the Tan's meticulously analyzed ideas and bring them into physical reality.

The Logical Tan could calm the often volatile or excitable Red by remaining practical and rational. In addition, while the Red is not usually interested in figuring out all the details of a project, the Logical Tan is willing to take responsibility for figuring out the details.

If these two are willing to allow for their differences and appreciate the elements that each brings into the relationship, they could create an interesting balance in their lives.

Red and Environmental Tan Relationship

See Environmental Tan and Red Relationship.

Red and Sensitive Tan Relationship

A Sensitive Tan is too gentle and meek to handle the power, energy and volatile personality of a Red. A Sensitive Tan is similar to the Blue personality in the sense that she tends to take things personally.

A Sensitive Tan wants to love, support and nurture someone. She would be completely intimidated and suppressed by the Red's powerful behavior. She wants to feel secure and emotionally bonded with her mate. The Red is much too independent to be a suitable mate for a Sensitive Tan. A Red also withholds his thoughts and feelings. The Sensitive Tan tends to feel emotionally disconnected from him. A Red would find a Sensitive Tan unchallenging and uninspiring. A Sensitive Tan does not live with the same physical lust for life as a Red.

Red and Abstract Tan Relationship

See Abstract Tan and Red Relationship.

Red and Green Relationship

A Green and a Red can be a very dynamic pair. Combining the Green's ability to plan and organize with the active physical energy and stamina of a Red can produce amazing results. A Red loves to put plans into action. The fire and vibrancy of a Red fascinates and challenges a Green. A Green appreciates and admires the Red's persistence, determination and willingness to work hard. The power of a Red is such that a Green cannot intimidate him with her mental prowess and skills. The Red is fascinated by the intelligence and mental agility of a Green, making him eager to put the Green's plans into action. With the Green's mental abilities and the Red's physical energy, they can accomplish extraordinary projects together.

The negative side of this combination is that they both tend to have strong tempers. A Red can become physically violent and want to strike out, while a Green can provoke and even injure someone with her sharp tongue. Since both are strong-willed, independent, and determined to have their own way, they can live in constant conflict. It can be a battle of the wills, with each determined to win. A Red is quick to lose his temper and a Green is quick to blame. Their discussions can quickly become intense shouting matches. However, this same fire and energy can make them a very lively duo.

A Green has a sexual appetite only when she is with a partner she respects, a partner she cannot dominate or run over. A Red does not tolerate being dominated by anyone. With the lustful appetite of a Red, this couple can experience quite an intense sexual relationship.

Both of these colors are very powerful, independent, efficient and strong-willed. They usually respect each other. A person would not, however, want to get in between these two during an argument.

Red and Blue Relationship

This is not a very compatible combination. A Blue tends to take the outbursts of the powerful and explosive Red personally and be in tears most of the time. A Blue is spiritual; she loves to contemplate God, the nature of the Universe and the meaning of life. A Red does not relate to this at all. A Red's idea of reality is what he can see, touch and taste.

A Blue doesn't enjoy being in her body very much, while a Red's greatest joy is living in a physical body. The Red has a lustful appetite for sex. A Blue wants to be cuddled, hugged and held, which is something that the Red is not apt to do because he feels it lacks intensity. A Red wants power and passion from his mate. The Blue is much more emotional and sentimental. A relationship between a Red and a Blue would be like oil and water, with the Red being reluctant to open up emotionally and the Blue needing emotional depth from her partner. The Red wants to explore physical reality, while the Blue wants to explore inner feelings and spiritual beliefs. The Blue wants someone who is very loyal, bonded and committed. While a Red is capable of loyalty and commitment, he is also very independent. When he gets a desire to go out and be on his own, he will just go. The Blue, taking this very personally, will feel hurt and offended by the Red's abandonment. A Blue enjoys talking about the relationship and about how she feels. A Red has no desire to talk about his feelings, let alone what he is feeling about the relationship. Blues tend to be natural mothers, while the Red in no way wants to be mothered or coddled. Instead, he wants to be admired for his physical strength, power and courage.

In general Reds are too powerfully explosive and emotionally unavailable for the sensitive, emotional Blue. While any relationship is possible, and a couple committed enough could make anything work, this combination has more than its share of challenges.

Red and Violet Relationship

See Violet and Red Relationship.

Red and Lavender Relationship

See Lavender and Red Relationship.

Red and Crystal Relationship

This relationship would be a very challenging one. A Red with a Crystal would be like "a bull in a china shop." The Crystal is much too sensitive and fragile to be around the power, intensity and energy of a Red. Crystals need too much solitude, peace and quiet for the rambunctious and energetic Reds. Crystals understand and need spiritual meditation. Reds understand and need practicality and down-to-earth physical labor. The Reds' tendency to express themselves physically, often even explosively, intimidates and frightens the Crystals. Crystals, if they express themselves at all, do so through gentleness, touch and sensitivity. The Red involves himself in all of the things Crystals abhor. The physical realities that Reds enjoy — getting their hands dirty, changing the oil in the truck, butchering meat — are too harsh, dirty and grotesque to Crystals. Sex with the robust, lustful Red would also be too intense for the Crystal.

The Red could help ground a Crystal, but that "grounding" would probably be too heavy and severe for the delicate Crystal. The Red would eventually tire of having to hold back his energy.

Red and Indigo Relationship

See Indigo and Red Relationship.

■ ORANGE

Orange and Red Relationship

See Red and Orange Relationship.

Orange and Orange Relationship

Since Oranges don't seek out long-term committed relationships, neither partner would initiate a marriage. Rather than marriage partners, these two would make better adventuring companions. The solitary Orange usually prefers to go mountain-climbing or skydiving by himself. He loves the freedom and independence of being able to challenge the environment on his own. However, Oranges do befriend other Oranges because they frequent the same environments. In many ways, Oranges are compatible, but compatible as friends, not as mates. Neither one of them would be interested in having intimate conversations, sharing their feelings, or bonding emotionally. There wouldn't be much basis or need for marriage, since neither one needs the commitment. They could, however, share the same interests and hobbies, such as auto racing, hang gliding or deep sea diving.

Very few other friends are willing to venture into the areas where Oranges love to go. Spending time with other Oranges may be their only chance for companionship. In addition, since they both enjoy planning and strategizing, it can be exciting for them to work on ideas together. (They must learn the art of cooperation first, however. The Orange is used to being independent and alone.) They each understand the other's need for personal freedom and space, and so don't have the smothering, needy or over-protective attitudes associated with some of the other LifeColors.

Both Oranges relate to the desire to challenge the environment, to experiment with danger and to live life on the edge. There is a possibility, however, that these two could become so competitive they would end up killing themselves by pushing too far.

Neither Orange wants to take on the mundane responsibilities of running a home, so home is not where either of them would spend much time. Since Oranges are so independent and self-sufficient, when the two partners disagreed, they could merely go their own ways without emotionally damaging each other. One of the greatest

222 / LifeColors

challenges in life for an Orange is the challenge of going within. Human emotion is the most frightening frontier of all for him. It is easier for an Orange to become angry at his mate and leave her rather than facing himself and finding out that he may actually be part of the problem. Oranges don't typically sit down to work out emotional or relationship difficulties. With neither partner invested in a long-term commitment, a relationship between two Oranges does not usually last very long. However, this type of relationship suits Oranges just fine. Their similarities can actually fulfill many of their mutual needs.

Orange and Magenta Relationship

A Magenta and an Orange would probably only have a short-term relationship, if they were to have one at all. These two are compatible at first, because the Orange's daredevil behavior excites a Magenta. The Magenta finds him fascinating for a while. The Magenta also appreciates that the Orange is independent. The Orange doesn't smother or depend on the Magenta, which allows her the freedom to go out and have a good time. However, since neither is interested in long-term committed relationships, they eventually drift apart.

With the zany creativity of the Magenta, and the Orange's cunning ability to strategize and materialize ideas, a good working relationship is possible with this pair. If the Orange wanted to jump over the Grand Canyon, the Magenta might be able to create a new invention to help the Orange accomplish the feat.

As a rule, however, these two are too different to be in a relationship with one another. An Orange is usually too serious for the fun-loving Magenta. While the Orange is away exploring, the Magenta is attending as many parties and social events as she can. They don't even make good roommates. When the Orange wants to get a good night's sleep before going off to climb a mountain, the Magenta wants to stay up late and entertain friends. The wild antics of a Magenta can disrupt the lifestyle of an Orange, usually causing bad feelings between them.

While Oranges and Magentas are both independent risk-takers, and both love to go beyond established limitations, they don't have much else in common. Each respects the other's daring and boldness, but neither can relate to the other's style. The Magenta feels that the Orange's need for physical danger is foolish and self-indulgent. The solitary Orange, who relishes his privacy, cannot relate to the Magenta's bizarre behavior and need to call attention to herself. While an Orange prefers a physical challenge and is cunning in the face of danger, a Magenta prefers a social challenge and is outrageous and defiant in the face of accepted social standards.

A Magenta and an Orange are seldom found in the same environment. The possibility of these two ever meeting in the first place is rare. Even though these two are fascinated by each other's independent and unique lifestyles, in time they find their differences too extreme and eventually go their own separate ways.

Orange and Yellow Relationship

See Yellow and Orange Relationship.

Orange and Logical Tan Relationship

See Logical Tan and Orange Relationship.

Orange and Environmental Tan Relationship

This pair has a bit more in common than a Logical Tan and an Orange, because both enjoy working with the environment. They also each have a healthy respect for the power of nature. An Environmental Tan can be fascinated with and have respect for the physical challenges that an

Orange is able to overcome. After awhile, however, the Environmental Tan often grows bored and uninterested in the Orange's relentless need to challenge the environment. The Environmental Tan feels the Orange is taking too many unnecessary, life-threatening risks. He sees more value in researching the environment with sensible tactics. Although they are both interested in planning, measuring and organizing their tasks, they each have different reasons for their calculations. An Environmental Tan sees the value in research to better the environment. An Orange calculates the risks involved in the task to ensure personal survival. If an Orange and a Environmental Tan were to set off on an adventure together, the Orange would eventually want to leave the Environmental Tan way behind. The Environmental Tan is too cautious for the daring Orange. The Environmental Tan, like the Logical Tan, can be too conscientious, security-minded, and stable for the adventurous Orange.

Neither of these personalities deals well with emotions. They tend to keep thoughts and feelings to themselves; neither prefers to express openly. In this relationship, verbal and emotional communication tend to be sparse — neither one usually instigates conversation. Sex would be somewhat of a convenience with these two. Neither one sees sex as a focus or priority. Both understand the need for physical release at times, but then they prefer to move on to more important matters.

Since both tend to be isolated thinkers and loners, these two make better roommates than marriage partners. In their marriage intimacy, emotions and communication would be lacking, since neither chooses to deal with such issues.

Orange and Sensitive Tan Relationship
See Sensitive Tan and Orange Relationship.

Orange and Abstract Tan Relationship

An Orange and an Abstract Tan are not compatible. They have nothing in common. An Orange tends to be a loner and does not need companionship, while an Abstract Tan loves people and enjoys socializing. Because the Orange is not usually emotionally or physically available to the Abstract Tan, the Tan tends to keep more and more to herself. This pattern continues until both the Orange and the Abstract Tan are living separate and isolated lives.

The childlike Abstract Tan needs someone who will communicate with her and take care of her. An Orange is indifferent to the Tan's theoretical concepts, and tends to be a private independent person who is not interested in being responsible for the childlike and dependent Abstract Tan. The gentle yet scattered Tan prefers to observe others and philosophize about life rather than to share in any of the daring physical exploits with the Orange. The Orange doesn't have the time or the interest to untangle the Abstract Tan's thoughts and ideas. He is more interested in planning his next adventure.

These two are happier with companions who are more like-minded.

Orange and Green Relationship

See Green and Orange Relationship.

Orange and Blue Relationship

See Blue and Orange Relationship.

Orange and Violet Relationship

While an Orange and a Violet would probably respect each other's independence and power, they would have different views about the purpose of life. Whereas an Orange is trying to conquer the world, the Violet is trying to save it. The visionary Violet believes there is a higher purpose for living on the planet, which involves inspiring and saving humanity. The brash Orange doesn't have the time or inclination to save the world. He prefers to be alone and adventurous.

While an Orange admires the leadership ability of a Violet, he resents the Violet if she attempts to lead him or tell him what to do. An Orange does not respect the visions of a Violet, feeling instead that the Violet is an impractical and unrealistic dreamer. To an Orange, "saving the world" is too high an ideal. Oranges respect the environment and want to see it protected, but they do not usually choose to involve themselves in any political battles. A Violet feels that the Orange is missing the greater purpose of life, which is helping mankind. Both of these personalities are very powerful, independent and courageous in their own areas of expertise, but they have disagreements as to the defini-tion of courage and the purpose of life.

The Violet is a natural performer who prefers to have an audience, while the Orange couldn't care less if people admire his spectacular feats of daring. Both the Violet and the Orange love to travel, but they have different reasons and purposes for traveling. The Violet loves to explore the planet to learn about different people and cultures. The Orange tends to be drawn to places where people rarely dare to even venture. The Violet is fascinated as the Orange tells of his adventures of climbing the highest mountain or jumping from a plane. The Violet is able to live vicariously through the Orange's stories. But as long-term mates, these two have very little in common. The spiritual causes to which a Violet feels drawn do not interest an Orange, while to a Violet, the daring exploits of an Orange seem to be an unproductive use of time.

Orange and Lavender Relationship
See Lavender and Orange Relationship.

Orange and Crystal Relationship

This relationship isn't very compatible. A Crystal is much too sensitive and delicate to be consorting with the rough, rugged and challenging Orange. An Orange wants to be outdoors confronting nature, exploring, climbing mountains and taking on the challenges of the physical world. The sensitive Crystal prefers to be in the quiet, gentle solitude of nature. An Orange is too harsh and brash for this fragile, soft-spoken personality. Being around an Orange too long can overwhelm and overload the Crystal's delicate system.

An Orange's lifestyle goes against a Crystal's way of life and her belief system. This loving being communes and becomes one with nature. She doesn't challenge or conquer it. The esoteric Crystal needs someone she can relate to on a sensitive, spiritual basis. An Orange has no desire to discuss spiritual topics.

The Orange is also too independent to meet the needs of a Crystal. He is rarely home, which would eventually upset the Crystal. Even though Crystals need to have a lot of time alone, the Orange would be gone far too much for the Crystal's well-being. The Orange would find the Crystal's need for quiet and solitude unappealing and unchallenging. The Orange craves excitement, adventure and challenges. These two individuals would have absolutely nothing in common.

Orange and Indigo Relationship

This is another couple who would have nothing to talk about and nothing in common. The Indigo's concepts about the universe appear to be too strange and foreign to an Orange, who likes physical reality, excitement and adventure. The Indigo prefers to deal with spirituality, love and ideas about "consciousness." An Orange has little or no interest in these topics. The Indigo may admire the courage and daring of the Orange, and respect her desire to go beyond accepted limitations. But the Indigo would find the Orange much too brash, independent and egocentric to be much of a companion.

An Orange tends to be a loner. An Indigo, while also enjoying time alone, usually enjoys quiet, personal time with close, intimate friends. An Indigo would be confused and bewildered by an Orange's need to conquer physical reality, since the Indigo believes that physical reality is just an illusion. An Orange lives too much in her body for the Indigo to be able to relate to her. The Indigo treasures life, believing that life has deep spiritual meaning. An Orange sees life as a physical challenge, an opponent to be conquered. An Indigo would love to be at the top of a mountain pondering the beauty of life. This is not why an Orange goes to the top of a mountain. An Orange prefers to conquer life, not to "appreciate" it. These two would find very little on which to base a meaningful relationship.

■ MAGENTA

Magenta and Red Relationship

Typically, this is a relationship that would have major problems. Reds usually like everything to be practical, down-to-earth and realistic. Magentas don't want anything practical, normal or realistic. They want their lives to be outrageous. A Magenta likes to shock people, which a Red finds totally embarrassing, unnecessary and ridiculous. These two colors would have absolutely nothing in common. A Magenta loves to constantly try new, interesting and bizarre things. She wants to go to parties and be outrageous. A Red does not like parties or trying anything new. This relationship is comparable to a tractor driver going out with a punk-rock star with purple hair. The common sense and practical accountability of a Red would make a

Magenta completely bored. She would lose interest quickly. With the Red's stubbornness and unwillingness to change, the Magenta — who loves to try wild and crazy antics all the time — would feel stifled. The Red's interest in sex, physical endurance and strength does not interest a Magenta at all. These two usually have nothing in common.

However, a Red will occasionally take on more of the wild and rowdy aspects of his personality, and in this case the Red will join the Magenta in attending parties and social gatherings. When a Red's behavior gets outrageous or uncontrollable, it is usually because of his temper or his sexuality. A Red can lose his temper easily and cause a scene. He also dislikes his sexual expression to be suppressed. He can often go to flagrant and boisterous extremes with his sexual behavior. A Magenta usually shakes up people's traditional rules and systems to make a social statement about non-conformity. A Red is more of a fighter.

While these two could enjoy attending wild parties together for a while, a typical Magenta and a rambunctious Red would probably eventually start competing with each other for attention.

Magenta and Orange Relationship

See Orange and Magenta Relationship.

Magenta and Magenta Relationship

While these two colors would probably have a great time together at first, they would eventually try to see which one could be more bizarre. This combination is not very practical. Neither one of them has the desire to be responsible for the home, or to support a relationship. Since Magentas tend to move from relationship to relationship very quickly, these two could have an interesting but brief experience together.

This pair would probably enjoy creating a bizarre, artistic work or invention together. They could have a great time shocking people by walking down the street wildly dressed with their hair different colors and shapes. They would enjoy attending parties together. Seeing a home that two Magentas had decorated would be an incredible experience. But having these two outrageous Magentas together would probably be too intense for any of their friends to handle. The more a Magenta is around another Magenta, the more bizarre and outrageous his behavior becomes. They tend to feed off of each other.

This relationship would be interesting and fun for both of them for a short period of time. However, since neither one of them would be a stable influence in the relationship, it would probably soon fall apart. Neither would want to pay the bills, take care of details or make a living. This couple would make great friends or roommates for a while, but soon they would want to move on to yet another adventure.

Magenta and Yellow Relationship

These two could be great playmates. A Magenta would constantly be entertaining the Yellow, who is always looking for fun, entertainment and excitement. They both love going to parties. They would have a great time together, as long as their goal was just to have a good time. However, when it comes down to being responsible, taking care of the home and going to work, there would be difficulty in this relationship.

A Yellow would respect a Magenta's ability to make money without conforming to society's standards, since the Yellow is also looking for the freedom to express himself creatively outside of the restrictive nine-to-five job. Since both of these colors are so creative, they could create wild, artistic, innovative inventions together. A Yellow, who loves to laugh, enjoys watching the antics of the Magenta. Since neither one of them is interested in a committed relationship, they would give each other the freedom to come and go when they want, to see other people and to have a good time.

Sex, for a Yellow, is a very playful experience. For a Magenta it is a sensual experiment, so these two could enjoy playing with sex together.

Neither one of these colors likes to be manipulated or told what to do, so they would allow each other the freedom to make their own choices. The main problem is that neither one wants to be the responsible one at home. This couple would most likely be childless because of the commitment involved in having children.

The childlike exuberance of a Yellow is fun for a while, but the Magenta does not appreciate being around children for long. The Magenta would eventually want to experiment with a different, more challenging or outrageous mate. While these two are great friends and playmates, they usually do not end up as long-term partners.

Magenta and Logical Tan Relationship

This would not be a likely pair. The Magenta's bizarre behavior would be too outrageous for a Logical Tan, who likes stability, reliability and security. All these qualities go against the beliefs and behaviors of a Magenta. A Logical Tan would become easily embarrassed by the Magenta's antisocial behavior. The open-minded and uninhibited Magenta could open up a Logical Tan's practical way of looking at life. And a Logical Tan could be a stabilizing and grounding force for a Magenta, who has a tendency not to be able to pay bills, keep a steady job, or even keep a household together.

Eventually however, the Logical Tan would most probably become frustrated with the unreliability and strange behavior of a Magenta. A Logical Tan desires logical, analytical and sensible behavior. It is those very rules, standards and disciplines set down by the Logical Tan that a Magenta loves to challenge. Everything the Logical Tan finds sacred, the Magenta shoots down. Even the most open-minded Logical Tan would find these challenges exhausting after a while.

This combination could provide an interesting balance for a short period of time, but this is not a very practical or realistic long-term relationship.

Magenta and Environmental Tan Relationship

See Environmental Tan and Magenta Relationship.

Magenta and Sensitive Tan Relationship

See Sensitive Tan and Magenta Relationship.

Magenta and Abstract Tan Relationship

The main reason that this relationship would not work out is that the Magenta does not want to take care of the dependent Abstract Tan. There are many other reasons why these two would be better off finding different mates. Even though the Magenta enjoys unusual people, the energy of an Abstract Tan is too scattered and chaotic for him. He eventually becomes annoyed and bothered by her inconsistencies. The Abstract Tan spends too much time in her head for the likes of the Magenta, who instead prefers to experiment and play with physical reality. When the Tan expresses her thoughts, they shoot out in all directions like fireworks. Trying to understand the Tan can be unnerving for the Magenta. Although the Magenta's behavior is bizarre, he feels that there is purpose behind his madness. He wants to wake people up and keep them from becoming stuck and complacent. The Magenta cannot see any purpose or justification behind the Abstract Tan's rambling, philosophical discussions. He can't understand how they apply to his life.

Both of these individuals enjoy parties and social gatherings. Neither one wants to be responsible for taking care of business. Their home is frequently cluttered, unkempt and disorderly. In their own way, these two are both overgrown children who want someone else to pay their bills for them.

Neither of them cares to have strongly committed or deeply emotional relationships, though the Abstract Tan does want someone around who can provide interesting conversations as well as a secure and supportive environment for her. The Magenta is too independent and wild to provide stability or security for the Tan. If the Abstract Tan tried to depend on the Magenta, he would rebel and leave. If the Abstract Tan attempted to communicate her various hypotheses and notions to the Magenta in her typical shotgun style, he would become perplexed, then annoyed, and then apathetic.

The Abstract Tan would develop theories regarding the Magenta's behavior, but the Magenta is not interested in being analyzed. (He wouldn't understand the Tan's explanations anyway.) These two would typically end up going in their own separate directions.

Magenta and Green Relationship
See Green and Magenta Relationship.

Magenta and Blue Relationship
See Blue and Magenta Relationship.

Magenta and Violet Relationship
See Violet and Magenta Relationship.

Magenta and Lavender Relationship

Lavenders and Magentas both tend to live in their own worlds. A Magenta's world is outgoing, adventurous and bizarre, while a Lavender lives in a pretty, fantasy world. A Lavender is more soft-spoken, intuitive and sensitive. They each tend to be the "unusual" personality in their color family. Other people have a hard time relating to either of these colors. Magentas and Lavenders would have a hard time relating to each other as well. The Lavender wants a partner she can relate to in a very loving and gentle manner. A Magenta is too brash, independent and outspoken for her. They would, however, both leave each other alone. Neither one would be insistent that his partner follow the other's belief system.

Because these two live so much in their own worlds, it would be very rare for them to cross paths. They wouldn't have anything in common other than their unique ways of looking at the world and at life. Even though they would be fascinated by their differences for a while, this pair would not be comfortable in each other's company for very long.

Magenta and Crystal Relationship

See Crystal and Magenta Relationship.

Magenta and Indigo Relationship

Magentas and Indigos are the avant-garde personalities of the aura spectrum. A Magenta is much too outrageous, loud and brash for an Indigo, however. An Indigo tends to be much more spiritual, quiet, intuitive and sensitive than a Magenta. They both challenge and question standard, accepted belief systems. A Magenta challenges them because she loves having the freedom to express herself. She believes people should be able to experience life in their own unique ways. The Magenta challenges oppressive or outdated social standards and behaviors.

An Indigo questions the accepted beliefs because he believes that they are limiting to the soul. An Indigo believes we are fully-actualized God-beings, here to experience life through our creativity and spirituality. The Indigo questions belief systems because they are usually of lower consciousness, or from a limited concept of reality.

A Magenta does not relate to an Indigo's spiritual ideas. The Indigo's ideas seem too esoteric and unrealistic. A Magenta prefers to express herself creatively and physically. An Indigo doesn't yet understand the physicalness of our being. The body is foreign to him. A Magenta is "free" sexually, experimenting with one person after another, just for fun and variety. To an Indigo, sex is something much more personal and spiritual. It is a soul-to-soul experience. A Magenta's sexual behavior would totally confuse and bewilder an Indigo.

A Magenta likes to be around people, to frequent parties and to attend social gatherings, but the Magenta ends up being a loner because most people can't relate to her bizarre behavior. An Indigo loves people, but finds very few whom he can relate to or trust. His spiritual ideas and heightened sensitivity are so advanced that most people can't communicate with him. Both a Magenta and an Indigo feel like outcasts.

A Magenta doesn't seem to take life as seriously as an Indigo does. The Magenta is not as sensitive. An Indigo out of his power can get so confused and lost in this physical environment that he withdraws into drugs or alcohol. This is a form of hiding out. A Magenta will withdraw for a while, but it is very short-lived. She can become a loner, but it doesn't seem to bother her as much as it does the Indigo. Both of them tend to be the "black sheep" in society, and so understand and experience compassion for each other.

These two individuals probably wouldn't be found in a relationship. They would both respect each other's need for independence. They would be fascinated by each other's belief systems and how they relate to other people. But they would be unable to relate to or live with each other's approach to life. An Indigo would be intimidated by the Magenta's bizarre behavior. An Indigo wants confirmation that what he intuitively feels is the intrinsic truth about life. A Magenta would not be able to provide realistic answers to this inquisitive and gentle soul. In the presence of the Indigo's serious and sensitive spiritual nature, the Magenta would not feel free to express herself outrageously.

■ YELLOW

Yellow and Red Relationship

Even though both of these colors are in the physical family, the Yellow's energy is much too sensitive for the power and strength of a Red. The Red would have a tendency to crush the carefree Yellow.

On the positive side, a Red could probably provide stability to the Yellow's life. The Yellow is so childlike that the Red often plays the role of the responsible parent.

They both love physical work, moving things around, and tactile sensation. Yellows are fond of being outdoors, working with the land, or working with their hands. They typically take jobs as gardeners, electricians, plumbers, athletes or other physically active workers. Reds also enjoy working with their bodies and with the physical environment. Consequently, Reds and Yellows are often found in the same environments and occupations.

Reds have a very intense emotional side. They release anger and frustration abruptly. Yellows tend to run away from anger. Since the Yellow is intimidated by the Red's power, strength and explosive nature, the Red would definitely be the dominating partner in this relationship.

Both of these personalities understand what it means to live in the moment. They both enjoy physical pleasure and immediate gratification. Sex between these two could be a lot of fun. Combining the passion and sexual appetite of a Red with the sexual playfulness and willingness of a Yellow could create a great physical relationship.

A Red tends to be much more grounded and responsible than a Yellow. A Yellow, however, can add playful and light-hearted fun to the life of the serious and intense Red. The Red would have to maintain patience and self-control so that he wouldn't intimidate or scare away the Yellow. The Yellow would have to stay in her power in order to withstand the intensity and strong temper of the Red. A Red would not approve of a lazy or irresponsible Yellow. He takes his work and responsibilities very seriously. He could become quite frustrated with the easygoing attitude of a Yellow.

If both the Red and the Yellow stayed in their power, this couple could provide a good balance for each other. Both enjoy physical activities, living and working with their bodies and being out in their physical environment. However, if either the Yellow or the Red slipped out of power, the Yellow would tend to feel like an abused child. Intimidated by the volatile temper and overwhelming power of a Red, the Yellow would want to run away. The Red tends to be too strong, heavy and overbearing for the sensitive and childlike Yellow.

Yellow and Orange Relationship

Both the Yellow and the Orange enjoy playing in their physical environment and in their physical bodies. These two often share some of the same interests, but they do not have the same emotional needs. The Yellow is frequently fascinated by the feats and skills of the Orange, and occasionally participates in similar activities. These two can be compatible if the Orange does not expect the Yellow to accompany him on all of his dangerous exploits. The Yellow would eventually become insecure and frightened of the physical danger that the Orange continuously faces. A Yellow fears the possibility of experiencing physical pain. The Yellow, being carefree and independent, is happy to go off and play with other people while the Orange goes sky- diving.

Problems can arise in this relationship when the Orange becomes too aloof. The Yellow needs to be around people more than the Orange does. The Orange is such an independent loner that he is not always physically or emotionally available to the sensitive Yellow, causing her to feel abandoned. Frequently, the Orange is also too powerful and intense for the childlike Yellow. The daring Orange wants to challenge life and conquer his environment, while a Yellow just wants to have a good time and play in it. An Orange takes his dangerous work very seriously. The Yellow rarely takes anything seriously. The Yellow also loves sex. An Orange is sexual, but sex is not one of his priorities. He is much more interested in going on an adventure. Again, the Yellow can feel abandoned and alone when her needs are not met by the self-absorbed Orange.

This couple can have a good time together if they share physical activities together. However, in the long run, this relationship will most likely drift apart, with the Yellow not finding the sensitivity and playfulness that she requires in a mate, and the Orange becoming bored with the responsibility of a relationship. Neither wants to pay the bills or take care of the domestic chores — they are much too concerned with having fun or going off on adventures.

Yellow and Magenta Relationship

See Magenta and Yellow Relationship.

Yellow and Yellow Relationship

Yellows play well together. A marriage between two Yellows will often feel like children playing house. These two have a great deal in common. They understand each other's need for sensitivity, fun, freedom, and time and space to be alone. They both enjoy being physically active, being outdoors, laughing, playing and generally enjoying life. Healthy, balanced Yellows can experience a joyful, energetic and fulfilling life together. Unbalanced or out-of-power Yellows, however, may experience problems regarding either financial stability, complications arising from negative addictions, or emotional insecurities due to the unwillingness to commit.

If one partner delves into any of the negative addictions, such as drugs or alcohol, it will probably cause problems for the other Yellow as well. Yellows have very little self-discipline when it comes to addictive substances. It will be twice as hard for one of the Yellows to stop if the other doesn't stop at the same time. If one continues the addictive behavior without the other, the playmates won't be playing the same game, which will cause disconnection and hurt feelings between them.

Great financial wealth will *probably* not be a part of this couple's lives unless they are lucky enough to get it "the easy way"—through the lottery, an inheritance, or a creative idea which happens in the right place at the right time. Usually, Yellows struggle with money.

One thing is most certainly guaranteed with this couple, however — their sex life (and many other parts of their life) will be fun and compatible.

Yellow and Logical Tan Relationship

See Logical Tan and Yellow Relationship.

Yellow and Environmental Tan Relationship

Even though the Yellow and the Environmental Tan enjoy many of the same physical activities, they are not the most compatible mates. Yellows are too irresponsible and immature for the solemn and practical Environmental Tan. Although he enjoys the fun, light-hearted spirit of the Yellow, the Tan is eventually worn out and frustrated by her careless behavior. The Yellow needs a playmate, someone who can laugh, be silly and enjoy life with her. The Environmental Tan doesn't really know how to play. His life is often burdened with responsibilities. Although the Environmental Tan can add stability and security to the Yellow's life, his seriousness can eventually become too heavy and burdensome for the carefree Yellow. She can suffocate under the weight.

These individuals both enjoy experiencing the physical environment. They are often found in similar locations, enjoying the same activities. If they are in a relationship with each other, they can at least share some of these same hobbies. However, the fun-loving Yellow is usually more reckless and free than the cautious Environmental Tan. They don't enjoy their sports with the same zest and enthusiasm.

If the Environmental Tan agrees to be the responsible and rational partner who takes care of all the details and pays the bills, then the Yellow has the freedom to bring fun and joy into the relationship. Both can benefit from this arrangement. The Yellow can bring light and hope into the often grim life of an Environmental Tan, while the Environmental Tan can offer financial stability and order to the Yellow's chaotic and frequently impoverished lifestyle.

While these two can provide elements missing in each other's lives, they are usually too different to enjoy each other's company for an extended period of time. The Environmental Tan is too regimented for the childlike Yellow. The Yellow doesn't want to abide by the Environmental Tan's rules and expectations. She prefers a mate who loves spontaneity and creativity. The Environmental Tan's personality doesn't allow him such frivolities. The Environmental Tan prefers a mate who is rational and responsible. He wants a companion who is an intellectual equal as well as a reliable and dependable partner.

These two are happier and more satisfied with mates who have personalities more similar to their own.

Yellow and Sensitive Tan Relationship

A Sensitive Tan and a Yellow provide a gentle balance for each other. The warmth and gentleness of the Sensitive Tan is safe and comforting for the childlike Yellow. A Sensitive Tan is understanding and accepting of the Yellow's playful behavior. Rather than judging or criticizing the Yellow, the Sensitive Tan's Blue aspect tends to mother and nurture him. (Yellows tend to attract mothering personalities to them.)

These two both enjoy helping people. They are both caring, thoughtful and likeable individuals. They both tend to be sensitive and considerate toward one another. The Sensitive Tan provides a loving and secure environment for the disorderly Yellow, while the Yellow brings lightness and joy to the often serious Sensitive Tan.

There are potential problems with this combination, however. Although the Sensitive Tan appreciates the Yellow's kindness, sensitivity and willingness to help others, she, like the other Tans, actually prefers a mate to be dependable, prudent and rational. She also values commitment. A Yellow usually has a fear of commitment and responsibility. A Sensitive Tan can occasionally feel frustrated by the Yellow's irresponsible and unreliable behavior. She finds herself being the stable, financial provider for the family, while the jovial Yellow is off somewhere being creative or playful. The Sensitive Tan quickly discovers that the Yellow is better at spending money than he is at earning it.

Reacting to the Yellow's irresponsibility, the Sensitive Tan can easily develop a mothering attitude. She feels that she must take care of the Yellow or everything will fall apart. At first, the Yellow enjoys someone taking care of all of his responsibilities. However, he eventually can become resentful of living with a mother instead of with a playmate. Although the Sensitive Tan is usually forced into the role of caretaker by the Yellow's unreliable behavior, neither partner is ultimately happy with that situation. To create a harmonious relationship, the Sensitive Tan must either adjust and learn to accept her role as the practical partner (without becoming the Yellow's mother), or the Yellow must learn to become more responsible and reliable.

If these goals can be achieved these two can make an excellent couple. Because the Sensitive Tan is such a patient person, she is tolerant of the Yellow's actions. She is the type of partner who can live peacefully with a Yellow.

Yellow and Abstract Tan Relationship

See Abstract Tan and Yellow Relationship.

Yellow and Green Relationship

See Green and Yellow Relationship.

Yellow and Blue Relationship

A relationship between a Blue and a Yellow is very common. The two personalities are very attracted to each other. The mothering Blue tends to be drawn to the child-like Yellow. Their relationship usually starts off well. The needs of the Yellow are more than met by the loving, nurturing Blue, who likes to take care of everyone. Her nurturing often includes taking care of the Yellow financially. A Blue is well-known for rescuing a "lost," down and upset Yellow, only to find once she nurtures him back onto his feet, he flees the nest. Blue/Yellow relationships have potential for success, provided that the Blue doesn't smother or over-mother the Yellow and provided the Yellow can take commitment seriously.

There are traditional problems that occur between a Blue and a Yellow. When a Blue is in love with someone, she wants to be around him all of the time. A Yellow needs his time and space to be alone. When the Yellow chooses to be alone, the Blue takes this as a personal rejection. She retreats, feeling unloved and rejected. The sensitive Yellow, not wanting to hurt anyone and wanting to avoid conflict at all costs, will usually run away. A Yellow also hates being manipulated by guilt, which is the weapon most commonly used by a Blue.

Blues and Yellows both love to help people. They are both very sensitive, giving and considerate of other people's feelings. They will tend to be a very pleasant couple, provided they make it to couple status at all. The number one priority for a Blue is a loving, committed relationship. And one of the greatest fears of a Yellow is commitment. The long-suffering, loyal, and monogamous Blue may have to wait years to hear the words she longs to hear from a Yellow — and wait she usually does.

A Yellow/Blue union is compatible when the Blue, who will do anything for a loved one, will laugh at the Yellow's jokes, allow him his freedom and time alone, and learn how to *receive* gifts from him. (Yellows love to bring little gifts home.) A Yellow needs to learn to allow a Blue to cry or talk about the relationship. He needs to learn not to run away. A Blue is never trying to hurt anyone. She just wants to know that she is loved.

A Blue must love the Yellow enough to help him believe in himself, rather than to create a dependency. A Blue must learn to allow the Yellow to be around her because he *loves* her, not because he needs her. Blues must learn to release the need to be "needed."

A Yellow must learn that commitment is not a confinement, but, rather, that it is a tool that promotes growth and deeper understanding. A Yellow needs to see that telling a Blue that she is loved and appreciated brings her joy. He does not have to see her need for love as a manipulative maneuver to trap and smother him.

While Yellows came to the planet to bring joy and to heal people, Blues came to bring love. They can be a wonderful team if they can understand and support each other's goals, needs and priorities.

Yellow and Violet Relationship

A Yellow and a Violet can be a fun, creative and inspiring team. Together, the Violet's vision and the Yellow's creativity can produce some fascinating results. These two are comfortable playing together. A Violet is one of the personalities who doesn't judge the Yellow's need to play.

Both of these personalities love people. Even though the Yellow may be shy until she gets to know people, both the Violet and Yellow enjoy socializing.

These two also enjoy sex. They are two of the most sexual LifeColors in the spectrum. Although the Yellow tends to be playful while the Violet prefers to be passionate, they can experience a good balance of energies together.

The Violet usually assumes the role of leader in the relationship. He takes his purpose on the planet much more seriously than the Yellow does. Actually, the only real problem that can arise with this couple is if the Yellow becomes consistently lazy, flaky or irresponsible. The Violet, who has a strong need to move forward and accomplish his goals and visions, can become frustrated and disappointed with the Yellow's tendency to procrastinate. A Yellow is frequently insecure and afraid to take risks. She prefers instead to be spontaneous and live in the moment rather than set goals and make plans. The Violet tends to be the dynamic force in the relationship. The Yellow adds lightness, fun and creativity to the relationship. Frequently, the Yellow prefers to ride the Violet's coat-tails, which means less work and responsibilities for the easygoing Yellow. This can cause the Violet to lose respect for her.

It is usually the Violet who is more capable of producing money. However, if the Violet is scattered and out-of-power, both the Yellow and the Violet can experience financial difficulties.

These two usually share many of the same interests — music, entertainment, physical exercise, sex, people and traveling. Although they have different purposes behind these interests, they tend to enjoy experiencing them together.

A Violet and a Yellow are typically a harmonious couple. They usually enrich each other's lives. As long as the Yellow doesn't become lazy, fearful or irresponsible, she can inspire the Violet with humor and creativity. As long as the Violet doesn't become too arrogant, serious or overbearing, and as long as he takes time out to play with the childlike Yellow, he can inspire the Yellow to reach greater levels of creative or healing abilities. He can teach her to take risks and experience more of her potential.

A Violet is here to help save the planet and change it for the better. A Yellow is a natural healer and is here to "lighten up" and bring joy to the planet. Together, these two can be an inspirational, creative team who can teach mass audiences through such mediums as film, art, music and other creative forms, or they can travel the world, reaching the masses together as healers. In power, they are a dynamic team.

Yellow and Lavender Relationship

Yellows and Lavenders play well together, but a marriage between them would be like two kids playing house. Neither is driven to accomplish anything, though the Yellow often enjoys fixing things around the house. Yellows are like children, while Lavenders tend to live in a fantasy world. The fact that a Yellow tends to live more in his physical body can help the Lavender by keeping her in her body more often. They can physically play together. A Yellow can help keep a Lavender grounded, and a Lavender can tell great fairytales and stories to entertain him. However, in the meantime, neither of them are paying the bills, taking care of business or making any money. They see life in the same childlike fashion.

Since both are sensitive and caring, neither of them wants to hurt the other's feelings. Both, when threatened with conflict, tend to run away or escape into a fantasy world. Neither of them is usually grounded enough to carry on an adult relationship with the other. This couple is similar to ice cream with chocolate syrup on top. It's beautiful to look at, it tastes good, but it's probably not the healthiest combination in the world.

A positive aspect of this relationship is that when the Yellow's creativity is combined with the fantastic imagination of the Lavender, the two can create wonderful children's books, stories or toys. They will, however, probably need to find someone else to carry out the actual details of writing and publishing the book.

Since neither of them manages money well, they tend to use it up very quickly. Unless they are independently wealthy or living off an inheritance, these two would be better off marrying responsible mates who can take care of them. They are a great creative duo, but not very practical marriage partners.

Yellow and Crystal Relationship
See Crystal and Yellow Relationship.

Yellow and Indigo Relationship
See Indigo and Yellow Relationship.

7. Relationships with the Mental Colors

■ LOGICAL TAN

Logical Tan and Red Relationship
See Red and Logical Tan Relationship.

Logical Tan and Orange Relationship
These two colors do not understand each other very well. An Orange usually finds a Logical Tan to be too security-minded, safe and complacent. A Logical Tan usually thinks that an Orange takes unnecessary risks. A Logical Tan enjoys calm, rational, mental tasks; an Orange needs to be physically active while challenging life. A Logical Tan does not see the logic or purpose behind an Orange's behavior. A Logical Tan prefers to settle down in the suburbs, have a stable nine-to-five job and commit to her family for the rest of her life. An Orange finds a Logical Tan's way of life to be synonymous with a slow, boring, tortuous death. This daredevil does not want the encumbrance of a relationship, the responsibility of a family or the tedium of a nine-to-five job. He doesn't want the burden of traditional commitments or responsibilities.

A Logical Tan does not usually respect or admire the risk-taking actions of an Orange. She judges them to be self-indulgent, impractical, dangerous and illogical. One thing these two individuals do have in common, however, is that they both like to calculate and plan every detail. A Logical

Tan can be impressed and fascinated by the cunning mind and organizational skills of an Orange, while the Orange can call on the detail-oriented Logical Tan to help him research all the facts and figures involved in the feat. They do not, however, enjoy the same lifestyles, hobbies or challenges.

Logical Tan and Magenta Relationship
See Magenta and Logical Tan Relationship.

Logical Tan and Logical Tan Relationship
This relationship has great potential for compatibility. Both are grounded, reliable, stable and methodical personalities. They share the same priorities. They both work for a living, have secure jobs and enjoy discussing intellectual topics.

A potential problem in this relationship is that it can become very predictable. Logical Tans frequently work at the same jobs, live in the same home and follow the same patterns their entire lives. There is no adventure in their lives. They have no motivation to change. This couple can become very habitual, doing the same thing over and over again. However, they can also be very content with their lifestyle. Growth takes place at a pace they find comfortable. It is safe, secure and reliable.

They both understand the other's need to see all the data and proof. They each appreciate the other's dependability. What may be missing in this relationship, however, is emotional expression. Both tend to keep their feelings to themselves. But having a mate who doesn't demand emotional intimacy is comforting and safe for a Logical Tan.

Logical Tan and Environmental Tan Relationship
This relationship is similar to one between two Logical Tans. This couple is very compatible, the only difference being that an Environmental Tan is more connected with

the physical environment. He wants to work with the environment and is more interested in physical activity than a Logical Tan. If an Environmental Tan decides he wants to go diving to investigate some part of the ocean, a Logical Tan won't usually join him. Not believing it is a safe activity, she sees no logical reason to participate. The Environmental Tan will usually experience these types of activities without his Logical Tan partner.

For the most part, these two are very much alike. Both are dependable, stable and grounded. They both choose to analyze data and work with details. They share the same priorities. They may be interested in different projects and activities, but their different interests may help the relationship continue to develop and progress. They can educate each other in different areas.

There may not be much passion or intimate communication in this relationship. Both tend to be reserved and keep their feelings to themselves. Their relationship often resembles a business relationship. All the details and responsibilities are handled on a daily basis, but rarely are there fireworks. Both can be content with these arrangements—neither feels compelled to be swept away by emotions.

Logical Tan and Sensitive Tan Relationship

See Sensitive Tan and Logical Tan Relationship.

Logical Tan and Abstract Tan Relationship

See Abstract Tan and Logical Tan Relationship.

Logical Tan and Green Relationship

See Green and Logical Tan Relationship.

Logical Tan and Blue Relationship

Blues desire a monogamous, committed relationship, and are often drawn to the stability and reliability of a

Logical Tan. Unfortunately, what typically develops in the marriage is a communication problem. Blues communicate from the heart — they want to bond emotionally with their mates. Logical Tans, on the other hand, process intellectually. A Tan prefers to analyze the situation and come up with a rational solution, while keeping his emotions and thoughts to himself in the process. This can frustrate the Blue, who feels shut out and isolated from the deepest part of her mate.

A Logical Tan does not intellectually understand the emotional unpredictability of the Blue. She seems to be too intuitive and too illogical for the methodical and rational Tan. The Blue is constantly wanting to "discuss the relationship" and to talk about "feelings." A Tan can eventually become too emotionally unfulfilling to a Blue. The Blue feels she is often talking to a wall.

In this relationship, the Blue needs to become more emotionally mature, so that she doesn't wear out her Logical Tan mate by constantly requiring outside reinforcement to validate her self-worth. She must trust in the knowledge that she is loved. (That is the greatest lesson for a Blue — in or out of a relationship.) However, the Tan must also realize that the Blue must have emotional gratification, and must learn the value of open discussions about feelings. If she is fulfilled emotionally, then the Blue will go to the ends of the earth for her mate.

If both are looking for a "traditional" marriage, in which the Blue wife loves and nurtures the Logical Tan husband while he goes off to work and supports the family, then this relationship can work. With a Tan, the Blue has the comfort and satisfaction of knowing she has a stable, reliable and committed mate. The Tan knows that he has a loyal, loving and devoted mate who will take care of him. The Logical Tan is the disciplinarian of the family, while the Blue is the nurturer.

While communication may be a problem, commitment and security are the rewards for this couple. Both fill different roles in the relationship. Tans and Blues must realize that they each see the world differently, process feelings differently and have different priorities. If a Blue can understand that a Tan needs to process information slowly and methodically (and if she can remain patient when he gets "stuck"), then she will have a secure marriage. If the Logical Tan can understand the emotional needs of a Blue, and if he can learn to trust what she "feels" regardless of the lack of "facts," then he will have a loyal, supportive and loving mate. (One way in which a Tan can learn to trust a Blue is for him to observe and analyze her track record. Since a Blue's intuition is almost always right, the Tan can learn to trust it.)

Logical Tan and Violet Relationship

Because the beliefs and behaviors of Violets and Logical Tans are at opposite ends of the spectrum, a relationship between them is challenging and only occasionally successful. Since the Logical Tan methodically and analytically processes every step between one and ten, she is appalled by the Violet's habit of trying to jump from one to fifty. A Logical Tan considers a Violet to be an unrealistic dreamer. It is common for these two to experience conflict with each other. When a Violet actually does accomplish his vision, however, the Logical Tan is awed and impressed by the Violet's power and insight.

While a Logical Tan is practical, analytical and methodical, the visionary Violet is often scattered, and far from "practical" in the normal definition of the word. In their relationship, problems can arise when the Violet wants to race forward, putting logic aside and risking everything on a dream. This usually upsets the Logical Tan, who values the security and the stable lifestyle she has worked so hard to establish. The Logical Tan can soon become frustrated and resentful of working so hard to financially support the Violet, who is off chasing dreams. Even the most patient Logical Tan will eventually want these dreams to materialize and produce a real income. The Violet may want to travel, but the Logical Tan argues that taking time off from work would be irresponsible and impractical.

A Violet has profound emotional depth and can be completely moved to tears due to his compassionate nature. He wants to communicate with his mate with the same intensity. A Logical Tan tends to hold back her feelings. She doesn't usually care to explain them to anyone. A Violet is passionate, sexual and creative, while the reserved Logical Tan tends to withhold in these areas as well. These two have a difficult time communicating on the same level.

Although Violets and Logical Tans have completely different needs, they can potentially benefit from each other if they stay centered and in power. The skeptical and cautious Logical Tan tends to ground the Violet and also to slow him down. The Logical Tan can also provide a stable and secure foundation to the relationship by adding common sense, reason and practicality to the Violet's ideas. When she trusts him, the Logical Tan can figure out the steps necessary to realistically actualize the Violet's dream. For example, the Violet can visualize an advanced form of media technology, and then the Logical Tan can develop the detailed technology to bring the vision into physical form. The Logical Tan can also provide a steady income so that the Violet can fly with his ideas.

The Violet can keep the Logical Tan's life from becoming stuck or predictable. The Logical Tan frequently gets enmeshed in repetition. The Violet can help the Logical Tan see life from other perspectives, thereby broadening her experience. The Violet can also help the Logical Tan explore and develop her emotions. While the Logical Tan can help the Violet keep his feet on the ground, the Violet can help to keep the Logical Tan from focusing only on the ground. They can provide a good balance for each other. However, it is more common for the Violet and Logical Tan's differences to frustrate and annoy one another.

Logical Tan and Lavender Relationship

This is an interesting relationship, one which could either provide balance for the couple, or cause them consistent frustration. A Logical Tan wants life to be rational, logical and practical. A Lavender's life is anything but practical. She instead lives in a world of dreams, visions and fantasies. This is judged by a Tan to be unrealistic and irresponsible. The Logical Tan must usually take care of the bills, go to work and handle the daily responsibilities in the relationship. This can eventually frustrate the Logical Tan, unless he accepts and agrees to the arrangement.

The gentle Lavender can provide creative and artistic aspects to the relationship. The Lavender can inspire the traditional and oftentimes short-sighted Logical Tan to see things from a different perspective. She may also free him from some of his habitual behaviors. A Lavender can help to keep her Logical Tan mate from becoming too rigid. Her fantasies and unique perspectives sometimes fascinate the otherwise analytical mind of a Tan.

In his power, a Logical Tan appreciates the sensitivity and gentleness that a Lavender adds to his life. Out of power, the Logical Tan becomes quite frustrated with the Lavender's inability to function within a practical, logical and economic system. The Lavender, who is much more sensitive and fragile than a Tan, can become quite hurt by the Logical Tan's inability to relate with her emotionally. Distressed by the situation, she withdraws into her own world. Communication between them then becomes difficult and sometimes impossible.

As long as the Logical Tan does not demand that the Lavender adhere to his set rules, laws and disciplines, the Lavender can feel free to be her creative self. The Lavender often appreciates the practical and responsible abilities that the Tan contributes to the relationship because his willingness to take care of business gives her the freedom to play. However, a Lavender can also find a Logical Tan too dogmatic and stifling for her taste.

What normally occurs with this couple is that they ultimately discover that they have no interests in common, and that their styles of communication differ dramatically. A Logical Tan usually keeps his feelings to himself and only discusses rational information. When a Lavender shares her experiences, her descriptions are beyond comprehension for the Tan. He doesn't relate to her world. This relationship often takes the form of a responsible, disciplining parent and a withdrawn, yet sensitive child. These are not the ingredients that can create a mature, emotionally-fulfilling and intimate marriage.

The success of this relationship depends on both the Logical Tan's and Lavender's willingness to allow the other person to bring his or her own unique contribution to the relationship. While one provides the secure and stable foundation, the other cultivates the emotional, creative and spiritual aspects of the union.

Logical Tan and Crystal Relationship

See Crystal and Logical Tan Relationship.

Logical Tan and Indigo Relationship

See Indigo and Logical Tan Relationship.

■ ENVIRONMENTAL TAN

Environmental Tan and Red Relationship

A Red and an Environmental Tan would probably have

more chances of success in a relationship than a Logical Tan and a Red. Both the Red and the Environmental Tan enjoy exploring and relating to the physical environment. Both tend to be the strong, silent type, and so would have an appreciation for each other. However, both also tend to keep their thoughts and feelings to themselves, and so an intimate and emotional bond between these two would probably be lacking. Sexually, this pair is more compatible than a Logical Tan and a Red.

The Environmental Tan, just like his Logical Tan counterpart, would be able to make plans and organize information. The Red would use her physical energy to implement the plans. Because of their complimentary skills, these two are a good working team. The Environmental Tan also has enough strength not to be intimidated by the explosive power and energy of a Red.

A problem that this couple can experience is that an Environmental Tan tends to live more in his head than a Red, and the Red may not be able to relate to everything that the Tan finds intellectually stimulating. On the other hand, the Environmental Tan's intellectual interests can add an extra dimension to the relationship. (See the section on Red and Logical Tan relationships to learn more information on the potential problems for this couple.)

Since neither are interested in sharing on an emotional or intimate level, these two would probably make better business associates than marriage partners. However, a successful relationship between them is not out of the realm of possibility.

Environmental Tan and Orange Relationship
See Orange and Environmental Tan Relationship.

Environmental Tan and Magenta Relationship
This combination is very similar to that of a Logical Tan

and a Magenta. The Environmental Tan is much too stable, reliable and logical for the outrageous behavior and challenging ideas of a Magenta. This couple has very little in common. They find each other's attitude and behavior unappealing. (See the section on relationships between Magenta and Logical Tan for more information regarding this couple.)

Environmental Tan and Yellow Relationship
See Yellow and Environmental Tan Relationship.

Environmental Tan and Logical Tan Relationship
See Logical Tan and Environmental Tan Relationship.

Environmental Tan and Environmental Tan Relationship
This can be a great business relationship, where each respects the ideas and power of the other. However, there is not much emotional expression, tenderness or intimacy between the Environmental Tans. They both tend to live their own lives independently. Because they both keep their emotions to themselves, their communication is not very intimate or open. They respect each other for their mental abilities, stability and common sense. However, there is not enough diversity between them to add depth to the relationship. This pair is too much alike. They make great friends or business partners, but they are traditionally not very emotionally intimate or sexually exciting as marriage partners.

Environmental Tan and Sensitive Tan Relationship
This couple has potential for compatibility. The Sensitive Tan desires a partner who has a sense of responsibility, reliability and inner strength, and the Environmental Tan embodies those qualities. A Sensitive Tan needs a mate who is capable of commitment and will support a family.

An Environmental Tan will choose to do this. Both prefer to communicate and relate with others on a very logical, mental level.

A potential problem is that a Sensitive Tan, who has traces of Blue in her aura, occasionally needs someone she can relate to on an emotional and intimate basis as well. An Environmental Tan is not usually emotionally available. At times, the Environmental Tan is too gruff and regimented for the Sensitive Tan. The Sensitive Tan appreciates the Environmental Tan because she feels she can rely on him to handle daily matters; however, her emotional needs are not always met. If the Sensitive Tan can accept the fact that the Environmental Tan can only give on certain levels, and if she can relax and fulfill her own emotional needs, then this relationship has potential for success.

The Sensitive Tan provides the quiet, nurturing home environment for the Environmental Tan. She also provides the softness and emotional tenderness that the Environmental Tan needs at times to balance him. A Sensitive Tan doesn't invade the Environmental Tan's need for privacy. Her style doesn't threaten the Environmental Tan. Instead, he appreciates her quiet reliability, her sense of responsibility and her subtle methods of nurturing. However, her gentleness is occasionally unchallenging to the Environmental Tan. He sometimes prefers a mate who is a bit more powerful and assertive.

Neither Tan is outgoing or risk-taking. Neither is an avid socializer, although the Sensitive Tan prefers to be with people more often than the Environmental Tan does. They both prefer to stay at home, creating a comfortable, secure and private environment for themselves and their family. They relate with each other's need for security and consistency. Both are fairly stable, neither has emotional highs or lows which threaten or upset the other. Communication between them tends to be safe and predictable.

In many ways, these two colors have the potential for a harmonious relationship. They have the ability to complement each other and to provide the security and stability they both need.

Environmental Tan and Abstract Tan Relationship

This is not usually a very compatible couple. The Environmental Tan, who wants order and discipline in his life, is exasperated by the chaotic and haphazard behavior of the Abstract Tan. She is too careless and forgetful for his taste. The Environmental Tan prefers a partner who is more powerful and can stand on her own two feet. The gentle Abstract Tan is looking instead for someone to take care of her. The Environmental Tan has no respect for her inability to be responsible and reliable. While the Abstract Tan has good intentions, she just usually has too many things going on in her mind at one time to follow through on many of them.

The Abstract Tan is usually intimidated by the Environmental Tan. She can be overwhelmed by his power and strength, and this increases her tendency to withdraw into her head. The Environmental Tan is a very private and solemn person who usually keeps his feelings to himself. While the Abstract Tan will discuss the concepts of emotions, she tends to detach herself from her own personal feelings. Consequently, this couple can be emotionally unavailable to each other. Although the Abstract Tan's cheerful and optimistic attitude could benefit the somber Environmental Tan, he tends to reject her. The Abstract Tan's exuberant and scattered energy usually bothers the quiet Environmental Tan.

Even though the Environmental Tan appreciates the Abstract Tan's conceptual understanding of unconditional love for humanity, he prefers a mate who can help him take care of business. An Abstract Tan prefers a mate who won't require her to be so responsible or reliable and who will be more understanding toward her unique style.

Environmental Tan and Green Relationship

See Green and Environmental Tan Relationship.

Environmental Tan and Blue Relationship

See Blue and Environment Tan Relationship.

Environmental Tan and Violet Relationship

This is a very interesting combination. Although it has potential, this relationship does not usually remain a long-term, compatible one. Violets are usually concerned about saving the planet on a humanitarian level. Environmental Tans tend to be concerned about saving the planet's physical environment. Both of them are concerned about the same goals, but from different perspectives. They can provide a good balance for one another. The Environmental Tan can bring practicality and reliability into the relationship, helping the Violet to focus and bring her visions into physical reality. The Violet can help the Environmental Tan see ideas and concepts beyond the limits of facts and proven information. Her visions can inspire and broaden the mind of the Environmental Tan.

Problems often occur when the two attempt to communicate. They have different styles. The rational, unemotional Tan tends to keep his feelings and dreams locked inside, while a Violet has great emotional depth and needs to relate with her mate on that level. To an Environmental Tan, a Violet appears to be an unrealistic dreamer, with her head too often in the clouds. Her ideas seem unreliable and impractical. To a Violet, an Environmental Tan often appears to be shortsighted, unemotional and overly cautious. A Violet requires passion and forward movement with her relationships. An Environmental Tan does not express passion or take leaps of faith easily, although he can learn to do so. His solemn behavior can eventually frustrate the Violet. Conflict and disagreements between this emotional visionary and the practical realist are common.

In a balanced, functioning relationship, the Environmental Tan is commonly the stable, consistent partner with the reliable job. The Violet focuses her attention on her dreams and visions, which can eventually elevate this couple into higher standards of living.

This couple will not compete with each other for attention, since the Environmental Tan has no desire to call attention to himself. He is delighted to leave the role of entertainer to the charismatic Violet. However, with the Violet constantly wanting to be the focus of attention at social gatherings, the Tan may eventually judge her as being either insecure or pompous and egotistical.

Although this couple has the possibility of providing a good balance for each other, it is more common for them to become frustrated with each other's differences. An Environmental Tan feels more secure with his traditional, proven methods of living. Supporting a Violet's dreams may cause him financial hardship until the Violet is able to prove herself successful. A Violet needs to fulfill her dreams and live her potential. A Tan can analyze the Violet's visions so much that it slows her down, or even causes her to give up. Being unable to live her dreams can cause the Violet unhappiness, depression and confusion.

Although these two have potential as a couple, their differences usually become uncomfortable and limiting for them both.

Environmental Tan and Lavender Relationship

See Lavender and Environmental Tan Relationship.

Environmental Tan and Crystal Relationship

An Environmental Tan and a Crystal would probably

not be able to create an intimate or emotionally bonded relationship together. Neither one typically seeks out relationships. The Crystal enjoys emotional communication, but is often too withdrawn to instigate conversation. The Environmental Tan is not interested in emotional discussions. Consequently, intimacy doesn't usually occur with this couple. Both of these individuals require time alone. Each tends to respect that need in the other, but these two can become too isolated.

Since an Environmental Tan does not display wild or outrageous behavior, the Crystal is not affected by his energy. The Environmental Tan can provide grounded stable energy for the fragile Crystal. However, the Crystal can also feel that the Environmental Tan is too emotionally unavailable, too practical, too stern and too rigid for her gentle nature. He doesn't usually understand the Crystal's spiritual beliefs or her need to go within to meditate.

Both of these colors appreciate nature, which gives them something to share together. However, the Crystal has a much more gentle, etheric and emotional approach to nature and life in general. The Environmental Tan tends to appreciate life by analyzing it. A Crystal can contribute beauty and softness to the technical Tan, while the Tan can add security and stability to the life of a scattered and insecure Crystal.

If these two each allow and accept the balance that each adds to the other's life, they can build a fairly complimentary relationship. However, since both of them tend to be introspective and quiet, what is often missing in this relationship is intimacy, emotional bonding, and open communication. The Crystal would probably have to adjust to the established, practical boundaries of an Environmental Tan's world, when she would be much happier living inside her own quiet inner world. Even though each of these personalities can provide the qualities that are missing in the other, an Environmental Tan is usually too rigid, too logical and too disciplined for the gentle, fragile, emotional Crystal.

Environmental Tan and Indigo Relationship
See Indigo and Environmental Tan Relationship.

■ SENSITIVE TAN

Sensitive Tan and Red Relationship
See Red and Sensitive Tan Relationship.

Sensitive Tan and Orange Relationship
This relationship can be challenging and uncomfortable for both partners. The Sensitive Tan tends to worry constantly about the safety and well-being of the Orange. The Orange finds the mothering behavior and the non-risking attitude of the Sensitive Tan to be boring and suffocating. A Sensitive Tan wants her companion to be at home doing practical, nurturing and safe activities with her. The Orange has no desire to fulfill the needs of a Sensitive Tan. Living with the quiet stability of a Sensitive Tan is slow death for an Orange, who prefers to be much more adventurous, bold and outrageous. The Sensitive Tan is usually consumed with dread every time the Orange walks out the door to go challenge the physical environment or attempt a daring feat. After a while, the stress is more than she can handle.

A Sensitive Tan needs to depend on her mate to be a provider. Taking on traditional responsibilities is not an Orange's idea of really living life, however. If the Sensitive Tan married an Orange, she would spend most of her time alone. She needs more companionship from her spouse than the Orange is willing to give. Often an Orange is drawn to a Sensitive Tan specifically because she is willing to stay home and take care of business, freeing the Orange to go out and be adventurous. Eventually, however, these mates are torn apart because the Sensitive Tan resents the abandonment and the Orange resents the suppression. These two do not usually meet each other's needs.

Sensitive Tan and Magenta Relationship

A Sensitive Tan prefers her life to be calm and quiet. Consequently, she is not comfortable with the outrageous behavior of a Magenta. A Magenta is much too bizarre, non-conforming and nontraditional for her. Instead, the Tan needs stability, responsibility and reliability from her partner. She needs someone who can provide security for her. A Magenta does not choose to fill this role.

A Magenta tends to find a Sensitive Tan too complacent. Although he knows that she will take care of the details, run the home and provide a loving, nurturing environment for him, eventually he becomes bored with her stability and predictability.

A Magenta needs a partner who is willing to be outrageous and fun-loving with him, and give him the freedom to be expressive. Although the Sensitive Tan doesn't stop the Magenta from expressing himself, his behavior often offends her. She is easily embarrassed by him. The quiet and respectful Sensitive Tan is much more interested in following the rules and complying with the standards set by society. Magentas love to challenge rules and live outside of society's standards. He feels no need to be quiet or respectful.

Although a Magenta may have some of his daily needs met by the responsible Sensitive Tan, he usually finds her to be uninspiring. At the same time, the Magenta does not usually fulfill the emotional or mental needs of a Sensitive Tan.

Sensitive Tan and Yellow Relationship

See Yellow and Sensitive Tan Relationship.

Sensitive Tan and Logical Tan Relationship

A Sensitive Tan and a Logical Tan can create a successful relationship. Both LifeColors have many of the same needs for security, stability and reliability. Because of the subtle Blue characteristics in her aura, the Sensitive Tan will often bring more intuition, sensitivity and warmth into this relationship.

A potential problem is that a Sensitive Tan wants love, affection and emotional sensitivity as well as dependability and accountability from her mate. While a Logical Tan can provide security and stability, he doesn't usually know how to be open on an emotional level. A Sensitive Tan will usually be patient, even though she misses the emotional bonding. While she appreciates that her Logical Tan mate provides security for the home by bringing home a regular paycheck, she is eventually disappointed with the lack of emotional communication in the relationship. Although the Logical Tan may not understand his mate's emotional needs, he appreciates that she at least is calmer and more rational than most other people. When a Sensitive Tan cries, there is usually a logical explanation behind it.

This is actually a good relationship. The Sensitive Tan provides emotional balance and warmth to the relationship, while the Logical Tan provides security and stability. The differences in their emotional make-up do not usually outweigh their many compatible qualities.

Sensitive Tan and Environmental Tan Relationship

See Environmental Tan and Sensitive Tan Relationship.

Sensitive Tan and Sensitive Tan Relationship

A relationship between two Sensitive Tans is very comfortable and compatible. These two individuals are content having a warm, secure home together. They are also very loving and supportive partners. They both understand the need for quiet, calm and privacy, and they can fulfill each other's need for commitment, security and nurturing.

Although these two are emotionally and mentally compatible, a relationship between them tends to become complacent. Each Sensitive Tan hopes and expects that their partner will take care of business and support them so that they can stay home and nurture the family. Although she enjoys a companion who is stable and realistic, a Sensitive Tan is usually happier with a partner who has a little more ambition.

While these two can communicate effectively with each other, the element missing in this relationship is passion. There is usually a lack of drive, ambition, dynamic power and sexual fireworks between them. Since Sensitive Tans do not like to take risks or initiate change, their potential for growth together is minimal.

Although this relationship is not very exciting, these two can be very secure and comfortable together. They often make better friends or roommates than marriage partners.

Sensitive Tan and Abstract Tan Relationship

A Sensitive Tan is one of the few personalities who understands and accepts the Abstract Tan's unique behavior. Both of these individuals process intellectually. They both prefer to work with details. The Sensitive Tan is fascinated by the Abstract Tan's ability to see all of the details simultaneously, and she is patient enough to allow him the time he needs to put all of the components together. The Sensitive Tan appreciates and shares the Abstract Tan's love of humanity. The Sensitive Tan will usually act on her love for people, while the Abstract Tan frequently spends more of his time speculating and conceptualizing about humanity's potential. The Sensitive Tan can encourage the Abstract

Tan to become more of an active participant in life, and help him design the steps to accomplish something with his ideas.

The Sensitive Tan is very supportive and nurturing toward the frequently misunderstood Abstract Tan. She enjoys his innocence and optimism, although at times she can grow tired of the chaos he creates. She typically finds herself cleaning up after him, helping him locate his missing car keys, and reminding him of appointments. Although she is a nurturer, the Sensitive Tan can become exhausted being the Abstract Tan's mother and caretaker.

If the Sensitive Tan can maintain her patience and understanding toward the Abstract Tan, and if the Abstract Tan can learn to focus his scattered energy and become more dependable, this couple can experience a compatible relationship.

Sensitive Tan and Green Relationship

Whether or not this relationship is compatible depends upon which roles the Sensitive Tan and Green partners are willing to play with each other. The patient and methodical Sensitive Tan can be a great secretary, bookkeeper, assistant or help-mate for the Green. While the Green conceptualizes plans, organizes information, and manages the business, the Sensitive Tan takes care of all the details. This can be very helpful to the Green. The Sensitive Tan respects the ambition and intelligence of the Green. She also enjoys the financial results produced by his efforts. In this relationship, the Sensitive Tan feels secure knowing that she will always be financially supported. In return, the Sensitive Tan provides a loving and comfortable home environment for the hard-working Green.

The powerful and dominating Green can often be too intense for the quiet Sensitive Tan, however. The ambitious and quick-thinking Green can make too many demands on her and take advantage of her willingness to help him. He can also be hard on her delicate emotional personality. Even though the Sensitive Tan is usually calm and logical, and can rationalize away much of the Green's behavior, she can also be easily hurt by his sharp criticism. The fast-paced Green can become impatient with the slow, methodical processes of the Sensitive Tan. Usually the Green expresses his frustration; even if he withholds his judgments, however, the Sensitive Tan is intuitive enough to sense his disapproval. She can try repeatedly to keep up with the Green's demands, only to become overwhelmed by his quick pace and high expectations.

The Sensitive Tan can also be disappointed by the Green's workaholic behavior. While she enjoys his substantial income, she wants home and family to be bigger priorities to him. She is not interested in amassing a great fortune and owning expensive possessions. The Sensitive Tan wants to share a loving, comfortable, secure and modest home with her spouse. For her a home without a mate and family is just an empty shell. The goal-oriented Green, however, does not usually share the Tan's modest desires.

While the Green appreciates the support he receives from the Sensitive Tan, he can also become bored with her. He desires a mate he can have mentally challenging conversations with. A Green loves to debate. He loves to be inspired by new and progressive ideas. Making changes, taking risks, and learning new information are all exciting to the Green. The Sensitive Tan is more comfortable with the same, familiar environment. She is hesitant to take risks and is intimidated by arguments.

On one hand, these two can provide balance for one another. The Green can support the Sensitive Tan, and yet keep her from becoming staid and complacent. The Sensitive Tan can assist the Green by taking care of the mundane details which he abhors. She can also teach him to relax and be more patient.

On the other hand, neither may completely fulfill the other's needs. The Green can intimidate or emotionally wound the gentle Sensitive Tan, while the Sensitive Tan can be too predictable and uninspiring to the energetic Green.

Sensitive Tan and Blue Relationship

See Blue and Sensitive Tan Relationship.

Sensitive Tan and Violet Relationship

See Violet and Sensitive Tan Relationship.

Sensitive Tan and Lavender Relationship

Although these are both gentle, loving personalities, they don't always fulfill each other's needs. Their relationship frequently evolves into a parent/child relationship.

A Sensitive Tan, who is one of the more patient and understanding individuals in the aura spectrum, desires a mate who is responsible and reliable. A Sensitive Tan needs a sense of security in her relationship. Being pragmatic, stable and responsible are not on the list of Lavender personality traits. Unless the Sensitive Tan is willing to be the practical and dependable provider in the family, she will be constantly worried about the Lavender's inability to be financially reliable. A Sensitive Tan feels safer with someone who understands the concepts of commitment and responsibility. The Lavender is too much of an irresponsible nonconformist.

A Sensitive Tan rarely understands the Lavender's preoccupation with other realities. She also becomes frustrated by the Lavender's frequent emotional withdrawals. She can feel abandoned and alone in this relationship. This couple does not communicate very well with each other.

The methodical Sensitive Tan wants a sense of order, logic and practicality in her life. The imaginative Lavender prefers to live in his fantasies and dreams. The realistic Sensitive Tan is concerned with paying the bills, buying food and maintaining a stable job. The fanciful Lavender is more interested in having the freedom to be creative. The Sensitive Tan's expectations and concerns can eventually smother and overburden the simple Lavender. Being forced to focus energy on responsibilities in physical reality is uncomfortable and even painful for the Lavender. He ends up escaping the demands of the relationship by retreating into his own world.

If these two can stay balanced and in power, they can work out an equitable arrangement that can benefit both. The Sensitive Tan is able to provide a stable environment for the ungrounded Lavender. If the Sensitive Tan is willing to take care of the day-to-day details and responsibilities her Lavender mate is allowed to be a creative dreamer. The appreciative Lavender then has the freedom to explore and bring back information from other realities to her. This information can sometimes help the Sensitive Tan see life from other perspectives and, therefore, broaden her horizons. The Lavender can lighten up the Sensitive Tan's usually predictable life with spontaneity and creativity.

Usually, the quiet, unobtrusive Sensitive Tan will not force a Lavender to conform to her standards. She basically supports and nurtures her mate. However, the Lavender's irresponsible behavior will eventually disappoint the Sensitive Tan. Ordinarily these two do not fulfill enough of each other's needs to make this a very happy or successful relationship.

Sensitive Tan and Crystal Relationship
See Crystal and Sensitive Tan Relationship.

Sensitive Tan and Indigo Relationship

Even though this relationship can often be comparable to a mother caring for a child, it does have potential. A Sensitive Tan does not always understand the surrealistic ideas or belief systems of an Indigo. An Indigo predominantly operates from his intuition and inner "knowing." He has no facts to support his beliefs. The Sensitive Tan usually wants life to be more practical and realistic.

Although the Sensitive Tan has a difficult time understanding the Indigo, she continues to be very loving and nurturing, almost parental, toward her Indigo mate. An Indigo feels appreciative of the quiet love and acceptance he receives from the Sensitive Tan. In power, the Indigo is a very loyal and committed partner, which the Sensitive Tan appreciates. These two typically have more of a mother/child relationship than a husband/wife relationship, and the Sensitive Tan usually ends up financially supporting them both.

For this relationship to be compatible, the Sensitive Tan needs to focus her attention on the Blue aspect of her personality, to enable her to bond with the emotional and spiritual Indigo. To be able to communicate with the Indigo, she must be willing to put the rational Tan aspect of her personality on the back burner and trust the intuitive part of her soul. She must also be willing to provide the economic stability in the relationships, while the Indigo explores his spirituality.

This relationship could be a challenge to maintain, because these two personalities have very different approaches to life and reality. Because they are both loving and sensitive individuals, however, they have the capability of working out their differences.

■ ABSTRACT TAN

Abstract Tan and Red Relationship

A relationship between an Abstract Tan and a Red is not typically compatible. Even though each personality has qualities that could provide balance to their relationship, overcoming their differences could be challenging.

The Red's energy is solid and reliable. He is a dependable, hard worker. The Abstract Tan's energy is scattered and often chaotic. She mentally travels in so many directions at once that she seems inconsistent and irresponsible. Even though the grounded Red could add a strong, stable foundation for the disorganized Tan, he would eventually be worn out by the Tan's random mental processes. The Tan's abstract theoretical discussions do not interest the practical Red. He instead prefers to work with tangible, physical reality. The Abstract Tan tends to live in her head, philosophizing and speculating over various concepts. Her tendency not to follow through or take action on her ideas eventually frustrates the Red.

The Red's personality is action-oriented. Although the Abstract Tan could benefit by having this practical worker in her environment, she could have trouble explaining her ideas to the Red. The powerful Red prefers to know what jobs need to be done so that he can take action on them. The scattered Abstract Tan would typically have the Red doing a myriad of apparently unrelated tasks until he became frustrated by her disorganized plans. For instance, if the Abstract Tan wants all of the living room furniture rearranged, she will tell the Red to move the couch over by the stereo system, and then ask him to repair the dishwasher. Later, as he is in the midst of his repair work, she will ask him to move the chair and the lamp to the place where the couch had previously been. The Red becomes frustrated as he jumps randomly from task to task. She should tell him where she wants all of the pieces to be placed so he can then move them all. The Red is happier when he can see the tangible results of his completed project before moving on to the next assignment.

The Red's frustration and quick, volatile temper can intimidate the sensitive and childlike Abstract Tan. She typically withdraws from him. Since neither of these personalities is adept at sharing their feelings, there could be a shortage of emotional and intimate communication between them.

Even though the Red enjoys the Abstract Tan's optimism and appreciates her unconditional love and acceptance, he eventually becomes irritated by her scrambled behavior. Although the Abstract Tan enjoys being taken care of by the reliable and responsible Red, she realizes that her inconsistent behavior disappoints him. Consequently, she feels that she is incompetent and a failure.

This couple would be able to provide some of the missing elements for each other. However, both are usually happier with partners who can understand and be compatible with their lifestyles.

Abstract Tan and Orange Relationship

See Orange and Abstract Tan Relationship.

Abstract Tan and Magenta Relationship

See Magenta and Abstract Tan Relationship.

Abstract Tan and Yellow Relationship

These two personalities are usually gentle and considerate toward each other, though they don't necessarily make practical or dependable marriage partners. They can feel safe with each other, since neither would ever want to hurt the other. If the Yellow doesn't understand the abstract theories of the scattered Tan, he usually just laughs them off rather than getting upset at her. However, in time the Tan's random mental speculations will begin to confuse and even bore the fun-loving Yellow. The Yellow prefers to spend time playing, exercising, playing sports and experiencing physical reality. Although participating in physical activities helps an Abstract Tan loosen up and get out of her head a little, she is not apt to spend as much time being physical as the Yellow would like. The Abstract Tan enjoys theorizing and philosophizing.

Both of these personalities are energetic and optimistic and they enjoy the company of other people. They are both curious and excited about learning new things. They are also both sensitive individuals who are very concerned about being liked by others. They have similar, childlike personalities. The Yellow prefers being physical and having fun, however, while the Abstract Tan enjoys mental speculation and theoretical concepts.

Both the Yellow and the Abstract Tan tend to be like irresponsible children, so as a couple they can experience financial difficulties. Neither wants to handle the responsibilities of running a household.

This pair could be fun playmates. However, both tend to need responsible partners who can take care of business.

Abstract Tan and Logical Tan Relationship

Although both of these personalities prefer to work with the details of a project, the Abstract Tan's random style of choosing priorities can drive the Logical Tan crazy. The Logical Tan can become frustrated trying to understand the thought processes of the Abstract Tan. Rather than retrain the Abstract Tan, if the Logical Tan can just stand back and let her accomplish each step in her own scattered way, he will discover that she eventually does pull the whole project together. The Logical Tan cannot expect an orderly and sequential process from the Abstract Tan. He will be disappointed if he tries to re-educate the Abstract Tan.

Neither of these personalities likes to delve into emotional realms. Consequently, they are safe with each other, although a sense of emotional depth and intimacy will be continuously lacking in their relationship.

The Abstract Tan's tendency to misplace possessions can concern or annoy the conscientious Logical Tan. In addition, the Abstract Tan's scattered behavior, her incongruous stories, and her unreliable, forgetful nature can put the Logical Tan's life into a chaotic tailspin. He doesn't enjoy a disorganized lifestyle. He can also be worn out by the Abstract Tan's inability to efficiently handle her finances. In this relationship, the Logical Tan can quickly become a critical parental figure.

The Abstract Tan does add a sense of unconditional love and acceptance to the Logical Tan's otherwise straightlaced life. Even though the Logical Tan doesn't always understand or appreciate her ways, he does appreciate her optimism and her love for humanity. She brings these elements, which are frequently lacking, into his life.

The Abstract Tan appreciates the fact that the Logical Tan is able to create a stable, practical and logical environment for the two of them. The Logical Tan is willing to be responsible, to work and provide for a family. The Logical Tan can provide a solid and reliable foundation for the flighty Abstract Tan, but he can also make her feel inadequate and incompetent because her style is so unusual.

The Abstract Tan can provide unconditional love to the Logical Tan and also help him to see humanity from a higher, more compassionate perspective. She can also throw his life into chaos and confusion with her undisciplined, disorganized behavior.

These two can at least be compatible friends. If the Logical Tan is willing to be the more responsible partner and if he can learn to be patient while the Abstract Tan puts the pieces of the puzzle together in a less than methodical manner, this pair has potential together. If the Abstract Tan can learn to stay a little more focused and organized, then the methodical Logical Tan can feel more relaxed and secure around her.

Abstract Tan and Environmental Tan Relationship

See Environmental Tan and Abstract Tan Relationship.

Abstract Tan and Sensitive Tan Relationship

See Sensitive Tan and Abstract Tan Relationship.

Abstract Tan and Abstract Tan Relationship

Life with these two as partners would most likely be total chaos. They could have wonderful, philosophical conversations about a wide variety of topics, but their home would be cluttered with clothes strewn everywhere, unpaid bills hidden under piles of unopened mail, and outdated memos reminding them of missed appointments.

Neither of these individuals would be dependable enough to take care of business. In addition, because they both usually have hectic schedules and are running in many different directions, they would rarely see each other. Even if they were to set up an appointment to get together, inevitably one of them would forget the appointment. If they tried to do things together, they would just be adding more to their already heavily-booked agendas.

Due to the fact that Abstract Tans try to avoid actually dealing with their own feelings, these two would not experience a great deal of emotional intimacy together. Even though they would be able to share their enthusiasm for knowledge, and their optimism and love for humanity, they would be more compatible as friends. As friends, they could get together sporadically to discuss ideas and concepts. As friends, there would not be the same pressure to get together that there would be if they were married. Both would be better off marrying people who could provide them with a stronger degree of stability and commitment. They each need partners who can take care of them and help stabilize and focus their lives. The Abstract Tans together are too scattered and unorganized to function very efficiently as a team.

Abstract Tan and Green Relationship

Even though each of these personalities has abilities which could help the other, they are generally not compatible. The Abstract Tan's scattered and disorganized lifestyle irritates the orderly Green. The Green, who takes great pride in the fact that her environment is clean, organized and elegant, is appalled by the Abstract Tan's disheveled surroundings and his obvious lack of respect for his possessions. The Green can panic every time the Abstract Tan goes near any of her priceless and fragile possessions.

The Green is fascinated by the Abstract Tan's ability to see an entire concept and each of the details simultaneously. However, she often becomes frustrated by the scattered Tan's inability to explain the concept to her in an organized and rational manner. She also becomes impatient with the Tan's inability to follow through with and complete many of his projects. Even if he does complete his many projects, they are frequently not done as quickly or as perfectly as the Green would like.

The Green is typically so intelligent, quick and organized that the Abstract Tan tends to feel slow, inadequate and inefficient around her. The friendly and sensitive Tan can also be so intimidated by the Green's power that he hides in his head, venturing out only briefly to talk about some new philosophical concept before retreating back inside where he is safe. While the Green may be fascinated by the Tan's ideas, she rarely sees any practical application for the Abstract Tan's unconditional love of humanity. She wants to know how the Tan's theoretical concepts apply to her daily encounters with work and life.

Even though the Green could provide structure and organization to the Abstract Tan's life, the Green eventually becomes frustrated and bored with the constant effort. Even though the Abstract Tan could bring an attitude of optimism, friendliness and love to the Green's often serious world, the Tan usually feels intimidated, misunderstood and unappreciated by the powerful Green.

The Green needs a mate who is much more powerful and ambitious and who can take care of himself. The Abstract Tan usually needs someone to help him organize his life and who will be patiently understanding and supportive of him. Neither of these personalities typically fulfills these needs for the other.

Abstract Tan and Blue Relationship

An Abstract Tan and a Blue are compatible in many ways. The Blue appreciates the Tan's understanding of unconditional love and acceptance for humanity. The Blue often wishes, however, that the Abstract Tan were more open and emotionally available on a personal level. As with all of the Tans, the Abstract Tan tends to live too much in his head for the Blue's liking. He is not as willing or able to experience the deep, emotional bond that the Blue desires in a relationship.

The Blue does appreciate the Abstract Tan's sensitivity, his friendly personality and his optimistic nature. While very few of the other LifeColors understand or tolerate the Abstract Tan's scattered behavior, the Blue loves and accepts this misfit. She understands how it feels not to be understood by others. Like the Abstract Tan, a Blue doesn't have the facts to support what she intuitively feels inside. She also has difficulty explaining her feelings logically to others. The Abstract Tan has difficulty explaining his ideas logically to people because his mental pictures are scrambled and chaotic. The Blue is usually loving and patient enough to give the Abstract Tan time to bring all of the details together. In return for the Blue's love and devotion, the Abstract Tan appreciates her and gives love back to her.

The natural mothering instinct of the Blue causes her to take care of the childlike and sensitive Abstract Tan. She shops for him, cooks for him, listens attentively to his abstract concepts, and picks up after him. She can be a very faithful caretaker. However, even the long-suffering Blue can become overwhelmed and exhausted by the Abstract Tan's chaos and untidiness. She occasionally tires of keeping him focused and organized so that he can stay on track. The Blue also desires to be taken care of by her mate. She can often feel abandoned and disappointed by the Abstract Tan, because his schedule is frequently so hectic and busy that he rarely has time for her. It is not that the Abstract Tan doesn't love and appreciate his Blue mate. It's just that he forgets to make her a priority.

When this couple is finally able to spend time together, the Blue enjoys hearing about the Tan's many philosophical ideas about love and humanity. The Abstract Tan enjoys the warmth, acceptance and attention he receives from the Blue. If the Blue becomes too emotionally needy, however, the fearful Abstract Tan may withdraw into the security of his own mind, leaving the Blue alone and emotionally unfulfilled. The Abstract Tan must organize his life a little more and make his Blue mate a priority in order to create a happy and successful relationship.

These two personalities are sensitive and loving enough to be able to create a harmonious relationship together.

They must each learn to stay in power and in balance, however, in order to accomplish this goal.

Abstract Tan and Violet Relationship

See Violet and Abstract Tan Relationship.

Abstract Tan and Lavender Relationship

See Lavender and Abstract Tan Relationship.

Abstract Tan and Crystal Relationship

Typically, an Abstract Tan and a Crystal do not make a very compatible couple. The chaotic, unfocused behavior of an Abstract Tan totally scrambles the Crystal's energy and causes her turmoil and frustration. The Crystal needs her environment to be quiet, clean, simple and uncluttered. The Abstract Tan's environment is far from being clean and uncluttered. Although both of these individuals are sensitive and mean well, neither wants to take care of or be responsible for the other.

Emotionally, they are both withdrawn. The Crystal quietly stays in her own inner spiritual world, while the Abstract Tan safely hides in his own head. They do not know how to experience intimacy with each other.

The Abstract Tan is very social and enjoys being around a lot of people. The Crystal shies away from people. Being around too many people shatters her sensitive and fragile soul. Though both of these individuals love to learn, they have different methods of obtaining information. The Abstract Tan loves to research and gather information from other people and outside sources. The Crystal quietly and calmly meditates for her answers.

The Abstract Tan, with his energetic and outgoing personality, doesn't know what to do with the delicate Crystal. If they were married, the Abstract Tan would tend to spend most of his time out of the house or constantly coming and going. The Crystal would be irritated by the Abstract Tan's erratic behavior and chaotic lifestyle. Frustrated, the Crystal would close herself off from the Abstract Tan, causing the sensitive Abstract Tan to feel rejected and unloved. To keep from being hurt any more, the Abstract Tan would then withdraw into his mental and philosophical world. With both partners isolated and alone, there would be no hope for communication or intimacy.

These two personalities would be happier with partners who were more similar, and more understanding toward their unique behavior and lifestyles.

Abstract Tan and Indigo Relationship

An Abstract Tan and an Indigo often create a harmonious relationship. They both have a similar quest for knowledge. They want information that will help them understand humanity and universal principles. These two are frequently misunderstood by others because their attitudes and behaviors are so unique. An Abstract Tan and an Indigo both experience unconditional love and understanding for humanity. Even though they are both sensitive, caring, childlike, inquisitive souls, they are usually slow to develop deep relationships. Both need to trust the people they become involved with. These two can trust each other because they understand and appreciate each other.

The Abstract Tan, who is frequently a storehouse of information, can provide answers for the inquisitive Indigo. She can patiently teach the Indigo many facts and concepts about physical reality. In appreciation, the Indigo completely loves and accepts the Abstract Tan. The Indigo isn't tremendously bothered by the Tan's many ideas and tasks, or by her scattered and disorganized behavior. The Indigo can gather information from a wide variety of the Tan's activities. These two can form a tight and devoted friendship. They can honor, trust and teach one another.

The Indigo wants to bond on a deep, soul-to-soul level with his partner. The Abstract Tan, however, is uncomfortable delving into such profound emotional commitments. The Indigo is usually patient and understanding concerning the Abstract Tan's fears. Given enough time and space to explore her feelings in her own way, the Abstract Tan may start to trust the Indigo enough to open up to him. If the Tan is never able to reach an emotional level at which she can bond soul-to-soul with the Indigo, the Indigo will still be accepting and loving, but also disappointed. The Indigo will always feel a void, being unable to connect with the Abstract Tan's soul.

Another potential problem is that neither is very adept at taking care of business. They both mean well, however, and if they learn to work out a plan together, they can make their lives together work. They can keep each other focused and on track. These two can make a very loving and compatible couple.

■ GREEN

Green and Red Relationship
See Red and Green Relationship.

Green and Orange Relationship
An Orange and Green combination could be a very fascinating one. Greens are the business-oriented planners and organizers. An Orange could benefit greatly from a relationship with this entrepreneur. An Orange enjoys working for organizations that can sponsor him in such occupations as race car driver or stunt man. A quick-thinking Green can create business deals to enable the Orange to work for such a company. When the Orange desires to climb Mt. Everest, the Green can help the Orange create the

backing and financial support to take the trip. The Green is also smart enough to be able to find ways that the trip can benefit the sponsor. An Orange is impressed by the Green's mental skills. The Green is fascinated by the Orange's mental cunning and his ability to plan and carry out daring feats. But while the feats interest the Green, she does not usually join him on his dangerous adventures.

A Green and an Orange would have respect for each other's skills. While they both love to calculate strategies, plan events and test their skills, each have different goals. A Green loves mental challenges, accomplishing projects and making money. An Orange loves the physical challenge of overcoming or outwitting his opponent. The Orange appreciates the money a Green can generate to enable him to pursue his desired challenges. This can be a great business partnership, with the planning skills and money-oriented ideas of a Green combined with the Orange's cunning and physical abilities.

Both tend to be very self-sufficient and independent. Neither one of them *needs* to be with the other person, but both of them are fascinated and appreciative enough to know the value each brings to the relationship. However, since neither one wants to be controlled or told what to do, a conflict may arise with this relationship. Their independence and desire to be in control could create power struggles.

With the intelligence, planning and organizational skills they both have, it would be easy for this pair to become financially prosperous, independent and free to do what they want. They would have respect for each other's mental capabilities, skills and abilities to take on challenges. For the most part, this couple has great potential together.

Green and Magenta Relationship

A Green and Magenta relationship can be quite fascinating. The creative and artistic imagination of a Magenta can fuel the business ideas and entrepreneurial abilities of a Green. The quick mind of a Green is fascinated by the unique ideas and thoughts of a Magenta. The Green has the intelligence, persistence and skills to pull off the Magenta's ideas. The Magenta, on the other hand, is fascinated by a Green's quick mind, her ability to see patterns, and her organizational skills.

The ability of the Green to take care of business and provide financial security enables the Magenta to be creative, outrageous and spontaneous. They both appreciate each other's ability to be independent. Neither one of them wants someone suffocating or depending on them.

This couple runs into problems when a Green needs to be admired and respected. The Magenta generally feels no need to respect or admire anyone, or to behave at all in a respectable manner. His behavior often solicits quite the opposite reaction from people. The Green can become very embarrassed with the disrespectful actions of a Magenta. A Green can also quickly lose respect for the Magenta because the Magenta does not choose to be as stable nor take life as seriously as the Green.

The Magenta, who does not like to be controlled or told what to do, can end up resenting the powerful and domineering attitude of an out-of-power Green. While a Green likes to tell people what to do, the Magenta rebels and challenges her control. Both of these colors are fiercely independent and strong-willed. This can cause problems and power struggles in the relationship.

A Green wants expensive, quality items in her home — the nicest furniture, the finest clothing and the most expensive jewelry. A Magenta prefers outrageous items, not necessarily expensive ones. A Green wants people to be impressed by her surroundings, while the Magenta prefers to shock people. This difference in attitudes can become quite frustrating for the Green. While they each recognize the ability of the other to fill needs in the partnership, this relationship could be very short-lived if neither feels his strongest desires are being met. While consistency and commitment are important to a Green, she is also one of the first to leave a relationship if it does not turn out the way she wants. These two may be better business associates than marriage partners.

Green and Yellow Relationship

While nothing is impossible, and any couple can work things out with enough commitment and determination, this relationship can be an incredible challenge.

At first, a Green is drawn to the light energy of a Yellow. The Yellow's easygoing attitude and sense of humor help to balance out the Green's intense and serious attitudes. After a while, however, the Green usually loses patience and tolerance for the Yellow's lack of ambition and drive. While pushing and demanding more from the Yellow, the Green quickly loses respect for him because the Yellow is not accomplishing something of value in his life. The sharp tongue of a judgmental, critical out-of-power Green can inflict incredible scars on the sensitive Yellow. Being insecure about his own abilities anyway, it is very difficult for him to meet the high standards of the Green perfectionist. Once a Green is frustrated, no matter what the Yellow does, it is never enough. To further exacerbate the Yellow's sense of inadequacy, when the Green is angry, she withholds sex and affection from her mate. Sex and physical touch are two of the greatest joys for a Yellow. If these two are out of power, the outcome of this marriage will probably be physical, mental and emotional humiliation for the Yellow and disappointment for the Green.

While a Green loves to give orders, a Yellow hates to be told what to do. The Yellow, often feeling browbeaten, will resort to covert and subtle ways of rebelling against the authoritative Green. This only serves to irritate and provoke the Green even more. Hence, a vicious cycle of oppressive parent versus rebellious child begins.

For a Yellow and Green relationship to work, the Green has to realize that the Yellow does not have the same goals or priorities as hers. If the Green wants financial prosperity, she will have to create it herself. In balance, the Green can "accomplish" while the Yellow creates or brings joy to the planet. If a Yellow can make people feel better, he feels that he has performed a valuable service. The Green needs to allow the Yellow to have his own unique goals.

A Yellow, on the other hand, needs to understand that the Green wants to experience life to its fullest degree, while accomplishing as much as she can. When she gets frustrated and angry, the Yellow needs to realize that the Green is angry and frustrated with herself. The Yellow may be able to help the Green realize her own potential and power, and not to be afraid of it. A Green just wants to be respected, admired and given acknowledgment for what she has done. Acknowledgment is the greatest gift a Yellow can give to a Green.

Since a Yellow hates to be told what to do, the Green can *inspire* him into his creativity instead of pushing him. A Green empowers people by *example*, and so could be an example to the Yellow.

In power, these two personalities can benefit from each other. The Green can take the creative ideas of a Yellow, formulate a plan and bring them into physical form. The artistic Yellow can benefit from the organizational and managerial skills of a Green. As long as this pair can stay balanced and allow each other their unique talents, they can accomplish great creative projects together. However, it's more common for the Green to grow beyond the Yellow.

Green and Logical Tan Relationship

These two personalities have potential for a good relationship, because they both process intellectually and share many of the same interests. They both enjoy discussing ideas rationally and logically. They are usually intellectually compatible. However, the Logical Tan typically processes information more slowly than the Green, and this can cause the Green to become frustrated and impatient. While the Logical Tan is processing the information slowly and methodically, analyzing each and every step, the Green has already arrived at a final solution. A Green does not want to go into all of the steps that the Tan insists are necessary. The Green usually mentally tunes out the Tan while he tells a story. She doesn't listen to all of the details, but is off somewhere else thinking about other plans. She reconnects to his story only when he has reached the punch line.

If the Green can realize the advantage of the Logical Tan's ability to be involved in details she can learn to appreciate him. With a Tan partner, the Green is free to plan ideas and concepts, while the Logical Tan fills in the details. If the Green becomes impatient and tries to dominate or push the Tan, he will move even slower. Their opposing behaviors can frustrate both of them. A Green also tends to have an "I told you so" attitude, which irritates a Tan and prompts him to resist her even more. There is a simple solution to help them with their differences. While the Tan is methodically and precisely analyzing every step, the Green should keep herself busy by mentally or physically working on other ideas and plans.

These two frequently experience conflict over money. A Green wants to make a lot of money quickly. A Logical Tan believes he has to work a long time for money. He must save, invest wisely and be patient. He wants to build a stable foundation. A Logical Tan, who does not like to take risks, will attempt to caution the Green. This only frustrates her. A Green is more of a gambler and risk-taker than a Tan. A Green likes to play the stock market. A Logical Tan prefers a savings account. A Green likes to spend money. She wants classy, expensive, quality possessions. A Logical Tan prefers items that are practical, functional and less expensive. A Tan is usually very frugal with his hard-earned money. These two often argue over the amount of money being spent in the home or in the business. A Green tends to overspend. She often lives beyond her means, which aggravates a Tan.

Out of power, Greens and Logical Tans both tend to be judgmental and stubborn. A Green likes to be right. A Tan won't move until the facts have been proven to him. Although they can usually discuss a problem rationally and intellectually, a Green can become sharp-tongued during an argument. While a Logical Tan tends to keep his emotions and thoughts to himself until he has analyzed the situation, a Green is quick to process and quick to lash out. Consequently, their "dialogues" can be one-sided. The Green can be so quick and powerful that the Logical Tan doesn't have time to come back with a response. The Green is usually the more domineering and powerful in this relationship. When the Tan feels overpowered, he withdraws in self-defense. This cuts off the communication between them, which further irritates the Green because she wants to be heard and respected.

To maintain harmony in this relationship, each must allow the other his or her own method of processing. When the Green wants a lot of money, she must learn to create it herself. She cannot push a Logical Tan to make more money for her. If she has a goal or an idea, she must either accomplish it by herself, or allow the Tan to slowly process and achieve it.

The Logical Tan needs to learn to compromise more often with the Green. He needs to trust the Green's track record and be willing to risk more often. He needs to respect the Green's quickness and intelligence. He needs to be careful not to be so detailed and technical that he slows down an entire project.

This couple has potential for success, provided the Green doesn't push the Logical Tan faster than he's willing to go, and provided the Logical Tan doesn't constantly slow down the Green. If these two can perceive their differences as assets, then they can work well together. The Logical Tan can take care of each detail so that the Green is free to create, organize and plan the strategies. Otherwise, their differences can create too much disharmony between them. The Green can appreciate the Tan's stability, or she can become impatient with it. The Tan can be frustrated by the Green's rash and impetuous behavior or he can respect her willingness to act on her ideas.

Green and Environmental Tan Relationship

An Environmental Tan is strong enough to hold his own with the intense Green. The Green is attracted to the mysterious demeanor of the Environmental Tan, and considers his self-confident and aloof behavior to be a challenge. The Environmental Tan is fascinated by the Green's sharp intelligence and her ability to take quick, decisive action. These two are capable of accomplishing almost anything together. The Environmental Tan is a powerful personality and, therefore, one of the few who cannot be dominated or controlled by the strong-willed Green. Occasionally these two can butt heads, but the Green tends to respect the strength and tenacity of the Environmental Tan.

Because they are fascinated by each other's style and presence and are excited by each other's power, they tend to be sexually attracted to each other. The electricity and magnetism between them creates energy which thrills them and can keep them tantalized for a long period of time.

They both respect each other's strong mental abilities. They are both intelligent and capable individuals who are self-motivated as well as independent. The Green and the Environmental Tan both want partners who are resourceful enough to take care of themselves. They admire each other's competence.

Problems arise when the Green becomes frustrated by the Environmental Tan's slow, deliberate movements. She is impatient with his need to cautiously analyze information before making decisions. The Environmental Tan does not want to be rushed. When out of power, the Green can become critical, demanding or intolerant. The Environmental Tan tends to withdraw inside himself, closing down any possibility for communication between them. This behavior irritates the Green even more — she wants to be heard and respected. No matter how angry and frustrated the Green becomes, the Environmental Tan cannot be forced from his shell. The Green's only course of action is to back off and wait until the Environmental Tan decides to emerge again. If the Green lashes out too often, the Environmental Tan will eventually learn not to trust her, and will remain permanently closed off from her.

The Green must learn to occupy her time with other projects while allowing the Environmental Tan the time he needs to process all of the details. Fortunately, these two are independent enough to work alone. They don't need each other to feel successful or fulfilled. Because both of these personalities tend to focus so intensely on their work, they can spend a great deal of time apart. It is helpful for these two to occasionally work on projects together, so that they can maintain communication and contact with each other. The Tan is more willing to calmly take care of the details of a project, which frees up the Green to develop ideas. The progressive Green can keep the Environmental Tan's life from becoming too rooted and mundane. She adds sparks and challenges to his otherwise routine life. The Environmental Tan can add a quiet stability to the often impatient Green.

Green and Sensitive Tan Relationship

See Sensitive Tan and Green Relationship.

Green and Abstract Tan Relationship

See Abstract Tan and Green Relationship.

Green and Green Relationship

This couple is potentially a very powerful, ambitious, successful and wealthy combination. They also have great potential to experience power struggles. Two Greens together may respect each other, but they may also butt heads. Greens like to be right. They hate losing arguments.

If both are in charge of their own respective areas in business, they can have a good partnership. If their jobs are clearly defined and delineated, and if they can learn to respect each other's power, intelligence and opinions, there can be admiration and compatibility between these two. The problems surface when their goals differ, or when one Green wants to dominate and control the other. A Green cannot tolerate being controlled but does, on the other hand, enjoy doing the controlling. Consequently, if one Green is married to another, they will each need to learn mutual respect and compromise in order to work out solutions.

When there is no respect between them, out-of-power Greens can be cruel to each other. They can also be very competitive. One is always trying to make more money or be more successful than the other. Since Greens like to be right, they tend to have frequent and volatile arguments. Greens are usually very strong-willed and tenacious.

If there is mutual respect and admiration, sex between these two can be quite powerful and dynamic. However, if there is a disagreement or an argument, they will each withhold sex until the argument is satisfactorily resolved.

One thing is certain, these two *will* have money, an elaborate home and quality possessions. They both have lavish and expensive tastes.

Greens love challenges. They can each encourage the other to learn, accomplish and advance. Life will not be boring for these two. Their biggest problems are that they can both be competitive, strong-willed, stubborn and argumentative. They are usually intellectual equals, however, so their psychological battles can be exciting for them.

Both Greens love to win, so for there to be harmony and balance in this relationship, they have to create ways for both to win. Since they are both so intelligent, finding a plan that allows both to win should be easy for them.

Greens need to admire and respect their partners. Fortunately, a Green is one of the LifeColors that another Green cannot run over. Mutual respect is a possibility with this couple. Although a business partnership may have a better chance for success than a marriage, as long as these two see each other as equals, they have potential for harmony.

Green and Blue Relationship

See Blue and Green Relationship.

Green and Violet Relationship

A relationship between a Green and a Violet has excellent potential. A Violet is one of the few colors in the aura spectrum that a Green can't run over. A Green is powerful and bright; while a Green can quickly process steps one through ten, a Violet can jump from one to fifty. Consequently, the Violet can stay several steps ahead of a

Green. The Violet can inspire and challenge a Green. However, in order for this relationship to succeed, the Violet must stay in his power, remaining focused and centered.

A Violet has visions and dreams he wants to accomplish. An out-of-power Green can thwart a Violet by criticizing his visions, claiming they are not rational or practical. The Green often perceives the Violet to be an unrealistic dreamer. When the Violet jumps to step fifty, the Green will often challenge him, and question his ability to accomplish that vision. If the Violet is not in his power, he will doubt his abilities to achieve his dream. The Green will then step on the Violet's idea and lose respect for him. When in his power, the Violet can stand firmly committed to his ideas, even if the Green challenges him. The Violet's power and commitment will usually inspire the Green and motivate her to develop the plan to accomplish the dream.

Another conflict that may arise within a Green and Violet relationship is the Green's desire to keep things orderly and efficient. An out-of-power Violet can get scattered and disorganized, causing the Green to lose tolerance and respect for him. Another potential problem centers on their sexual attitudes. While a Violet is sexual and passionate, a Green can often be aloof and protective. When the Green is upset, she often puts up emotional barriers. Their sexual appetites can differ. When both are happy and feeling respected, however, sex between these two can be intense, passionate and fulfilling.

Greens and Violets are the wealthiest people on the planet. But one of the conflicts that can arise between a Green and Violet is over their intention and purposes regarding money. A Green will do a job just because there is money in it. (An out-of-power Green can set up oil platforms even if it damages the environment.) However, a Violet has to believe in what he is doing. There has to be a higher purpose to it, and he has to enjoy the work. A Violet often judges a Green to be too materialistic, too cold, too calculating and too concerned about money. A Violet wants money, but only because it gives him the freedom to do what he really wants. A Green wants money for material possessions and power. She wants classy clothes, elegant cars and expensive homes. A Violet questions the value of material possessions. If they can accept their differences, this couple has the potential of making enough money to make them both happy. The Green can have her quality possessions, while the Violet can afford to travel and be philanthropic.

One of the many positive aspects of a Green and a Violet relationship is that the in-power Violet will allow the Green to be powerful. He is not intimidated by her need to control. A Violet will listen to a Green, and then do things his own way anyway. Violets, being charismatic leaders, don't care about ordering people around. This accepting attitude creates less conflict between a Green and a Violet. However, when the Violet is out of power, this couple can experience power struggles because both want to be in charge. A Green must be in a relationship with someone she respects. As long as the Violet stays in his power and focuses on bringing his dream into reality, the Green will respect him.

Because both Violets and Greens want to be self-employed or have their own businesses, they can make good partners. Even though the Violet has a vision, he is not always sure how to accomplish it. The Violet's vision can be planned, organized and implemented by the efficient Green.

It is possible for this couple to achieve and maintain balance and harmony in their relationship. When the Violet sees a vision, the Green needs to support it and to develop a plan to manifest it. In other words, the Green needs to trust the Violet's vision. This can be challenging when it doesn't look practical. However, the Green has the capacity to make dreams practical and financially rewarding. In turn, the Violet needs to learn to focus his attention so that he doesn't frustrate the Green's need for order and discipline. A Violet doesn't want to be limited or restricted, but he does need to stay focused. While a Violet has a tendency to want to do ten projects at once, a Green partner can help him stay on target and focus on one project at a time.

A Green and Violet relationship has great potential for being dynamic, powerful, harmonious and productive provided the Violet maintains focus and equal power, and the Green stays set on accomplishing her goals and feeling good about herself. It is a good relationship as long as both partners stay in their power, centered and balanced.

Green and Lavender Relationship

For the most part, a Green will be fascinated by the fantasies and creative aspects of a Lavender, but he would eventually become frustrated with her inability to take action and accomplish something. Their partnership could be a productive one if the Green could take the Lavender's creative ideas and put them into practical use. If the Green doesn't expect intellectual challenges from the Lavender, but instead accepts her creative ideas as stimulation, the two can work together. If the Green becomes angry or frustrated, his energy is too intense and threatening to the sensitive Lavender. She would retreat into her fantasy world to escape his fury.

In power, this pair could add balance to each other's lives. The Green could add a practical and logical aspect to the Lavender's ungrounded and lofty fantasy world, while the Lavender could add a fun and creative aspect to the Green's work-oriented and often stressful life. The Green would have to find intellectual conversation with other friends, not from his Lavender cohort. In this relationship, the Green would be the domineering, controlling mate.

Generally, these two are not the best marriage partners for each other. The Green is usually frustrated by the Lavender's lack of ambition and concentration as well as her unreliable behavior. The Lavender is usually intimidated and overwhelmed by the Green's intense power and drive. The emotional needs of the Lavender would probably not be met by a Green. A Green is not relaxed and open with his emotions. He prefers to stay in control, which could leave a Lavender feeling alone and unfulfilled. They would be more successful as business partners than as loving, intimate, sexual mates.

Green and Crystal Relationship

See Crystal and Green Relationship.

Green and Indigo Relationship

See Indigo and Green Relationship.

8. Relationships with the Emotional Colors

■ BLUE

Blue and Red Relationship
See Red and Blue Relationship.

Blue and Orange Relationship
This relationship would probably drive a Blue crazy and suffocate an Orange. The daring, life-risking behavior of an Orange would put the mothering Blue into a constant state of worry about the physical safety of the Orange. An Orange tends to be independent and adventurous. A Blue wants her mate to be at home, being loving and emotional with her. The solitary Orange tends to keep his emotions to himself. An example of a Blue/Orange relationship is a loving, nurturing woman married to an adventure-seeking policeman. The Blue is never sure if the Orange is going to come home at night or if he is going to be shot in the line of duty. After a while, the stress and the emotional drain is more than the Blue can handle.

An Orange prefers physical activity. A Blue prefers spiritual and emotional work. The sturdy Orange likes to live in his physical body and challenge his environment. The spiritual Blue does not usually focus on her physical body. The Blue likes to discuss spiritual and emotional concepts, while the Orange is not interested in these topics at all. The independent Orange doesn't choose to talk about his emotions, while emotions are the life source of a Blue.

An Orange is a loner. A Blue needs to be around people. While a Blue is a giver, an Orange seems to be more con- cerned with himself than with his mate or family. An Orange can often take advantage of the generous nature of a Blue.

This couple has very little in common. If they were married, the Blue's role would be to pack food for the Orange as he prepared to go off mountain-climbing. Not being a daredevil or a physical person, the Blue would choose not to accompany her mate. Instead she would stay home alone and suffer until the Orange returned. The Blue would spend too much of her time alone if she were married to an Orange.

This relationship is generally not compatible. Blues and Oranges do not have the same interests in life. They do not associate with the same types of people, nor do they share the same life purpose.

Blue and Magenta Relationship

This relationship can be quite challenging for a Blue. A Magenta is usually too bizarre for her. Because the Blue is very loyal, bonded and committed in her relationships, however, she will usually continue to love the Magenta regardless of his outrageous behavior. She tends to stand by him and to make excuses for his behavior, despite her embarrassment. The Blue remains loyal to her mate, even when he is unfaithful or hurts her in some way.

A problem this couple may face is that while a Blue is very monogamous, the Magenta looks at most relation- ships, even marriage, as brief encounters — something to experience, enjoy, learn from, and then move away from. This attitude can emotionally devastate a Blue.

A Magenta, although appreciative of the unconditional love he receives from the Blue, can also tend to abuse or take advantage of that love. A Magenta does not relate to the deep, emotional, spiritual needs, or the belief systems of the Blue. Although a Magenta may not try to change a Blue's belief system, ideals or spirituality, he also may not necessarily understand or agree with them.

Both of these colors enjoy being around people; they frequently attend social functions together. The Magenta's deviant behavior at these functions, however, often embarrasses the Blue, causing her to feel unaccepted by her peers. While a Blue enjoys other people, she also likes to spend time alone with her mate. She enjoys cuddling, hugging and being introspective. These activities do not interest a Magenta. He instead prefers to be around people, and to cause trouble by being outrageous. Since the Magenta prefers to be independent and uncommitted, the Blue can tend to feel abandoned and rejected in this relationship. The Blue is better off in a relationship with someone who can be more loyal, supportive and committed. The Magenta is happier exploring many relationships and maintaining his freedom.

Blue and Yellow Relationship

See Yellow and Blue Relationship.

Blue and Logical Tan Relationship

See Logical Tan and Blue Relationship.

Blue and Environmental Tan Relationship

Although a relationship between an Environmental Tan and a Blue is common, it is not always a very compatible one. While their daily, practical needs are met, their deepest needs and desires go unfulfilled.

The loving Blue is attracted to the stable and responsible qualities of the Environmental Tan. She sees in his quiet and calm personality the willingness to commit to a long-term, serious relationship. The hopeful Blue perceives that this Tan is both reliable and responsible. She knows she will be able to depend on him to be a good, solid provider and a faithful mate. The Environmental Tan assesses that the Blue is a warm, loving and loyal mate. He is drawn to her willingness to be supportive and her dedication to their relationship. He knows he can trust her. This relationship often reflects the typical marriage of the 1950's, in which Dad was the bread-winner and disciplinarian while Mom nurtured the children and took care of the home.

Eventually, communication becomes a problem with this couple. The Blue wants to discuss feelings and to bond emotionally with her mate. The Environmental Tan has difficulty expressing his feelings. He prefers to keep his emotions to himself and resents any attempts to invade his privacy. When an Environmental Tan is upset, he withdraws into the quiet solitude of his own mind to figure out a solution. The sensitive Blue, who wants to share every thought and feeling with her mate, feels shut off from him. She interprets his actions as a personal rejection. For the Blue, communication and sharing should be a major part of a successful relationship. The Blue loves affection, but the reticent Environmental Tan is not openly demonstrative. Feeling this is an indication that she is unattractive and undesirable, the Blue retreats in sorrow to her room.

The spiritual Blue enjoys sharing thoughts about love, God, religion, emotions and relationships. The pragmatic Environmental Tan is more concerned with physical reality — economics, government, data, logic and tangible substances. These two do not usually share the same basic beliefs about life.

The logical Environmental Tan believes that the Blue is too emotional and vulnerable. He cannot relate to the Blue's frequent torrent of tears and emotional moods. The Environmental Tan wants a partner who will quietly stand beside him and not make emotional demands on him. He needs his privacy. He also needs a mate who is practical and can deal with the necessities of life. A Blue is not always practical. She is ruled by her intuition and her emotions.

While their basic needs for security, trust, loyalty, stability and commitment will be met, some of their deeper needs can remain unfulfilled. The Blue's quest for emotional bonding and deep, spiritual levels of communication is often unrequited with this mate.

The Environmental Tan experiences frustration over the continuous emotional insecurities and neediness expressed by the out-of-power Blue. When he sees that the Blue is hurt and disappointed, the Environmental Tan assumes he has failed one more time. He frequently feels guilty and inadequate. He feels that being an intelligent person, a committed partner and a dependable provider should be enough to make his mate appreciate him.

While in power, this couple has the capability of creating a balance for one another. The Blue provides the emotional nurturing while the Environmental Tan keeps the relationship grounded and practical. However, they usually do not relate well to each other's inner needs.

Blue and Sensitive Tan Relationship

This couple is quite compatible. Both colors require emotional bonding, stability and commitment. The Sensitive Tan can add emotional stability to a Blue's life. An out-of-power Blue has a tendency to get moody, experiencing very dramatic, euphoric highs and very severe depressions. A Sensitive Tan is much more calm with his emotional reactions. Both are very loving, giving and nurturing people. While the Sensitive Tan is much more practical in the relationship, the Blue provides the emotional release. The Sensitive Tan gives the love and emotional bonding that the Blue so desperately desires. While tending to keep his emotions to himself, he is not opposed to expressing how he feels to the loving Blue. The Sensitive Tan, however, does not want to discuss his emotions all the time. The Blue partner must be understanding, and learn how to become more balanced with her emotional needs. Both of these personalities love people. The Sensitive Tan, however, requires much more time alone. He needs peace, quiet and order in his life.

The Sensitive Tan may have a difficult time understanding the emotional depth of a Blue or the extent of her emotional depressions. The Blue's emotional reactions are not usually logical; consequently the Sensitive Tan does not always understand the causes behind her irrational and erratic behavior. A Blue may experience hurt feelings because the Sensitive Tan is not always emotionally accessible to her. He is not quite as free expressing his feelings. However, the Sensitive Tan is usually gentle, calm and realistic enough to help a Blue out of her depression.

Even though both of these colors are highly intuitive, the Sensitive Tan is the one who is usually able to produce facts and information to support his intuitive thoughts and feelings. A Sensitive Tan can add practicality to the spiritual idealism of a Blue. The Sensitive Tan can take care of the details of running a home or supporting a family, while the Blue is then free to be the loving nurturer of the family. Both of these individuals believe in long-term commitments, and so this relationship has strong potential for fulfillment and success. If this couple marries, their relationship will probably last for life.

Blue and Abstract Tan Relationship

See Abstract Tan and Blue Relationship.

Blue and Green Relationship

A Blue and a Green are not usually compatible. They have very strong conflicting goals, priorities and methods of processing life. The workaholic Green tends to put his career before his relationship, which the Blue interprets as a personal rejection. The loving Blue feels that people, love, family and relationships are much more important than money, possessions, and reaching the top of the corporate ladder. Although the Blue enters the relationship supporting the Green's ambitions and goals, she eventually becomes hurt and resentful when she learns that money and business are consistently his priorities. The Blue can even become a workaholic herself trying to win acceptance and approval from her Green mate. She soon learns, however, that no matter how much they accomplish or how hard they work, the Green still wants more. Her emotional needs are rarely taken into consideration by the driven and ambitious Green.

The Green does not usually relate to the emotional needs of a Blue. Although the Green acknowledges that the Blue is more giving and patient than he is, he often loses respect for her because he considers her to be an emotional "doormat." The trusting Blue is easily taken advantage of and abused. The Blue typically sacrifices her own needs to help others. The Green is usually more self-centered and demanding. If these two go to a restaurant and the Green is dissatisfied with the quality of his meal, he will send the food back and demand better service. The apologetic Blue is embarrassed by the Green's behavior. The Green is too intolerant, outspoken and unforgiving for her comfort.

The sensitivity and moodiness of the Blue can irritate the powerful and self-controlled Green. He believes that such displays of emotions show weakness of character. The Blue, who craves warmth and affection, is frequently disappointed by the aloof and emotionally-disciplined behavior of a Green.

Both of these personalities value commitment and endurance. However, while the Blue will continue to hold on through emotional pain and suffering, hoping that some day her patience will pay off, the Green tends to be more logical. If he doesn't see the potential value in a relationship, he will leave it.

If the Green can learn to balance his life so that he spends some of his time with his mate as well as his business, then the appreciative Blue will lovingly support him in reaching his goals. When a Green is frustrated, he tends to either coldly and abruptly withdraw, or to become verbally abusive. Either behavior devastates the sensitive Blue. The Green must learn to communicate his feelings in a less hostile manner. The Blue, meanwhile, who can easily be hurt by his sharp tongue, needs to learn not to take the Green's outbursts so personally. His abrasive behavior usually signals frustration with himself rather than with his mate. The Blue can instead learn to leave him alone until he figures out a solution by himself or until he asks her for assistance.

The Green must learn to appreciate the Blue's ability to be so loving and generous rather than criticize her for it. If the Green can learn to become more emotionally available and less judgmental, he will have a very loving and devoted Blue mate. If the Blue can learn to fill more of her own emotional needs, she can grow intellectually with the Green, as well as be financially supported in style.

While any relationship can work if there is enough love, commitment and determination between the two partners, this relationship would require a lot of effort to be successful. Patience, compromise, education and understanding are necessary components in this relationship. If these two are willing to work against the odds, they each have the capability to learn and grow in this relationship. If, however, they don't want to work quite so hard, there are other partners who are more compatible, and can better fulfill their emotional and intellectual needs.

Blue and Blue Relationship

A Blue can bond emotionally very well with another Blue. Two Blues often experience an instant connection. They tend to think and feel the same way. Blues can be best friends within their relationship. They can cry together over the same romantic movies. Blues understand each other's emotional needs, trust each other's intuitive thoughts, and share each other's spiritual beliefs.

Blues are very moral, monogamous, loyal and committed, so extramarital affairs will probably never happen in this relationship. In addition, neither wants to hurt the other by leaving. Although divorce is also rare with them, should it occur, these two Blues will remain good friends throughout their lives. They will always stay connected on some level by writing, calling, or visiting each other. Blues tend to put a lot of energy into their relationships; consequently, they tend to stay in relationship for a long, long time.

Out of power, Blues are very moody and tend to take things personally. A harmless comment can send a Blue into an emotional tailspin. Because they can each be so emotionally vulnerable and needy, constant emotional reinforcement is required. Fortunately, Blues are typically open and available to each other, so loving support and affection usually flow generously between them. Blues understand each other and are willing to lovingly fill each other's needs.

A potential problem can arise when one Blue plays the victim or martyr so often that the other Blue tires of having to take care of him. If they both play the victim at the same time, both will want to be rescued. The partner who rescues will become the martyr and the other will feel guilty. A vicious cycle of victimhood, martyrdom and guilt ensues. A Blue's natural weapon of guilt is very effective when used on another Blue. One Blue can become quite manipulative toward the other when she starts using guilt.

Both Blues need to learn to receive as well as they give. When one Blue attempts to give to the other, the second one must learn to receive to enable the first Blue to feel fulfilled. Since Blues usually feel guilty asking for what they want, the other's intuitive abilities come in handy. Blues are each able to know the other's needs without any verbal communication. These two connect easily from the heart.

To stay balanced and in harmony, two Blues both need to realize that they are loved, that they don't need each other's repetitive reassurance to reinforce a sense of value or worthiness. They must both learn to love themselves as much as they love each other. Because Blues emotionally and intuitively understand each other so well and are both willing to give love, they tend to create very harmonious relationships together.

Blue and Violet Relationship

See Violet and Blue Relationship.

Blue and Lavender Relationship

While both of these colors are very sensitive, loving, considerate and compassionate, neither one wants to be the party responsible for supporting a home. The responsibility would end up falling into the Blue's lap, since she is the ultimate "doer" and "mother." A Lavender wants someone to take care of him so he can live easily and effortlessly in a fantasy world. The Blue, who usually enjoys being needed, ends up feeling more like a mother than a wife. The Blue wants the Lavender to relate with her on a deep, emotional, bonded level. However, a Lavender is intimidated by such deep, intense emotions, so he tends to withdraw from her.

The Blue tends to nurture, love and support the Lavender. She is usually accepting and forgiving enough to let him do what makes him happy; however, her needs are not always met. A Blue wants emotional commitment and stability. A Lavender does not exhibit those traits. A Blue, when she is out of her power, is filled with self-pity and plays the victim or martyr, which is too intense and serious for a Lavender. The Lavender usually escapes into a fantasy world, leaving the Blue with no one to listen to her or support her. A Lavender just does not relate to the Blue's heavy, emotional behavior.

In a marriage relationship, the Blue cannot depend on the Lavender for the emotional security and depth that she needs. The Lavender eventually feels trapped or smothered by the Blue. These two personalities are more emotionally compatible as best friends than as mates.

Blue and Crystal Relationship

See Crystal and Blue Relationship.

Blue and Indigo Relationship

This can be a very loving and nurturing relationship. A Blue is one of the colors that understands the spirituality of an Indigo. A Blue also wants peace, love and harmony on the planet, just as the Indigo does. A Blue is able to be very loving and accepting of the Indigo's need to understand and to search for answers.

An Indigo needs people who can understand and support his quest, not reject, criticize or try to stop him. The Indigo treasures the unconditional love that he receives from the Blue. The Blue can often find herself taking care of the frequently misunderstood and sometimes frightened, childlike Indigo. She has compassion for the Indigo's plight.

Because Blues and Indigos are both intuitive, they appreciate each other's inner knowing, and neither asks for supporting scientific facts, data or details. The Blue also appreciates the depth to which the Indigo bonds emotionally, soul-to-soul, with his mate. These two colors are both very loving, warm and committed in their relationships.

One of the few problems that can arise in this relationship is when an Indigo loses his center and withdraws inside himself. This is frustrating to a Blue, who wants to maintain emotional communication with her mate. The loving and patient gentleness of a Blue can usually bring the Indigo out of himself and back to center.

It is challenging for an Indigo to relate to a Blue who is out of her power because victimhood, martyrdom and self-pity are concepts he does not understand. A Blue tends to use guilt to manipulate people. An Indigo does not respond to guilt or any other type of manipulation. Communication can fall apart at this point. It is very important for both the Blue and the Indigo to stay in their positive power as much as possible for this relationship to reach its fullest potential.

It is natural for a Blue to want to nurture and support the people she loves. An Indigo thrives on the emotional support and loving strength of a Blue. An emotionally balanced Blue can also help facilitate the Indigo's search for truth on the planet.

■ VIOLET

Violet and Red Relationship

This combination would be very interesting. With the strong leadership ability of a Violet and her ability to see the future, she would give direction and vision to the Red's ability to bring ideas into physical form. With the Violet's head up in the clouds and the Red's ability to keep his feet on the ground, this couple could create a good balance for each other. The charisma and dynamic energy of a Violet would be fascinating and attractive to a Red, usually causing him to be sexually drawn to the Violet. A Violet is fascinated by the Red's ability to get things done.

Both of these personalities tend to be passionate, with a healthy sexual appetite. A Violet is sexual, but sex tends to be a universal, spiritual experience for her. For a Red, sex tends to be a very physical, lustful experience. Both would have their own unique experiences while making love.

The downside of this relationship is that the Red may consider the Violet's visions to be unrealistic dreams and have a hard time respecting them. The Red likes to see and touch physical reality. Plans must make sense to him. A Violet tends to live in the future, seeing upcoming trends. Reds tend to live in the moment, the here and now. A Violet is often into etheric ideas and concepts. The Red may mistrust what the Violet sees.

The Violet loves music and traveling. The Red is much more grounded and practical, preferring the comfort of home, while working on realistic and applicable projects. The Violet chooses to be a leader, while the Red shirks leadership duties, preferring to be a worker instead. He is relieved to have someone else assume the leadership role. Both of these individuals tend to be independent. The Violet enjoys the attention of others, however, while the Red is more of a loner. A Red tends to want to stay on the fringes at parties. Only when he knows people well will he take part in the conversation, provided the conversation is practical and down-to-earth. A Violet's topics of conversation tend to be of lofty ideals, spiritual possibilities and saving the planet. These conversations do not interest a Red. They seem impractical to him. The topics of their conversation would be quite diverse, with neither appreciating or understanding the other's point of view.

A Violet out of her power can become pompous or arrogant and she may try to tell the Red what to do. This would not go over very well with the Red, who would abruptly tell the Violet what he thought. While the Violet may respect his honesty, she may also find his abrupt attitude abrasive. A Violet is usually very accepting of other people. A Red is much less flexible. His behavior may appear to be too rigid and short-sighted to a Violet.

The charisma, power and sexual energy of a Violet and a Red can be very well-matched. However, the belief systems — one being spiritual and etheric, the other being physically oriented — can be quite different. There is also disparity in their display of emotions. A Violet has great emotional depth and tends to be expressive. A Red has emotional depth, but tends to keep it inside, until he has an emotional outburst. If the Violet is able to lift herself up above the Red's temper and see the bigger picture, the two can be compatible again, once the Red has calmed down.

If these two can get along with each other, the Red has the power and physical energy to carry out the visions of the Violet. The Red tends to take action, while the Violet continues to dream up ideas. This couple can be well-matched and compatible, provided they do not discuss spiritual beliefs or their concepts about reality.

Violet and Orange Relationship
See Orange and Violet Relationship.

Violet and Magenta Relationship
A Magenta and a Violet usually fascinate each other. The Violet's futuristic vision inspires the Magenta's quick and creative mind. While the Violet can often see an extraordinary invention in the future, he does not always know how

to create it. The Magenta can take the Violet's vision and actually create the invention using materials at hand.

Each of these colors need to respect the individuality and the independence of the other. The Violet can be more accepting of the Magenta's outrageous behavior and attitudes than most of the other LifeColors. The Violet can also find a Magenta's behavior quite bizarre. However, because people often find the Violet's ideas and visions unrealistic, he can relate to the Magenta.

It is possible for this couple to experience power struggles because each wants to go his own direction. This is fine if they are friends, but not if they are married. Going in different directions could cause them to drift apart. Neither one wants to be dominated by the other or give up his own dream. Because both of these colors enjoy being the center of attention, there can also be competition between them at social gatherings or around their friends.

This couple can enjoy an exciting sexual relationship. A Violet and a Magenta both like options when it comes to sexual partners, so an open marriage could be quite possible in this relationship.

A Violet enjoys his world on a spiritual and emotional level, while the Magenta experiences her world on a very physical, tangible level. A Magenta does not share a Violet's desire to save the planet, but she does not usually question him or try to prevent him from accomplishing this task. A Violet is not interested in shocking people's moral standards or social behavior. He is more interested in inspiring and leading people to a better life. A Magenta is more excited about shaking people up and helping them find their own unique styles and beliefs. A Violet envisions people living in unity and harmony on the planet. A Magenta wants each person to be an individual, living his own desires and dreams. While a Violet tends to see the bigger, universal picture and how everything works together, a Magenta tends to focus on what is in front of her and how she can make it unique and different. She tends to live more in the moment.

A Violet's visionary capabilities and his ability to keep moving forward fascinate a Magenta, and keep her attention for much longer than most of the other colors are capable of doing. A Violet tends to take his mission on this planet very seriously, however, while a Magenta chooses not to take anything seriously. This relationship, oddly enough, has more potential of succeeding than many of the other relationships in the aura family. As long as they do not compete for attention all the time, and as long as each allows the other the freedom to live life the way he or she chooses, this pair is compatible.

Violet and Yellow Relationship

See Yellow and Violet Relationship.

Violet and Logical Tan Relationship

See Logical Tan and Violet Relationship.

Violet and Environmental Tan Relationship

See Environmental Tan and Violet Relationship.

Violet and Sensitive Tan Relationship

This is a potentially strong relationship. The Sensitive Tan can support and nurture the Violet while the Violet provides the inspiration and vision to keep the relationship moving forward. Problems can arise when the Violet sees further than the Sensitive Tan is willing to go. Often the Violet has great ideas and business plans, but the Sensitive Tan fears taking a financial risk based on the Violet's unsubstantiated visions and dreams. However, when the Sensitive Tan feels that their combined income is stable and secure, she is more willing to allow the Violet freedom to experiment with his dreams.

The emotional depth and passion of a Violet can sometimes overwhelm the shy and reticent Sensitive Tan. A Sensitive Tan has the ability, however, to adapt and even to expand her own emotional boundaries to some degree. A Sensitive Tan does not always understand the Violet's desire to save the planet or to reach humanity. Although the risks involved in his vision may frighten her, the dedicated and loyal Sensitive Tan will tend to stand by her mate.

While the Violet wants to be the center of attention, the Sensitive Tan is content to stay in the background and emotionally support him. Consequently, these two do not compete with each other. Violets are natural leaders, while most Sensitive Tans are natural followers.

If the Sensitive Tan criticizes or mistrusts the Violet, the Violet may become unsure of his own visions and thereby become scattered, insecure and confused. The Sensitive Tan will then have to work even harder to encourage the shaken Violet to produce or to move forward with his career. The Violet, in turn, must learn to be patient and understanding with his Sensitive Tan mate. She does not see the bigger picture as easily as he does. She needs time to see the logic behind his dream, and the steps that are necessary to take in order to fulfill it.

The Sensitive Tan can provide the stability for the relationship and also fill in the necessary details to accomplish the dream. When the Violet wants to jump from one to fifty, it is more beneficial for the Sensitive Tan to help him plan the steps to get there rather than to oppose his ideas and dreams. This pair will accomplish more if they work together.

Violet and Abstract Tan Relationship

This relationship has potential for being successful, because the Violet is one of the few personalities who doesn't care about the order in which the Abstract Tan finishes her tasks. If these two are out of power, however, their relationship could be chaotic. Both of these individuals can see the entire picture at one time, and yet they can't always explain the steps that are involved to anyone else. They both understand how it feels to be scattered and overwhelmed and to go in too many directions at once.

Both of these individuals have a love for humanity and a love of knowledge. They enjoy searching for information that will unlock the doors of the universe. The Abstract Tan prefers to contemplate and discuss universal concepts, while the Violet prefers to take action and actualize the ideas and theories. The Violet's dynamic energy often inspires the Abstract Tan to find ways to manifest her ideas. The Violet can see his visions, but dislikes having to take care of all the details along the way. The Abstract Tan doesn't mind taking care of details as long as she can do them in random order. Being able to take care of the details of a project makes the Tan a good partner for the Violet.

At social gatherings, the outgoing and friendly Abstract Tan loves talking with a variety of people. She is able to learn interesting and valuable bits of information this way. The Violet, on the other hand, prefers to be the center of attention at parties. He can quickly become bored if the topic of conversation is not meaningful or interesting to him. The Violet prefers to discuss world affairs, politics, spirituality, universal principles, the media, travel, music, the environment or other topics that address the current transformation of consciousness on the planet.

Because both the Violet and the Abstract Tan can become scattered and disorganized, they must be careful not to feed off of each other's confusion and chaos. The Violet can quickly become intolerant of the Abstract Tan's unfocused behavior. Because the Violet can usually see the completed project in his mind's eye way ahead of anyone else, he can become frustrated and impatient with the inconsistent and unreliable pace of the Abstract Tan. The Abstract Tan, feeling his disapproval, withdraws from him. She detaches herself from her emotions so she won't be affected by the Violet's judgments and criticisms. The Abstract Tan will need to learn responsibility so that the Violet doesn't always have to take care of her.

The Violet wants passion and emotional depth from his mate. The Abstract Tan is overwhelmed by such intensity. Therefore, the Violet can be somewhat disappointed by the emotional qualities of this relationship. In their power, both of these personalities are accepting of each other's differences. Consequently, if they both stay focused and in power, they can be a good team. The Violet can be the dynamic, visionary leader, while the bright and perceptive Abstract Tan can help him maintain an optimistic faith in humanity. With their combined humanitarian idealism, this pair can help to change the planet.

Violet and Green Relationship

See Green and Violet Relationship.

Violet and Blue Relationship

A relationship between a Blue and a Violet has great potential. Blues have so much love to give that they can overwhelm most of the LifeColors in the aura spectrum. Violets, however, love being the center of attention and are capable of great emotional depth. This relationship can be very compatible. While the Blue gives all of her love and affection to the Violet, the Violet appreciates the attention and returns love to her. A Violet can be very demonstrative with his affections. A Violet is compassionate and understanding enough to allow a Blue to be overly emotional.

Both colors desire to help other people. The loving Blue finds meaning and satisfaction in supporting the Violet's vision to save the world. When the Violet envisions a grand dream, the Blue, who trusts her inner knowing, can usually sense whether or not the Violet's dream is right. They can be a very powerful team when the Blue supports and nurtures the Violet's dreams and visions. While some of the other LifeColors, such as Greens, tend to challenge the Violet's visions, the Blue usually encourages him. Both the Blue and the Violet personalities are intuitive. Spiritual growth and understanding are priorities for them.

A Blue loves the open, emotional communication that flows from a Violet. A Violet is willing to share his feelings with the devoted Blue. A Violet will openly reassure her that she is loved. A Violet is one of the only personalities who understands the Blue's emotional depth and insecurities and is willing to give her enough sincere love to bring her back to her center and her power.

When a Violet gets scattered and overwhelmed, a Blue usually comes to the rescue. When the Violet takes on too many projects, the Blue will jump in and help him. When the Violet loses his direction, the Blue intuitively helps the Violet find his center and refocus his energy.

One of the potential problems between a Blue and a Violet is that an out-of-power Violet can become very self-centered, egocentric and arrogant. A Blue, who tends to be so giving and loving that she can turn into a "doormat," can be taken advantage of or used by a Violet. His selfish and abusive behavior can hurt and confuse the loyal Blue. Her friends are often dismayed by how much emotional abuse she will take from the Violet because she loves him so much.

Another potential problem that may arise between a Blue and a Violet is in their sexual relationship. The Blue is very loyal, monogamous, and committed, and she desires the same commitment from her mate. A Violet, among all the LifeColors, has the most potential for being unfaithful in his relationships. A Violet is very sexually attractive, his chemistry radiates a sexual energy. If his appetite is not fulfilled at home, and often even when it is, he tends to stray. This, of course, can devastate a Blue.

For the most part, however, Blues and Violets are highly compatible. They are both spiritual, loving, emotional and generous toward other people. A Blue desires a mate she can deeply and emotionally bond with. A Violet has the potential of creating this passionate bonding. These two personalities are willing and capable of fulfilling many of each other's needs. They are also able to help each other stay balanced and in power.

Violet and Violet Relationship

A partnership between two Violets can be extremely dynamic and powerful. When two Violets are in the same room together describing and sharing visions, the high energy in the room is contagious. Violets are also very sexually compatible. The sexual chemistry between them is powerful and passionate. They are drawn to each other like magnets. It can almost be overwhelming. Together, they can inspire and empower each other's visions. With their passionate energy, the two of them together could accomplish almost anything on the planet.

There are a few potentially negative aspects of Violets being in relationship with one another. Because both enjoy being the center of attention, they can become quite competitive around each other. Both can also become very scattered as they try to accomplish too many projects at the same time. This also creates little opportunity for them to devote time to each other. (This problem can be seen quite often in the entertainment business. It is very common for two Violets in the entertainment world to be married, yet living very busy and separate lives.) Violets are also prone to extramarital affairs.

Another potential problem with two Violets is that while they are both great at "seeing" future projects, neither is efficient at planning all the details. If at least one of the pair stays focused and in his power, the projects will be handled.

For the most part, a Violet/Violet relationship is dynamic, charismatic and powerful. They are both passionate about music, sex, traveling and inspiring humanity. They have a great number of interests in common. They must make sure that they spend time together, however. By becoming too busy, they risk traveling in separate directions.

Violet and Lavender Relationship

See Lavender and Violet Relationship.

Violet and Crystal Relationship

See Crystal and Violet Relationship.

Violet and Indigo Relationship

This relationship has tremendous potential, provided the Violet does not become so overpowering and dictatorial that the Indigo ends up rebelling or leaving him. With the Violet's visionary abilities, he is able to relate to the Indigo's New Age beliefs. The Violet can actually see the future that the Indigo intuitively feels is coming. Violets are leading the way into the Indigo Age. Indigos appear to be surrounding themselves with Violets who have the leadership ability, power and strength to clear the way for the Indigo Age on the planet. The Violet clears the path, leading the way and keeping the Indigo safe from people who are not supportive or in harmony with her spiritual ways. The Violet also has answers to the Indigo's many questions.

Even though the Violet wants to be the center of attention, there is no competition in this relationship, because the Indigo prefers to stay quiet. A Violet has a much more passionate desire to be in the public eye than the Indigo does.

There are only a few areas where conflict could arise with this couple. The two have different social needs. An Indigo prefers to connect with a few close, intimate friends, bonding on a soul-to-soul basis with each. A Violet loves performing and surrounding himself with crowds of people. A Violet, out of his power and wanting to be the center of attention, will try to dominate the Indigo. An Indigo, however, will not be dominated, controlled or manipulated in any way. This could cause power struggles and a strained relationship. If they both stay centered they will support and accept each other.

For the most part these two create a highly spiritual and visionary team. Both of them have a curiosity about other people and cultures. They enjoy traveling. They both have a great amount of compassion for people everywhere. What they both feel, sense and see as the higher truth can broaden the horizons of many people on the planet. The Violet and the Indigo together search for truth and higher consciousness. In power, they both have an inner sense of what is moral and right. This team works well together with common goals. They both want peace, compassion and spiritual enlightenment on the planet.

■ LAVENDER

Lavender and Red Relationship

Lavenders and Reds have absolutely nothing in common. Lavenders exist in a fairytale world. They are not interested in physical reality. They live in their imaginations more than in their bodies. Reds enjoy physical existence and expressing themselves through their bodies.

Lavenders are too fragile and childlike for the volatile and lustful Reds. Reds relate to power, vitality, strength and courage. They love moving heavy mass in the physical world, working with the earth and expressing their sensuality. Lavenders love fantasy, spirituality, sensitivity and creativity. These two wouldn't know how to communicate with each other. They don't have any interests or beliefs in common, nor are they assertive conversationalists. Lavenders would not be able to relate to the powerful and lustful personality of Reds. The Reds would think that the Lavenders should be locked up in a mental institution.

Lavender and Orange Relationship

Oranges and Lavenders have absolutely nothing in common. Lavenders live in a fantasy world and are not willing to spend much time in physical reality. Oranges live completely in the physical environment. Understanding why one would risk his life or face physically dangerous challenges is beyond a Lavender's comprehension. A Lavender prefers to escape into a fairytale world, and not to take on physical challenges at all. A Lavender is much too sensitive, vulnerable and mild for the physical prowess and daring of an Orange. The Lavender is much too etheric and unrealistic for the grounded, physical Orange. An Orange might be temporarily fascinated by the childlike Lavender, but this fascination would quickly pass. The Orange would end up ridiculing the impractical Lavender. Both of these personalities also have a great need to spend time alone, so neither would tend to instigate this relationship. The ungrounded Lavender often needs someone to take care of her. An Orange prefers to be single, independent and free from responsibilities.

These two colors would rarely be found in the same environment, so there is very little chance of them even meeting. If they did, neither one would understand the other.

Lavender and Magenta Relationship

See Magenta and Lavender Relationship.

Lavender and Yellow Relationship

See Yellow and Lavender Relationship.

Lavender and Logical Tan Relationship

See Logical Tan and Lavender Relationship.

Lavender and Environmental Tan Relationship

Occasionally, an Environmental Tan and a Lavender provide a good balance for each other. The Lavender helps to lighten up or soften the Environmental Tan, and the Environmental Tan adds logic and stability to the Lavender's life. For the most part, however, these two frustrate each other. An Environmental Tan is too grounded, practical and emotionally inflexible for a Lavender. An Environmental Tan judges the Lavender as being unrealistic and irresponsible. He doesn't relate to the fantasy world in which she lives. He prefers three-dimensional reality. A Lavender would only fascinate the Environmental Tan for a short period of time and then he would expect her to become more practical and realistic. The Environmental Tan usually tries to clip the wings of the Lavender.

The Lavender does not find any joy or excitement in an Environmental Tan's lifestyle. She is not able to explore life emotionally or spiritually when she is with him. A Lavender becomes bored with the Environmental Tan's inability and unwillingness to see life from other perspectives.

This couple has very little in common. Neither one is able to relate to the other's perspective of the world.

Lavender and Sensitive Tan Relationship

See Sensitive Tan and Lavender Relationship.

Lavender and Abstract Tan Relationship

While both are sensitive and kind individuals, this pair would not be able to take care of each other or maintain an intimate relationship. The Abstract Tan is usually too scattered and confused to be able to be responsible for the ungrounded Lavender. The Lavender spends most of her time daydreaming or fantasizing in her own world. She is not present in physical reality long enough to take care of the household responsibilities. The Abstract Tan is just too busy and disorganized to remember to pay the bills. Each of them hopes that the other will take care of everything. Consequently, nothing gets accomplished.

Neither of these personalities is comfortable with emotions; as a result, they do not develop an emotionally intimate or bonded relationship. While the Abstract Tan likes to share his thoughts and philosophies with others, these two rarely understand each other's language. Although the Abstract Tan is often fascinated by the Lavender's descriptions of other realities, his already scattered mental processes can be blown out trying to understand her.

Both of these individuals are better off with partners who can add stability and focus to their lives. They need to be with people who are willing to take care of them.

Lavender and Green Relationship

See Green and Lavender Relationship.

Lavender and Blue Relationship

See Blue and Lavender Relationship.

Lavender and Violet Relationship

A relationship between a Lavender and a Violet is highly compatible. The Violet is the powerful, independent force who goes out into the world to take care of business, while the Lavender is free to stay at home and create a loving home environment for the Violet. A Lavender sometimes adds her creative ideas to the Violet's visions. A

Violet has great emotional depth, and can be very accepting of others when in his power. The Violet can allow the Lavender the freedom to spend time in her fantasy world. He is much more understanding of her behavior than many of the other LifeColors are. There is not competition between these two. The Violet wants to be the leader and the center of attention, and the Lavender shies away from attention and responsibility. The Lavender appreciates that the Violet takes charge.

A problem arises if the Lavender spends too much time in her fantasy world when the Violet needs emotional depth and communication from her. The Violet enjoys companionship. The Lavender is not always available to him. Nor is she able to lend much guidance or direction when the Violet becomes lost or scattered.

A Violet seems to have much stronger sexual needs than a Lavender does. However, a Lavender can usually handle the sexual power and chemistry of a Violet. She merely moves into her fantasies when she is with him.

When they are in power, a Violet and a Lavender can complement each other's lives. The Violet adds power, depth and progressive movement to the sometimes directionless and scattered Lavender. The Lavender adds fantasy, lightness and fun to the Violet's intensity and power. The Lavender adds creativity and imagination to the Violet's visions, while the Violet can actualize the Lavender's fantasies. Neither one demands a great deal of time or attention from the other person. These two colors are emotionally and spiritually compatible as long as the Lavender spends enough time in her body to be a companion to the Violet. They both allow each other the space needed to explore their inner feelings, fantasies and visions.

Lavender and Lavender Relationship

Two Lavenders together is a case of "nobody minding the store." While sharing stories with each other of wonderful adventures in other dimensions can be enjoyable for these two, their irresponsibility can get them into trouble. Neither wants to stay focused in this reality long enough to take care of the everyday responsibilities. Each Lavender looks to the other to take care of business. Each can become disappointed and even resentful if the other doesn't fulfill the role of caretaker and provider.

A Lavender fares better in a relationship with a mate who is reliable, responsible and action-oriented — this type of relationship gives the Lavender the freedom to travel on his inner journeys. Although Lavenders are sensitive and gentle toward each other and they allow each other time to be alone, they need mates who can provide them with some sense of stability, not add to their ungroundedness.

Lavender and Crystal Relationship

Both of these personalities tend to be too withdrawn and emotionally unavailable to have a close, intimate relationship with each other. They both spend too much time in their own worlds to be able to effectively communicate with each other. Neither one would have a grounded or practical influence upon the other.

Although they are both gentle, sensitive and intuitive beings who enjoy the pretty, delicate and fanciful things in life, neither is powerful or ambitious enough to deal with the real world. Neither wants to get a stable job to support the home, or enjoys taking care of the day-to-day responsibilities. Their home environment would be quiet because both would be off meditating or exploring inner worlds. However, paying the rent on their peaceful home could be a problem.

Crystals and Lavenders are safe with each other, because neither one makes strong demands on the other, or is looking for an intense love affair. Neither one overwhelms or intimidates the other. They appreciate each other's gentle nature.

These two can be quiet and considerate roommates; they don't have much to offer each other, however, in an intimate marriage relationship.

Lavender and Indigo Relationship

See Indigo and Lavender Relationship.

■ CRYSTAL

Crystal and Red Relationship

See Red and Crystal Relationship.

Crystal and Orange Relationship

See Orange and Crystal Relationship.

Crystal and Magenta Relationship

A Magenta and a Crystal are not very compatible. A Magenta's behavior is much too offensive and bizarre for the sensitive, quiet Crystal. A Crystal requires calm and gentle behavior from her mate. If a Magenta discovered that a Crystal did not like bugs and squirmy things, the Magenta would probably bring home giant bugs and decorate the entire house with them, just to shake the Crystal up. This attempt at humor would eventually fragment and shatter a Crystal.

A Crystal's priority is to get in touch with her spirituality and her own intuitive understanding. A Magenta has no time or desire to deal with an inner, spiritual level. He would become easily bored with a Crystal, although at first he would be tempted to try to figure out what made her tick.

Excitement, crowds, and parties are what thrill a Magenta. A Crystal, on the other hand, prefers a peaceful, calm home environment, a healing atmosphere, and a few close friends. A Crystal would be overwhelmed by a Magenta's outgoing and outlandish behavior. The Magenta would become indifferent and uninterested in a Crystal's point of view. These two would rarely be found in the same places, let alone marry or have friends in common. Neither of these personalities would understand the other.

Crystal and Yellow Relationship

A Yellow and a Crystal are both very sensitive, loving personalities. What these two have in common are their natural healing abilities. They both enjoy healing, working in gardens and connecting with nature. They are both physically and psychically sensitive through touch, especially through their hands. Both the Yellow and Crystal understand the need to have quiet time alone.

Problems arise, however, because a Yellow is often too energetic, much like a rambunctious young child, and can upset the delicate nature of a Crystal. While the Yellow wants to be outside playing and having carefree fun, a Crystal wants to be quietly meditating and reflecting on life. A Crystal is very soft, gentle and introspective, while a Yellow is more fun-loving and outgoing. After a while, the Yellow may become disinterested in the Crystal's need to have peace and quiet. A Yellow needs physical activity and play. While a Crystal enjoys the natural enthusiasm and carefree attitude of a Yellow, eventually his energy would exhaust her and she would need to withdraw from him.

Neither of these childlike personalities wants to go to work or be responsible for paying the bills. Although they would be kind and sensitive to each other, they wouldn't be grounded enough to financially support each other. Each of them would also tend to shy away from the responsibility and commitment of marriage. They would prefer to stay innocent and childlike throughout their entire lives. Both would be better off finding partners who could support them financially and be more emotionally stable.

Crystal and Logical Tan Relationship

Because both the Logical Tan and the Crystal prefer to keep their thoughts and feelings to themselves, they tend to be isolated and separate from each other. There is usually very little communication between these two.

A Crystal is usually too fragile for a Logical Tan. The Tan's rules, standards and beliefs are too limiting for her. A Logical Tan has difficulty understanding the Crystal's spiritual personality, as well as her need to be introspective and commune with God. A Crystal seems like a fine piece of china to a Logical Tan.

A Crystal needs to be able to trust and bond emotionally with her mate. A Logical Tan does not tend to bond on an emotional level with anyone. He prefers instead to have an intellectual companion, someone he can discuss factual, logical ideas and information with. Sharing emotional intimacies is threatening to a Tan. A Crystal has no desire to discuss the problems of the world or the current economic conditions, while these are areas that interest a Tan. A Crystal prefers instead to spend her time and energy contemplating spiritual ideas and the purpose of life. A Tan is much too analytical and logical to be able to relate to the spiritual Crystal.

If these two were to marry, they would spend most of their time in separate rooms at opposite ends of the house. While this could make them very compatible roommates, it does not do much to create an intimate and loving marriage relationship.

If this couple can stay in their power, however, it is possible for them to provide an interesting balance for each other. The Tan can provide a stable environment and financial security for the Crystal. The Crystal can bring gentleness and beauty into the Tan's often logical and mechanical world. The Crystal can inspire the Tan to consider inner and spiritual ideas rather than only focusing on logic and data. The Tan can help the Crystal stay more grounded and learn to feel safer in a physical world.

If they slipped out of power, they would probably withdraw from one another, making it difficult to maintain or continue a relationship.

Crystal and Environmental Tan Relationship

See Environmental Tan and Crystal Relationship.

Crystal and Sensitive Tan Relationship

A Sensitive Tan and a Crystal are both very sensitive, nurturing, compassionate and quiet people. They both prefer to keep their feelings and thoughts to themselves. Because they are calm, loving and caring, they tend to be gentle with each other. A Sensitive Tan often wishes that the Crystal were a bit more practical and logical, but she is loving and accepting enough to let the Crystal be who he is.

One of the challenges for this couple is that a Sensitive Tan, with her Blue aspect, needs an emotional commitment from her mate. A Crystal, however, doesn't want anyone depending on him or turning to him for emotional support. If a Crystal withdraws too often from meeting the emotional needs of his mate, the Sensitive Tan can feel abandoned. Nevertheless, if the Sensitive Tan can stay balanced and secure, understanding that the Crystal is giving as much as he can, this couple can be compatible. The Sensitive Tan must learn not to demand too much from the fragile Crystal, and the Crystal needs to learn to be more giving toward his mate.

Another problem that may arise is that a Crystal does not like to be practical or pay attention to details. The responsibility of maintaining the home, business or family tends to fall on the shoulders of the Sensitive Tan, who may find these responsibilities burdensome after a while. A Sensitive Tan prefers a mate who is a reliable partner, who shares the duties and responsibilities of supporting a family. A Crystal is not typically a proficient provider — he can barely support himself. An agreement must be made between these two regarding the division of obligations.

For the most part, however, these two make a compatible couple. They respect each other's sensitivity and need for quiet, reflective time. They are loving and considerate toward each other. A Crystal and a Sensitive Tan both want a calm, secure home and a pleasant, understanding relationship.

Crystal and Abstract Tan Relationship

See Abstract Tan and Crystal Relationship.

Crystal and Green Relationship

A relationship between a Green and a Crystal can be too harsh on the Crystal and too frustrating for the Green. A Green is ambitious, outgoing and driven to accomplish. A Crystal is introspective, quiet, calm, peaceful and not motivated to accomplish. She has no concept of earning money. A Green's energy can be too powerful and intimidating for the easily-frightened and scattered Crystal. A Green thrives on action and challenges that would overwhelm a Crystal. She needs solitude, meditation and harmony to feel centered. The Green does not understand the spiritual needs or relate to the spiritual personality of the Crystal. The quiet Crystal would be overrun by the strong, business-like attitude of the Green. She would tend to shy away from his intensity. A Green needs a partner who can match his power, someone he can have challenging, intellectual discussions with. A frustrated and angry

Green, who can be very abrupt and brutally honest when he communicates, could very well devastate the sensitive and fragile Crystal.

If this couple were to work out at all, it would only be if the Crystal were to add some of the Green's energy into her aura and become more powerful, stepping out into the world with more dynamic force. (A Crystal's tendency is to hide out.) The influence of a Green could actually help the Crystal become more secure and self-confident. If the Crystal was not overwhelmed by the Green's energy it could add power, direction and stability to her life. The Green would also have to be in power, and not be too abrasive or demanding on the Crystal.

Both of these colors have a need to be independent and to have time alone, so they would understand and respect this need in each other. A Green is one of the few personalities who could handle the Crystal's withdrawing without feeling rejected. Although both of these personalities enjoy having their environment clean, tidy and organized, these two basically prefer different things in their environment. Where a Green likes elegant furniture and fine, expensive art objects, a Crystal likes simple possessions. On the positive side, the Green would take care of business, allowing the Crystal time to stay quietly home alone. The Green does not mind having a career and making money.

A Green may be fascinated by the Crystal's spiritual ideas, though he would question and challenge many of them. Emotionally and sexually, both of these colors tend to be aloof. A Green prefers a partner who can be powerful and passionate. The intensity of having sex with a Green could overwhelm a Crystal if she were not careful. Only if the Crystal could take on the Green's energy and match his standards would they be compatible. More often, the Green tends to dominate the Crystal, becoming easily frustrated by her lack of drive and ambition. A Crystal does not challenge or inspire a Green and the Green tends to intimidate and overwhelm the Crystal.

Crystal and Blue Relationship

This relationship has the potential to be very harmonious. A Blue is loving and sensitive enough to accept the Crystal's emotionally fragile nature. The Blue can support and protect the gentle Crystal. Both the Blue and the Crystal have an appreciation for the esthetic things in life, and so they can create a harmonious and beautiful environment together. However, the Blue must also be very patient and understanding, as Crystals are often withdrawn and tend to keep their emotions to themselves. A Crystal has deep emotions, but doesn't share them with the rest of the world. The Blue, who wants to be able to connect and communicate with her mate on an emotional level, can often become frustrated by the Crystal's need for solitude.

Occasionally, problems can arise with this couple. When the Blue loses her center and sense of self-worth, she becomes needy and moody. The Crystal then typically withdraws into his own world, which leaves the Blue feeling abandoned and unloved. A Crystal is not a rescuer. When a Blue loves someone, she wants to be around him all the time. A Crystal needs to spend a great deal of his time in solitude to meditate, cleanse and balance himself. A Blue needs to be careful not to smother the Crystal with her emotional needs. The Crystal needs to emerge from hibernation more frequently to be with the Blue. A Blue loves having people around her. She always has an abundance of friends. A Crystal tends to shy away from people and social activities. The Blue may need to learn to go to social gatherings herself and allow the Crystal time to stay home alone.

The Blue, being a natural nurturer, can help the Crystal become clear and centered by loving and protecting him. His energy is fragile and easily shattered. The Blue can help create a safe home environment for the Crystal. If she tries to over-mother the Crystal, however, he can feel invaded. He often just wants to be left alone.

For this couple to be compatible, the Crystal must learn to express appreciation to the Blue. The Blue must learn when to gently give love and when to be still. She needs to learn not to feel personally rejected when the Crystal needs time alone. A Crystal does appreciate unconditional acceptance and love, which the Blue is very capable of giving when she is in her power. For the emotional Blue to feel fulfilled and appreciated, the Crystal just needs to share his feelings with her more often. Together they can be a very gentle and loving couple.

Crystal and Violet Relationship

This relationship has both positive and negative aspects. These two can provide a good balance for each other, though each can feel that the other does not meet his needs. The Violet needs to be out saving the world. The Crystal tends to withdraw from the world. A Violet has a desire to be the center of attention. A Crystal withdraws from having any attention focused on her at all. Though both are very spiritual, they live in two separate worlds. The Crystal lives in an inner world. The Violet lives very much in the outer world and wants to help improve it.

A Violet loves music and traveling. A Crystal prefers quiet solitude and staying at home in her own little haven. The Violet can offer a balance to the introspective Crystal by bringing home information concerning the outside world. This can enable the Crystal to become a little more well-rounded and better educated. If the Crystal can absorb some of the Violet's energy, she can become more powerful and less fragile. She must, however, be careful not to also take on the scattered attributes of an out-of-power Violet.

In this relationship, the Violet is definitely the powerful leader. The Crystal appreciates the fact that the Violet is out in the world, taking care of business and being productive, so that she is allowed to stay home and be financially supported. When the Violet comes home after a day of saving the world, the Crystal has created a very serene, nurturing environment for him. This couple can be very compatible, when they fulfill these needs for each other. If the Violet can refrain from being so powerful that he intimidates the fragile Crystal, she can show her appreciation by creating a loving home for him. Often, though, her typical emotional and physical withdrawal leaves the Violet no partner to interact or communicate with. In order to have those needs met, the Violet should depend upon communicating with others in the outside world.

Crystal and Lavender Relationship

See Lavender and Crystal Relationship.

Crystal and Crystal Relationship

While two Crystals can be compatible, with similar needs and beliefs, they have very little to learn from each other. They both understand the need for meditation and quiet solitude. Their home can be very peaceful, simple and quiet. Because they both tend to be withdrawn and introspective, however, neither one would be the first to instigate a relationship. They understand each other's need to work with nature for inner balance. They both want peace and harmony in the home; however, neither one wants the responsibility of traveling outside of the home to work for a living. Crystals are often shy and lack self-confidence. They are not very social. They tend to stay isolated in their own worlds, hiding in their own rooms. This relationship has very little potential for growth or development considering that neither one has anything to bring back to the other from the outside world. They are both better off finding mates who are more self-confident and can take charge.

Crystal and Indigo Relationship

See Indigo and Crystal Relationship.

■ INDIGO

Indigo and Red Relationship

Reds and Indigos would have very little in common. Indigos sense that life and matter are energy. A Red would feel that an Indigo dropped from outer space. Reds could not relate to the Indigos' different approach to physical reality, or their inability to see life as tangible.

Indigos are much too sensitive, soft-spoken and introspective to deal with the explosive physical energy, power and strength of Reds. Indigos tend to challenge humanity's limited concepts of physical reality. Reds prefer to see reality as entirely physical.

Indigos have a difficult time dealing with their physical bodies. Reds relate mainly to their physical bodies. Sexuality to an Indigo is a soul-to-soul experience, where two souls can soar together on a higher spiritual level. For a Red, sex is a lustful, physical and tangible experience. A Red would not be able to understand the language, ideals, philosophies or etheric beliefs of an Indigo.

The apparent aloofness of an Indigo would not bother a Red, since Reds tend to be loners anyway. But should they strike up a conversation, they wouldn't have much to say to each other. The Indigo is much too etheric for the physical, grounded personality of a Red. The Indigo is too much of a New Age child for the practical, sensible, realistic Red.

Indigo and Orange Relationship

See Orange and Indigo Relationship.

Indigo and Magenta Relationship

See Magenta and Indigo Relationship.

Indigo and Yellow Relationship

The friendly Yellow and the sensitive Indigo can be great friends. The Yellow's playful attitude interests the curious Indigo. Likewise, an Indigo's view of life is a novelty for the Yellow. A Yellow is so easygoing and playful that she enjoys the Indigo's different approach to life and his unusual beliefs about reality. With her creativity and curiosity, the Yellow can have a great time exploring some of the Indigo's ideas. Both LifeColors are sensitive and want people to like them, but they are also both stubborn — neither likes being told what to do. Because of this, they understand and respect the other's need for space and freedom. Neither has a desire to control the other.

While both are sensitive and considerate of the other's feelings, the Indigo wants to relate to his mate on a very deep, soul-to-soul level. A Yellow tends to take relationships and sex rather lightly. A Yellow can have meaningless, playful, sexual encounters with one person after another. An Indigo cannot even consider such behavior. A Yellow believes that life is to be lived in the moment, with the freedom to make spontaneous choices. While an Indigo also believes that life is to be lived in the moment (for that is all that there is), he also believes it is to be lived from deeper levels of compassion and commitment.

A Yellow tends to live in her body and relates mostly to physical reality, while an Indigo has a challenging time relating to his body at all. The Yellow wants to be more physically active, while the Indigo wants to focus more on understanding spiritual truths, moral issues and ethical concepts. The Indigo prefers to be more contemplative and subdued. During these times, the Indigo needs to retreat to his spiritual studies and allow the Yellow to go outside and play. The Indigo has to understand that it is not the Yellow's need or purpose to focus so intensely on higher concepts. The Yellow can help the Indigo understand his body better while also adding a dimension of fun, play and enjoyment to the Indigo's experience. The Indigo can teach the energetic Yellow about some of the inner spiritual aspects of life. These two personalties can provide a good balance for one another.

An Indigo and a Yellow enjoy the nonjudgmental, accepting natures of each other's personalities. But when the Indigo needs to know that he can trust and depend on those closest to him, the Yellow is not always there when he needs her. A Yellow does not enjoy the heavy responsibility of people depending on her. This can create ill feelings and disappointment for the Indigo. He can develop a lack of trust in her. The Yellow needs to learn to be more dependable and responsible within relationships. Because neither of these two LifeColors wants to hurt the other, and neither enjoys conflict, the Yellow and Indigo couple are intent on maintaining a harmonious relationship.

Indigo and Logical Tan Relationship

These two personalities have great difficulty understanding each other. The Indigo challenges most laws and limiting concepts on the planet at this time. The Logical Tan believes laws and standards are not only common sense, but necessary for our very survival. This pair can be in constant conflict with each other. An Indigo needs someone she can relate to on an emotional basis. Emotional bonding is not a priority for a Logical Tan; he tends to keep his feelings to himself. The Indigo's ideas seem unrealistic, impractical and often bizarre to the Logical Tan. A Logical Tan needs everything to be logical and analytical, with supporting proof and data. Everything for a Logical Tan must be a factual, realistic experience. Life for an Indigo involves energy, emotions, spirituality and higher concepts. A Logical Tan is the typical disciplinarian, while an Indigo is the antithesis of discipline. An Indigo challenges old ideas, standards and accepted ways of doing things. This upsets a Logical Tan's structured way of life. An Indigo is very far from the Logical Tan's ideals with her New Age concepts, spiritual ideals and unique ways of looking at life.

If these two were in their power, with the Logical Tan open-minded enough to at least discuss different ideas, they could possibly be friends. The Indigo could help the Logical Tan explore other possibilities. The Logical Tan could help the curious Indigo understand three dimensional reality by giving her facts and information. (However, the Indigo would probably believe the Logical Tan's facts were not conclusive.) An Indigo believes that there's more to reality than physical appearances. A Logical Tan wants the Indigo to be more realistic and practical, not question reality in the face of "obvious" facts. The Indigo's inability to conform or to be practical and logical eventually upsets a Logical Tan, whose purpose is to figure out and analyze three-dimensional reality. An Indigo wants to show people that their limited concepts of three-dimensional reality are probably not reflective of its true nature. Most likely, these two would be constantly questioning and refuting each other's beliefs.

Indigo and Environmental Tan Relationship

This is not one of the most compatible relationships. An Environmental Tan grasps his sense of reality from his physical environment. An Indigo seems to understand life beyond physical reality. An Environmental Tan wants life to be logical, analytical and grounded. An Indigo is the first one to challenge the traditional, rational belief systems. The Indigo challenges rules that are there just because that's the way things have always been done. An Environmental Tan, however, prefers to follow rules and live by set standards. He becomes agitated by chaos.

Both personalities, however, have a high regard for nature. They are inspired by the beauty and magnificence of trees, animals and the earth. This could be a common ground for their discussions. With an Indigo constantly challenging the belief systems and behaviors of the Environmental Tan, this appreciation of nature may be the only common ground they have. An Indigo is too different, too New Age and too spiritual for an Environmental Tan. While an Environmental Tan wants structure and discipline, an Indigo wants people to free themselves from their limitations. These two would be better off if they found mates who shared their same beliefs.

Indigo and Sensitive Tan Relationship

See Sensitive Tan and Indigo Relationship.

Indigo and Abstract Tan Relationship

See Abstract Tan and Indigo Relationship.

Indigo and Green Relationship

These two personalities are absolutely fascinated by each other — up to a point. At first, an Indigo is a curiosity for a Green. The Green, who loves to be quicker and smarter than everyone else, is fascinated by the Indigo's advanced ideas and concepts. However, the Green is also constantly challenging and questioning the Indigo. The Green becomes frustrated if the Indigo is not able to produce rational explanations to support his beliefs.

Considering that a Green has a strong need to control her life and the lives of those around her, and that an Indigo refuses to be controlled, there could be conflict between these two. Although a Green can be frustrated by an Indigo, she also respects his refusal to be dominated.

The inquisitive Indigo can learn a lot from the intelligent and well-informed Green. But the Green must be careful not to be too harsh or too pushy with the sensitive Indigo. An Indigo's emotions run deep and he needs to be able to trust the people around him. A Green can be very impatient, always in a hurry. An Indigo needs to move at his own pace. He will not be rushed, pushed or forced into anything. Another problem arises when an Indigo's desire to emotionally bond with his mate runs into a Green's protective walls. The Green has to be in control, causing her to protect herself emotionally.

The Green is definitely the money-maker in this partnership. An Indigo does not choose to deal with money. He can explore creative ideas instead, while the Green takes the ideas and transforms them into physical and practical form.

Conflicts can arise between a Green and an Indigo because of their different views and attitudes regarding people, money and business. An out-of-power Green can often operate outside of the moral belief system of an Indigo. Out-of-power Greens do not think twice about stepping on others as they climb up the corporate ladder. Indigos believe such actions are contrary to the spiritual nature of evolved beings on the planet.

This team can be very effective at facilitating each other's growth. They can also butt heads, however, and become frustrated. A Green usually does not have the same spiritual goals or understandings as an Indigo, and this frequently causes them each to go in different directions. Although the information that each brings back to the relationship can enhance and inspire the other, a Green has a tendency to be too powerful, bold, and brash for an Indigo. While an Indigo in his power is one of the few LifeColors who can stand up to a Green's power, an Indigo who is out of power can become easily crushed and intimidated by a Green. Broken and bruised, the Indigo then retreats within himself and finds it difficult to regain trust for the domineering Green.

Indigo and Blue Relationship
See Blue and Indigo Relationship.

Indigo and Violet Relationship
See Violet and Indigo Relationship.

Indigo and Lavender Relationship
Spiritually and emotionally, these two have similar characteristics. Both are very sensitive and gentle, as well as emotionally fragile. They both believe that there is more to life than physical reality and they allow each other the room to explore that belief. These childlike souls both live from their intuition rather than from logic or intellect. Since they both are highly creative, developing artistic projects together could be fulfilling and profitable for them.

Neither the Lavender nor the Indigo wishes to control or dominate anyone else. They are each very accepting and undemanding toward others. They allow one another the space they each need to live their own lives. They understand the need to be individualistic. They are both typically misunderstood by other people, so their mutual understanding is appreciated.

While they are both sensitive individuals, and are compatible in many ways if they stay balanced and in power, they don't always have much to offer each other. An Indigo needs to be with someone who can explain physical reality to him. He has trouble understanding life on the planet at this time. A Lavender is not usually capable of providing answers to the inquisitive Indigo because she doesn't spend much time in physical reality. The Lavender could actually give the Indigo a warped sense of the world by describing the fantasy world she experiences.

The Lavender is not usually capable of reaching the emotional depths that the Indigo requires from a mate. The Indigo wants to bond with someone on a soul-to-soul basis.

The Lavender prefers life to be less serious. The Lavender spends so much of her time withdrawn in her own world that the Indigo tends to feel alone and abandoned.

Although the Indigo may be intrigued by the Lavender's other worlds, he is more interested in learning about this one. The Lavender cannot relate to the intensity of the Indigo's quest for answers, so she usually floats into other dimensions, leaving the Indigo to search on his own. An Indigo gains little understanding from a Lavender about life on this planet.

While these two are both gentle souls, neither has a very practical sense of surviving in the physical world. They are nice to each other, but they would be better off with partners who could provide them with support, stability and direction.

Indigo and Crystal Relationship

The Crystal and the Indigo have very similar needs and beliefs. Their energies are very compatible. Although these two are both very gentle and sensitive beings who are easily affected by other people, they can be very soothing for each other.

Their priority in life is to connect with their spiritual sources and knowledge. The Indigo has a great desire to understand and live his life by higher principles and higher consciousness. The Crystal's life also revolves around her spirituality. They can have wonderful, enlightening discussions about spirituality and inner reality. Both share the need to spend quiet, reflective time in meditation. They understand the importance of going within to find answers. They also both understand the need to feel emotionally secure and protected, and they prefer spending time with sensitive and trustworthy people. The Indigo and the Crystal feel that they can trust one another. While they are both sensitive and fragile personalities who have highly charged physical and emotional systems, their energies are compatible with each other. The Indigo seems more capable of dealing with the intensity of the outside world, however, so it is usually he who brings worldly information home to the vulnerable Crystal.

The Crystal's natural ability to be a clear channel for universal energy has a very healing and energizing effect on the Indigo. It helps him stay centered and connected with his sensitive physical body. They both understand that they are unusual individuals, and they allow and accept each other's uniqueness.

Both the Indigo and the Crystal have great emotional depth. While the Indigo has a need to bond strongly on a soul-to-soul level with others, however, the Crystal has a fear of connecting so intensely. She has a fear of being hurt or shattered. The delicate Crystal often withdraws so far within herself that communication becomes difficult or even impossible. Even though the Indigo is gentle and understanding, he can feel lost and abandoned if the Crystal withdraws too often. Usually, these two are sensitive and patient with each other's needs. They can help each other stay secure and balanced, and consequently the Crystal can stay more open to the Indigo. Because both operate so much from their intuition, each one typically "knows" what the other needs to feel safe.

Out of power, they can both tend to spend more time in an inner spiritual world than in the outside physical world. Should either one withdraw too often, this couple could lose trust in each other. If, however, they maintain their spiritual understanding and their gentle communication with each other, these two are very emotionally, spiritually and physically compatible.

Indigo and Indigo Relationship

Two Indigos together are definitely able to understand each other. However, they can create a very challenging relationship because neither one, at this time, has a grasp on physical reality. They are not able to provide answers for one another. Even though they are emotionally and spiritually compatible, the two Indigos would make better friends than marriage partners. Although they both have spiritual understanding, they do not have much ability to deal with life on a three-dimensional level. Both of them experience similar difficulties making their way in the world.

Indigos do make very compatible friends. Neither tries to run the life of the other because they each respect the other's individual experience of life. They are able to bond with each other on a deep, soul-to-soul level. Their emotional and spiritual understanding is very compatible. Their inability to take care of everyday responsibilities, however, can cause difficulties. Neither usually wants to stay home to handle the details.

Emotionally, Indigos are more compatible with each other than they are with any of the mental or physical colors. These two can provide great comfort, appreciation and understanding for each other. However, they would each need to go to outside sources to find out more about the world. Since they would each have similar questions, they could share their newly-learned information and educate each other.

Even though they are compatible, it is better for Indigos to have others to protect and provide for them. It is more beneficial for an Indigo to be with another emotional/spiritual color, someone who has a grasp of the physical world.

9. Conclusion

■ ADDING COLORS TO YOUR AURA

You are constantly adding and changing bands of colors in your aura, though you are usually unaware that you are doing so. With the exception of the inner LifeColor bands, the other outer bands in your aura change colors frequently. The various colors reflect your state of consciousness at that time. If, for example, you decide that you must become more responsible and hard-working, that you must earn more money and accomplish a greater goal, the color green will begin to develop in the outer bands of your aura. Your LifeColors usually remain intact, but your behavior temporarily shifts into more Green aspects. You may find yourself uncharacteristically more driven, more concerned with money and occasionally more frustrated with other people's lack of ambition.

There are a few methods that can help you add different colors to your aura. You can imagine or visualize the desired color around you. Inhaling and visualizing that you are breathing the color *into* your body will help you become the personality of that color. Your thoughts and imagination are the most powerful tools that you have for creating what you want. Declaring and imagining that you have a certain color in your aura instigates the process, and that color begins to develop.

When you decide to add certain qualities and behaviors into your life, the corresponding color begins to evolve in your aura. If you decide, for example, that you are going to relax and have more fun in your life or maybe design some creative, artistic project, the color yellow will begin to emerge in your aura. If you decide that you want to start helping the planet by becoming involved in some environmental or political cause, then the color violet will appear in your aura. The more determined and dedicated you are with these new concepts and the more action you take in those directions, the brighter and more intense the color becomes.

Even if you unintentionally develop a certain behavior, the corresponding aura color will develop as well. For example, if you suddenly become outraged and angered, the color red will begin flashing in your aura. If you become pregnant and notice mothering instincts developing, the color blue will most likely also become apparent in your aura.

To consciously add colors into your aura, you must either visualize the specific color around you, or work to develop the behaviors and qualities that are associated with that color. If you desire to be more loving and nurturing toward your family, either visualize the color blue around you or start behaving in a more loving way. Either of these methods will add blue in your aura.

Be aware of the fact that if you add a certain color to your aura, you may easily experience that color's out-of-power characteristics as well as the in-power traits. If you add violet, you may become scattered and overwhelmed by the number of new projects you have recently undertaken. If you add blue to your aura, you may discover that you are suddenly a great deal more emotional. By adding yellow, you may find that you are unmotivated to accomplish anything or have an unusual craving for sweets.

When introducing new colors into your aura, you must learn to stay balanced and in power with the new personality traits, just as those who have had these LifeColors since birth have had to do. Once you develop a balance of all of the individual colors, they form the perfect "white light."

People often ask if adding green to their aura will stimulate healing. Many healers use the color green in their work. They paint their offices green or ask their clients to visualize the color green. This is not related to the LifeColor Green in a person's aura. Healers use the color green in their work because it lies in the middle of the color spectrum, and therefore promotes the balance that is necessary for self-healing.

■ LEARNING TO "SEE" THE AURA

We all came into this lifetime with the ability to see the aura. As we grew older, we learned not to see it. Infants and animals still see the aura because they have not been taught otherwise. That is why a dog will differentiate between strangers, growling and barking at one person yet befriending another, and a baby will smile and reach out to one person, but cry and pull back from another. We may each see the colors in the aura differently, just as we probably taste foods differently. Not all people experience the same taste when eating liver or asparagus, for example, as evidenced by the fact that some people actually enjoy the taste of these foods.

People often learn to see the aura through different methods. Trusting what you see or feel is the biggest step. Those in the physical family often sense the aura first through their physical bodies. Some people are able to feel the heat from a person's aura through their hands. You may experiment with this tactile sensing method by holding the palms of your hands approximately three feet from a person's body, and slowly moving in toward the body until you feel the sensation of heat or energy. In the beginning, you may only experience the sensation in your hands when you are a few inches away from the body. However, with trust, patience and practice your sensitivity will increase, and you can learn to feel a person's aura from a greater distance.

People in the mental family frequently learn to identify a person's LifeColor by comparing his language and behavior with the information that they have learned about the individual LifeColors. For example, they will conclude that someone who is an exercise fanatic, who has a childlike, playful personality and who doesn't like to work probably has a Yellow LifeColor. Those in the mental family can be some of the least trusting of their intuitive abilities. They feel more comfortable analyzing the facts regarding a person's lifestyle, behavior and occupation, and often learn to "see" the aura intellectually.

Many from the emotional family intuitively sense a person's LifeColor before they physically see it. They can feel whether the person is an insecure and sensitive Yellow, an emotionally depressed Blue, or a powerful Green just by "tuning in" to him. Blues, for example, are able to become quiet inside, ask their higher selves about another person's LifeColor, and usually receive the correct answer. Because Violets are such visual personalities, they tend to actually see the aura before most other people do. Their "third eye" seems to be more developed. Many Indigos, the New Age children, have retained their ability to see and interpret the aura.

A simple exercise to help you see the aura is to have a person stand in front of a white background, then focus your eyesight just above the person's head. After a while, you will be able to see a soft white glow around the body. Many people assume that what they are seeing is an optical illusion, an afterimage of the physical body. (For example, if you stare at something red for a while and then look away, the opposing color green will appear before your eyes. This is an optical illusion.) To prove to yourself that you are actually seeing the aura, ask the other person to concentrate his energy and imagine an intense beam of light shooting out from the top of his head. You should be able to see the white glow at the top of his head expand and fluctuate.

One incidental note: People frequently report seeing the colors gold and pink in the aura. The aura color gold can be seen around highly-evolved spiritual masters and usually signifies a very high vibration. The color pink is often seen in the outer bands of people's auras. Pink signifies that the person has a desire for love and romance in his or her life.

The key to being able to see the aura is to *ask* your higher source to help you see it and then to trust what you see. Make sure that you are not afraid to see the aura, because fear can hold you back. Are you concerned that your friends and family will think that you are crazy? Are you afraid that they will stop loving you? Are you afraid of your own power, or your psychic abilities?

We are moving into an era in which we will become aware that we are unlimited beings. We have many more abilities than we believe that we have at this time. The ability to see the aura is a natural one that we have forgotten how to use. It can be easy to re-awaken that ability.

Learning to see the aura will help us understand that we have more talents and abilities than we realize. It will also help us better understand ourselves and others. If we are ever to experience peace and harmony on the planet, understanding each other and accepting our differences as well as our similarities are major steps toward reaching that goal.

For information about Pamala Oslie's workshops
please write Pamala Oslie, c/o New World Library
58 Paul Drive, San Rafael, CA 94903
or call (415) 472-2100.

NOTES

NOTES

NOTES

NOTES

NOTES

NOTES

NOTES